HUMMINGBIRD

a heart-felt account of one woman's
emotional journey through life

from loss, fear and risk to
self-discovery and joy

Deborah Goodman

ISBN-13: 978-1484057032

Cover image and design by Amy Kate Wolfe
www.amykatewolfe.com

I dedicate this book to anyone who isn't happy, whatever the reason.

~ * ~

In memory of my father Kenneth Roy Goodman, my Aunty Babs, my brothers Nigel and Philip and my dear friend Alan.

~ * ~

Contents

Acknowledgments

This book would not have been possible without the help of my mum. Her support has been invaluable and she has willingly and consistently provided me with the information that I needed to complete the first part my story. This has been an emotional undertaking for her and I thank her for her love.

I extend this thanks to my brother Stephen and to Jane for their support of my project and to my dear friend Andy for believing in me. His encouragement, support, kindness, patience and constructive comments throughout this project have been invaluable.

Special thanks go to my ex-boyfriend Richard for his love, support and loyalty throughout the most difficult years of my life and for choosing to remain a friend.

To my closest friends (in alphabetical order): Angie, Carole, Catherine, Daxa, Jane, Jenn, Jo, Lavender Man, Louise, Owen, Sonya, Stuart and Sue for listening to my worries and for always being there to catch me when I fall. For their laughter and joy, their loyalty and love and for their wisdom and understanding. And, of course, not forgetting all of the other good and dear friends I've ever known in my life up to now.

I thank the other members of the Treatment Triangle – Kim and Jan – and my wonderful clients for giving me the opportunity to do the work I love and for their extended friendship and support of my fundraising. Also, for their genuine interest in my life and my book.

A particular note must be added for my client and friend Carmen, who gave me the first £20 towards my laptop, so that I could - and would - write my book in the first place.

I thank the people who read and commented on my draft for their honest and constructive feedback; and Dave Shannon for not only his friendship, but for the many hours he spent proof-reading my book. I should mention here that it was my decision to capitalise God and the Universe throughout – it just felt wrong not to.

I thank Amy Kate Wolfe for designing me a fabulous book cover.

And finally, I thank my parents for giving me life and the Universe for giving me joy.

Introduction

One day, a couple of years ago, I was talking to a client of mine called Margaret about my trip to India.

"I have a book you would love," she told me. "I will lend it to you."

The next time Margaret came to see me, she placed in my hand a book called Eat, Pray, Love.

I read it... and I loved it... and then I gave it back to her.

"Why do you think this book was a bestseller?" I asked Margaret as I returned her paperback.

"Because, Deborah," she answered, "women like to read other women's stories."

And so it was that I decided to write down my own story – so that other women could read it and enjoy it (and hopefully some men, too).

You may find my story interesting. You may be inspired by my journey of self-discovery and healing.

Hopefully you will connect with some of the things I talk about.

But definitely – most definitely – you will need to get yourself a tissue.

This is my story. The elements of my story that directly relate to me are pure fact. The elements of my story that relate to other members of my family are based on fact and are my closest interpretation of those facts.

I'm by no means an expert on Huntington's disease, on yoga philosophy, on cellular healing or indeed on some of the other subjects I talk about in this book.

The only thing I'm an expert on is me. And even that is debatable, as I'm learning more and more about myself and my life all of the time.

I only know what I think I know about my life. I have seen my life only through my eyes. They are not the same eyes that the other members of my family saw my life through and so each version of the truth is still the truth, but from a different perspective.

I'm just telling you how it was and is for me, and my interpretation of my world.

You could say that, just like Eat, Pray, Love, my story has three parts to it. Part 1 is about my early life – how I grew up with a 50 per cent risk of developing a devastating and debilitating terminal illness, and the effect that the hereditary illness had on my family and my life.

The second part of my story is about my healing path. It's about how, on the verge of a breakdown, I realised that I was probably not going to develop Huntington's disease and that I had to find a way to live my life with joy instead of sadness. This realisation took me on an amazing journey of self-discovery, not only on an emotional level, but also physically to India, China and Africa. Some of the names of the people in this book have been changed with respect to their identities, but they are all real.

The final part of my journey is about my life now and about how we can all choose to live with a positive attitude and reconnect with the joy that is within us all.

Chapter 1

Hummingbird

All journeys have secret destinations of which the traveler is unaware – Martin Buber

In November 1999, I went on holiday to Costa Rica. When I left for my holiday that year I had no idea that a little baby hummingbird would turn my life around so unexpectedly and so profoundly.

I was 37 years old and I was struggling with the sadness in my life. The holiday was to be an amazing adventure for me.

My tour guide, Larry, had rescued a baby hummingbird that he'd found in the forest. He was looking after the tiny bird – which he'd named Confucius – and he was feeding it with a syringe. Everyone on the coach tour fussed over Confucius; he was so cute!

Two days into the tour, something significant happened. Confucius became sick and started to have a fit.

"It's cruel to let him suffer like this," Larry told us. "I have to put him out of his misery."

As I sat next to Larry on the coach and watched as he squeezed the air from the tiny lungs of the little hummingbird, my own deep feelings started to emerge from the core of my being.

Thoughts of my brother's suffering came tumbling to the foreground, accompanied by a wash of emotion for all the suffering that myself and my family had endured over the past 30 years.

My dear brother wanted to end his own life and the death of Confucius was too much for me to bear.

The sadness of my life came pouring out, overflowing with no control and no restraint, and I wondered if it would ever end. I had no idea then that it was to be a significant turning point in my life and that, when the tempest eventually died down, I would be left with a rainbow of love and joy – brighter and better than I'd ever seen before.

Larry didn't give his actions a second thought. When he realised that the hummingbird was suffering and was going to die, he compassionately ended its suffering.

I silently sobbed. I wished that my brother Nigel could be allowed to die. I wished that his loved ones could be there with him, holding his hand when he went.

Chapter 2

When I was a little girl and life was 'normal'

"How much longer are you going to be in there?" I called through the bathroom door as I crossed my legs and willed my eldest brother to hurry up and finish his daily cleansing routine. Being one of seven people living in a house with one bathroom had its difficulties at times, as you can imagine. Oh sure, we had another toilet, but it was outside in the cold and, as a little girl, I was always worried about the spiders out there. What if one dropped on my head whilst I was peeing or worse still… Oh, I didn't want to think about it.

'Hurry up, pleeeeeaaassssse, I'm gonna pee my pants!' I sighed with relief as I heard the lock slide back and looked over my shoulder to make sure that no-one would slip in before me, around me, under me or perhaps even through me!

The three-bedroom, semi-detached council house in Chepstow Avenue, Hornchurch was a busy place in those days and I learned to be quick off the mark.

Chepstow Avenue sat happily between Plumpton Avenue on the right and Goodwood Avenue on the left, depending on which way you were facing. A little further afield were Kempton Avenue, Newmarket Way and Ascot Gardens. It was no wonder that the estate was known as the racecourse estate.

The parallel roads were cut in half by a central drive – appropriately named Central Drive – which had roundabouts at each junction separating the two halves of the roads. The roads either side of ours were rather long. Our road, however, was quite short due to the primary school that was situated at the bottom of it - a great convenience for me and my siblings as we had only a few minutes' walk to the classroom each day.

Entering the house through the front door, we'd see a narrow hallway with linoleum flooring leading to a small kitchen. Immediately to our left was a door leading to the lounge (we called that the front room) and then another door after that leading to the dining room which looked out onto the garden. On the right of the hallway was the staircase leading to the three bedrooms.

At the front of the house upstairs, my parents had a double bedroom and my sister and I had bunk beds in the little box room. My three brothers shared the third room at the back, next to the bathroom, but it wasn't an ideal situation. Like my sister, my eldest brother Stephen was a sensible and mature person and the two younger lads were boisterous and noisy. They couldn't have been more different to their elder sibling.

Mum got up early every morning to light the coal fire in the kitchen that heated the water for everyone to wash with. On chilly winter mornings, she would light the fire in the lounge and, when it had warmed the room a little, I would jump out of bed, grab my clothes and dash downstairs as quickly as I could to dress in the warmth of its glow.

I was the fifth and final child born to my parents in 1962.

Mum was just 18 when her first baby arrived. To everyone's surprise, he came out rather quickly.

With a nurse on either side she was escorted to the labour ward.

"The baby's coming," she told the nurses as they walked her down the corridor.

"You'll be okay, Mrs Goodman," they assured her. "You have plenty of time to go yet."

"I'm going to have the baby," she insisted with some urgency… and then out he came, right there and then, in the hospital corridor.

"I did tell them," she recalled later on as she cradled her firstborn gently in her arms.

Seven years my senior, Stephen and I didn't have too much to do with each other when we were young; he was much more sensible than I ever was and he seemed so much older than me.

The second child to join the family was Nigel. Born almost six years before me, he was full of fun. I liked my brother Nigel. I liked him a lot.

The third son and middle child was Philip. Mum tells me that Philip used to be a happy young lad. "He was always smiling when he was little," she recalls.

My mum was eager to have a daughter and so, with three boys already in tow, she decided to keep on trying. To her delight, just over a year later, my sister was born.

"Why do you think mum had five children?" I had asked my Auntie Jill one day, as I sat on her bed at the hospital. Five children had always seemed

Hummingbird

a bit excessive to me.

Jill was my mum's younger sister and she was undergoing treatment for breast cancer.

"Well, Deborah," she told me. "Your mum had a fibroid that was misdiagnosed as a pregnancy, so she stopped taking precautions because she thought she was already pregnant and that's when you were conceived."

"Oh, I see!" I laughed. I thought it was quite amusing, and was thankful that mum had developed a fibroid. If it wasn't for that fibroid, I wouldn't be here now, and you wouldn't be reading my story. Thank you fibroid, oh thank you!

Sadly, that was one of the last conversations I had with my Auntie Jill as she passed away shortly afterwards. She was only 50 years old.

From the information my Auntie Jill gave me, I realised that I wasn't exactly planned, but I certainly never felt unwanted in any way. My mum just got on with the job of looking after her five children, the same as she would have with just four.

I was born at home in the middle of the night. Well, maybe not *exactly* in the middle of the night (Mum can't remember the exact time) but it was definitely night-time, much to Stephen's displeasure.

"Wake up, boys!" Dad was excited that the fifth baby had been born. "It's a girl! You have another sister - come and see her."

Stephen reluctantly opened his eyes. "Oh, no," he groaned, just wanting to sleep and definitely not wanting to get up out of bed for yet *another* baby. "Do I really have to?"

My arrival completed the family and Stephen was thankful that I was the last of the babies.

In the early days we had a fairly normal life, I guess, with the usual scraps and family issues.

My dad worked hard as a mechanical engineer to keep the money coming in and, as well as having a part time job, mum worked tirelessly to keep her house and children in good order. We always had a freshly cooked meal on the table and we always ate it all up.

"Oi, get off!" someone at the dinner table would inevitably shout, as my hand would reach across to the plate of an unsuspecting sibling the minute their back was turned. If there was something for dinner that I particularly liked, I was often after some more. As we all sat down around the table my siblings would argue over who was going to sit next to me.

My sister was 15 months my senior and by nature the more sensible one of the two of us. I was tall for my age; I was as tall as my sister. Maybe it was all that extra food I was getting. To save money, mum used to make our dresses and sometimes clothe her daughters in identical frocks.

"Are you twins?" we were often asked and we'd giggle. Sometimes, for my amusement, I'd lie and say yes.

In the school holidays, my parents would take us on the train for daytrips to the seaside and, on a few occasions, we spent a whole week away in a chalet or a beach house. Mum and dad must have saved extremely hard to take us all on holiday.

I have vague recollections of summer days when dad would take us blackberry picking on our bikes, and mum would sometimes take us to the Leys open air swimming pool in Dagenham where we'd swim and sunbathe on the grass.

I remember that dad had a motorbike with a sidecar and we'd take it in turns to go out for a ride with him around the country lanes of Hornchurch and Upminster. Philip and Stephen both had tandems and I used to enjoy riding on the back of the two-seater bikes, allowing my brothers to do all the hard work!

As far as I can recall, up until 1969, all seemed pretty normal in Deborah-world.

Chapter 3

A shocking diagnosis

When I was seven years old, things started to change. Dad became absent-minded and clumsy and his personality began to alter. He'd light a cigarette and leave it burning in the ashtray, forgetting that he had been smoking it. He'd leave the tap running, forgetting that he was planning to have a bath or wash the dishes. He would put the kettle on to make a cup of tea and then totally forget to make it. My parents began to argue frequently and I started to feel a lot of tension in the house.

There came a point where my mum didn't recognise her husband anymore as the kind and caring man who doted on his family and helped her to manage them on a daily basis. She knew something was wrong with my dad, but he wouldn't talk to her about it. He insisted that he was fine.

Mum became increasingly frustrated with the situation. Dad started to lose one job after another and he was forgetful with his money. Financially they lived from week to week and on each payday mum put aside the money for the rent and the bills. She would then spend the rest on food and try to keep a little bit back each week for emergencies, clothes and treats.

One day, dad arrived home without his pay packet. He'd worked for five long days and had absolutely nothing to show for it. His whole week's wages were missing.

"Well, you must know what you've done with it, it can't have just disappeared," said my mum, unable to believe that there would be no money for us that week.

"I had it when I left work," said my dad, clearly confused. "I don't know what's happened to it."

"How am I supposed to feed us all?" Mum screamed at my dad. "What are we supposed to live on, fresh air? This is getting ridiculous, I don't know how much more of this I can take."

Calming her voice a bit, she looked him in the eye. "I think there's something wrong. You're not yourself anymore. You've become clumsy and forgetful. It's not like you to be like this. What's happened to you? Please come and see the doctor with me. He'll be able to help you. Help us.

We can find out what the problem is."

"There's nothing wrong with me!" Dad yelled back. "Stop saying that there's something wrong. There isn't. I'm perfectly okay. I'm just tired of you nagging at me all the time. Just leave me alone for goodness sake!"

This wasn't like my dad. Not knowing which way to turn, my mum finally went to the family doctor on her own for advice. "There's something wrong with my husband," she told him, desperate for some help. "He's become forgetful and moody. He gets aggressive, argumentative and he's getting really clumsy. I'm finding it difficult to cope with and it's getting worse. And now he's losing his money and we haven't got anything to live on."

"Get him to come and see me," the doctor suggested.

"He won't come, Doctor, he doesn't think that there's anything wrong with him."

Putting down his pen, the doctor sat back in his chair and looked directly and boldly at my mum.

"Mrs Goodman," he said. "If your husband says there's nothing wrong with him then there's nothing wrong with him. If the marriage is breaking down, I suggest that you should go home and be a good wife."

My mother left the surgery disheartened and disgusted. She was angry that her GP didn't believe her. She knew there was something wrong, but she couldn't get the doctor to listen to her. She was finding it difficult to cope with my father and to look after the house, her job and five children without my dad's help. The arguments got worse, as did the whole situation, and the pressure was building to breaking point.

Mum was worried about her husband, but with five children to feed and clothe, the rent and bills to pay, she couldn't afford to carry on like this forever. So, about two years after things started to go wrong between my parents, my mum left my dad.

She packed our bags and took me and my sister to stay with her parents in Romford, leaving my three elder brothers at home with my father.

I liked it at my grandparents' house; it was a calm and peaceful place to be. For a few days we didn't go to school and I felt like I was on holiday. During the day we went to play in the park over the road. We had it mostly to ourselves until school turned out and then we met other children to play with.

"We don't live here," I told the other children boastfully. "We're staying with our nan and we're not going to school!" It was exciting, not going to school. The other kids were envious and I liked that, it made me feel a bit special.

Then mum spoilt our fun. "The school is kindly sending a car for you tomorrow, so I'll get you up early and make sure you're both ready on time. It'll take about 20 minutes to get there."

The other children at school wanted to know why we were travelling in a car each day, but I didn't tell them that I was not living at home. I liked having a secret, even though I was a bit sad that I wasn't at home.

After five weeks at my nan's house, we packed up and returned home to find that my dad was no longer there. He'd agreed to move into a men's hostel so that mum could bring me and my sister back home. Dad was really sorry to leave us all, but his first priority was his children. He wanted to be sure that we were all together and that we would be looked after properly.

The woman who ran the hostel was a kind and compassionate lady. She contacted my mum and confirmed her fears. It was obvious to her that there was definitely something medically wrong with my dad.

"He's registered with a local doctor here," she told my mum. "Would you like me to make an appointment for you both to go and see him?"

"Yes, please, I'd really appreciate that." Mum thanked the lady and when the appointment was made and confirmed, she took my father to see the GP.

My mum explained things to the doctor as dad sat beside her. "He keeps saying that things will get better," mum said. "But nothing gets better, Doctor, it just gets worse."

The doctor listened attentively and was extremely helpful. He asked my father if he would be prepared to go into a psychiatric hospital for a rest and an assessment. My father agreed.

The mention of the psychiatric hospital reminded my mum of what her husband had told her when they'd first met - 18 years ago - when she was just 15 years old.

"My dad died in Warley Hospital," he had said.

Warley Hospital was a long-stay psychiatric hospital in Essex.

Mum cast her mind back. She remembered that she had been intrigued at the time and had asked dad's eldest brother what their father had died of.

"He had a nervous breakdown due to the war," she was told and she had no reason to doubt or question it all those years ago.

When my father was initially admitted to the psychiatric hospital his condition was undiagnosed and he was having treatment that wasn't correct or appropriate for him. He was taking the wrong medication and was even given electric shock treatment.

Mum told the doctor at the hospital that my dad's father had died in Warley Hospital and the doctor obtained my grandfather's medical records. The documents recorded that my Grandfather had suffered from Huntington's chorea, an incurable and hereditary illness.

The doctor informed my mum that because of the hereditary nature of the illness, it was likely that my father was suffering from symptoms of the same disease.

"Well, why didn't anyone tell the family?" my bewildered mother asked the doctor.

With a compassionate sigh, the doctor looked at my mum. "I saw the records," he told her. "It was written on them that the family was not to be told."

My mother's jaw dropped. She felt as though any hope she had left for her husband was being sucked out of her. *Family not to be told.* If she hadn't have been such a lady, she probably would have sworn.

"We've been through so much lately," she told the doctor, clearly angry and upset. "It's been a living nightmare: the arguments, the break-up, the upset. My poor husband. I feel so bad; I didn't know. If we'd have known what was wrong, I could've done something sooner. I can't believe they'd be so stupid. Didn't they realise how wrong that was to keep it from the family?"

"I'm going to send you to see a neurologist," the doctor told her calmly. "Now that we know what the problem is, he will explain everything to you."

Mum left the hospital with her mind going over and over, eager to see the neurologist and discover more about Huntington's chorea.

Still reeling from the information she'd been given, she confided in her eldest son, Stephen, who was eager to find out more about Huntington's chorea. In those days, we didn't have computers. Computers, smart phones, Google, laptops - he had none of the modern-day information technology we take for granted to help him with his research. It's hard to believe it now, but we didn't even have a telephone in the house back then.

Luckily, Stephen had studied first aid and he kept a copy of *Bailliere's Nurses' Dictionary* at home. The first thing he did when he found out about dad's illness was to go straight to his room and look up the condition. Taking the medical dictionary off the shelf, he hurriedly thumbed through the pages to find the entry he was looking for. Staring at the words in disbelief, he sat back on his bed, trying to get his brain to make sense of what he was reading.

The dictionary informed him that the hereditary factor of the disease meant that he was also at risk of the illness – and so were all his brothers and sisters.

Chapter 4

The ticking timebomb

"Could I have your urine sample please, Mrs Goodman?" the assistant asked my mum when she arrived at the neurologist's office.

"I haven't come about me, it's about my husband," she informed the assistant.

"The doctor needs to have your urine sample," the lady urged, clearly not listening to what my mother was saying. "Everyone has to give a urine sample before they're seen by the doctor."

"It's a bit pointless, really," mum said, still trying to explain.

"If you haven't got one," the insistent woman continued following her usual routine, "I need you to take this bottle into the toilet for me." She held out a sample bottle for mum to pee into.

Eventually, after persuading the assistant that she actually didn't need to give a urine sample to enable her to discuss her husband's condition with the neurologist, my mum was shown into a room to see the doctor.

"Please have a seat, Mrs Goodman," the doctor said as she entered his office.

Mum sat down in the clinical room. Feeling anxious and upset, but eager to know more about the illness, she prepared herself for the worst, not knowing how bad the worst would actually be.

"I want to tell you as much about Huntington's chorea as is currently known, so that you fully understand the implications of this illness. Is that okay, Mrs Goodman?"

She looked at his kind face. "Yes. Of course. I want to know as much as possible, please. Anything that you can tell me will be really helpful, thank you."

The neurologist continued.

"It is a condition of the central nervous system that affects the part of the brain that controls our movements," he said. "Someone with HC may look as though they're drunk, as their gait is affected and they typically have uncontrollable jerky movements, which is where the name *chorea* comes from. It's derived from the Greek word for dance.

"It causes the eventual loss of speech, the ability to swallow and leads to double incontinence. Understandably, a sufferer often becomes depressed and moody. They usually get increasingly thinner and frail due to the continuous movements and the enormous effort it takes to eat. And they can sometimes experience dementia."

The specialist paused for a moment to give my mum a chance to digest this information. He could see that her head was nodding slightly as he spoke and her facial expression showed her level of concentration as she listened intently, engrossed in his words.

"I have to tell you, Mrs Goodman," he continued, "that it's highly likely that this is what is wrong with your husband. In fact, I would say that it's almost certainly the case."

Mum's head was still nodding, showing that she understood, but she listened quietly until he had finished speaking.

"Unfortunately, your husband has inherited it from his father. We don't know what causes Huntington's chorea yet and there is no cure for it."

Her head stopped still and my mum finally broke her silence.

"Oh, I see. How long do you think he's got, Doctor?"

"The disease duration is typically about 15 to 20 years. Huntington's chorea is passed down in the genes from parent to child. I'm sorry to say that every child of an affected parent has a 50 per cent chance of developing the disease later in life, usually in mid-life, but sometimes earlier and, in some cases, when they're older. In a way, it's quite straightforward. Either a person has inherited the gene or they haven't, which means that they will either get the disease or they won't."

Mum sat still for a moment, allowing all this to sink in. Then, leaning forward a little, she spoke in a clear and calm voice. "So, let me get this clear in my mind. What you're saying to me is that, not only has my husband got it, but that all my children have a fifty-fifty chance of getting it, too? Is that what you're saying to me? They're all at risk? 50 per cent? *All* five of them?"

"Yes, Mrs Goodman, I'm afraid that any or even all of your children could have inherited the gene from your husband. I'm so sorry to have to tell you this."

"Isn't there a test they could have to see if they've got it?" my mother asked.

"I'm sorry, there isn't a test available at the moment," he said. "If, or rather when, they find the gene responsible, they may be able to do a test – and hopefully find a cure – but they haven't got that far with their research yet."

"Can it skip a generation?" she asked, clutching at straws and hoping that the answer would be a positive yes.

"No. I'm sorry, it doesn't seem to skip a generation. As far as we know, a person cannot be a carrier of the gene without the disease developing."

It was devastating news.

The only bit of good news that mum was given that day was that an association had recently formed to help people with Huntington's chorea and their families. The neurologist gave mum the phone number of the group.

Mum left the building, found a phone box and rang my dad's brother Harry to tell him the bad news. He was also at risk and, if it turned out that he had inherited the gene, so were his three children. Mum was by now convinced that her sister-in-law was showing signs of the illness and she voiced her concerns. My uncle Harry agreed that it was likely that his sister also had the illness.

My mother had to tell my father what was wrong with him and the implications of the diagnosis. There was no easy way to do it. Understandably, he was extremely upset and was worried about how many of his children the illness would eventually affect.

After my dad had been told, my mum went to see her parents, who were growing increasingly concerned about their son-in-law and the effect his behaviour was having on their daughter and their grandchildren.

At my grandparents' house, my distraught mother sat with her head in her hands.

"I just don't know how to tell the other children," she said, as they talked about the diagnosis. "What do I say to the girls? How am I supposed to explain it all to them? And what about Nigel and Philip? How are they going to take it?"

She really couldn't imagine how she was going tell us and it dominated her thoughts for days. She needed to find the right moment and, more importantly, the right words.

My brother Nigel was the next of the children to find out about the family illness from my mum.

Hummingbird

His reply was simple and straightforward. "If it happens to me, I'll shoot myself."

Next to be told was Philip, who didn't say anything at all. "He went very quiet and wouldn't speak about it," my mum recalls.

Then there was just me and my sister left to tell. The question though was *how*?

It's funny how fate sometimes takes over and forces our hand when we just don't know how to move forward with something.

We went to see dad at the hospital; me, my sister and my mum. There was a woman at the hospital – another patient – who had befriended my father. Dad had spoken to her about his illness and how worried he was about it affecting his children.

When the woman saw that my dad had visitors, she came over to talk to us.

"How do you feel about knowing you could get this disease?" she asked, directing the question to me and my sister.

"What? What's she talking about, Mum?" I asked, with a confused look on my face.

Mum took a deep breath in. The inevitable had been forced upon her. With a slow, controlled breath out, she sighed. "Don't worry about it, Deborah. I'll talk to you when we get home and explain it all," she said.

Later that day, my mum took me and my sister into her bedroom and sat us down on the bed. I was eight years old and my sister was nine.

"You know your dad isn't well," she said, with all the strength that she could possibly draw from inside her battered, bruised and thoroughly beaten up emotional self.

Aware of her sadness, we nodded our bowed heads respectfully.

In a soft, gentle voice, she continued. "Well, the doctors have told us that he has something called Huntington's chorea. I'm afraid that they don't know how to make him better."

"Will he die?" I asked.

There was no point in lying to us. Mum swallowed hard. "Eventually, yes. But he isn't going to die just yet; you'll have a lot of time to see him still. Years even."

"Is he going to stay at the hospital?" I asked.

"Yes, he has to stay at the hospital. I'm sorry, I can't look after him here. I wish I could," she told us regretfully, "but I can't."

Mum looked at our sad little faces. With tears in her eyes she continued. "I have to tell you the truth; I need to be honest with you. The illness is passed down through the family. Your granddad had it and dad got it from him. He didn't catch it like you catch a cold; he inherited it. Like you have inherited the colour of my hair; it's in our genes. It's what makes our bodies unique to us. Special. It's what makes you part of me and part of your dad.

"But that also means that you both might get it, too. Inherit it, like your dad inherited it from his dad."

"What about the boys? Could they get it, too?" we asked her, just as worried about our brothers as we were for ourselves.

"Yes, they could do. You all have a 50 per cent chance of developing the illness later on in your lives. When you're as old as your dad is now."

She held out her arms and she hugged us tightly.

Choking back the tears, she gently whispered, "That's a long, long time away yet, so you're not to worry, okay?"

"Okay, mum. It's sad though, isn't it?" I said, feeling the pressure of her hug increasing a little.

"Yes, it's very sad," she answered. "But it's a long way away and it may never happen, so we have to enjoy our life whilst we can, yes?"

We both nodded. "Yes," we said.

And so the day came when I first learned about Huntington's chorea.

Back in my room, I laid down on the top bunk bed and thought about what my mother had told me. Staring at the tiny red roses on the wallpaper, I didn't quite know what to think or feel.

The odds didn't look good. A one-in-two chance we had either inherited the gene or we hadn't. It was pot luck, just like the toss of a coin.

Heads or tails. 50-50.

The odds were the same, however you said them.

I was only eight and I couldn't even imagine being as old as my dad. It was so far ahead of me that it seemed like another existence entirely, so I put the information as far back in my mind as I could manage to put it. I went downstairs, ate my supper and carried on as usual.

Chapter 5

A difficult time

Mum continued to work and look after her family. Her father helped her out financially and supported her in any other way he could

In her spare time, mum tried to find out as much about the disease as she could. She rang the Huntington's Chorea Association and arranged to go to one of their meetings.

She went to her first meeting by herself and was amazed to see so many people there. The association had arranged for a speaker to attend and to talk about all the research that was going on into Huntington's chorea, which she found extremely interesting and helpful. It gave her some hope to know that someone, somewhere was looking for a cure.

"Maybe they'll find a cure before my children are affected," she thought to herself. "I hope so. Please, God, I hope so."

Mum was one of the earliest members of what is now known as the Huntington's Disease Association (the name of the disorder was changed from Huntington's chorea to Huntington's disease in 1990). The meetings were held in London every six months. Stephen started to accompany her whenever he could and my sister and I would go, too. But Nigel and Philip never went. I think that Nigel just accepted it and didn't need to know any more than the bare facts. He would deal with it if and when he had to, but until then, he didn't want to let it interfere with his life.

I have no idea how Philip felt about any aspect of the situation, because he never discussed it with me. If I were to guess, I'd say he probably buried his head in the sand, because he didn't know how to deal with it or how to express his feelings about it. I don't know for certain why he didn't want to go to the meetings.

Mum took us to see dad at the hospital as often as she could. My sister and I wanted to see our father, and so did Stephen, but Nigel and Philip were not so keen to visit him there. None of us liked seeing dad in a psychiatric hospital. It was extremely upsetting for me each time I went and it always left me feeling very low, but I felt it was my duty to go and I also wanted to be there for my mother. I felt so sorry for both my mum and my dad.

So, so sorry for them.

Stephen was extremely supportive. He bought my dad clothes and took him out of the hospital grounds whenever he could.

I wish I could remember things about my dad in more detail before he became ill, but so many of my memories are still hiding in the depths of my mind somewhere. It's reassuring to know from my family that he was a kind and caring man, a great dancer – maybe I get my love of dancing from him – and a loving father.

Understandably, my dad didn't cope with the illness very well. He was depressed and extremely upset.

"I just want to be with my family," he told us one day. "And I want to see the seaside again."

I'm not sure that he ever saw the seaside again after that.

It broke my heart because there was nothing I could do to make anything any better. Most of the time I didn't even know what to say to him. What *could* I possibly say to this poor, suffering man?

There were times when dad was so desperate to come home and see his family that he'd leave the hospital – sometimes in his pyjamas – and walk for nearly four miles to get to my nan's house or he'd get two buses and arrive unexpectedly on our doorstep.

We were all worried about him coming home. Dad was vulnerable travelling all that way on his unsteady legs, unsupervised. We worried that he'd come all the way home and that nobody would be there. What would he do then? He could be waiting for hours on the doorstep. And the other problem was that, once he was there, he never wanted to go back and would refuse to leave. Understandably, he just wanted to be at home with his family.

Mum got so distressed and angry with my dad when he turned up at the house. She couldn't look after him and her five children and earn enough money to keep the house and family going. The feelings of guilt were almost unbearable, but there was nothing she could do. Eventually, as the arguments got too much to bear, mum wouldn't let him into the house at all.

Whenever I heard my dad outside, I retreated to my bedroom. Pulling the net curtain aside, I would look to see what was happening in the front garden.

"I can't have you here," I heard my mum saying to my dad, with desperation in her voice. "You mustn't come here, you have to stay at the hospital where we can visit you. I'm sorry, I just can't cope with having you here anymore."

Her voice was full of anger and pain. She was overcome with sadness for her poor husband and the strain showed in her tone: "You shouldn't be travelling on your own!"

"I just want to be with my family," he'd tell her. His voice was angry and sometimes pitiful.

Mum didn't have a car or any means of getting him back to the hospital. The only way to return him was to leave her family and take two bus rides with an argumentative man who didn't want to get on the bus in the first place.

Whenever my dad turned up at the house, I would always hope that Stephen was at home, because he was good at dealing with the situation. If Stephen was there, he'd persuade my dad to go back to the hospital with him on the bus.

Living next door to us was a lovely Irish lady called Isa who had, over the years, become a great friend of my parents. Isa got on well with my dad and she would talk to him and try to make him understand that he had to go back to the hospital. Sometimes he would listen to her and sometimes he didn't want to listen to her.

Mum would knock on Isa's front door.

"He's here again," she'd say to her friend, who had been a great support to her since my dad had become ill. "Can I use your phone, please? I'm going to have to call the police."

The police were extremely helpful. Of course, my father didn't want to go back to the hospital with them and he'd resist as they tried to get him into their car. It used to break my heart as a little girl to see him struggle with them. I would will him from my bedroom window, "Dad, please get in without a fight. I don't want you to get hurt. Please, Dad, please".

One afternoon, after a normal day at school, I walked out of the safety and comfort of the classroom and into the crisp autumnal air. Feeling the cool breeze on my body and the sunshine on my face, I made my way happily towards the roundabout and prepared to cross the road for the very short walk home.

I wasn't the only child who heard the commotion but whilst others stopped to look, I was frozen to the spot by the sight ahead of me.

It was my dad. The police were trying to get him into their car and he was resisting and struggling against them.

Unable to move and not wanting my dad to see me, I watched from a distance, the nerves in my solar plexus tightening and my tummy churning over. In the background, I was aware of the voice of another kid calling attention to the disturbance.

"Look," he said excitedly. "That man's being arrested!"

The other school kids were all watching too; physically and emotionally distanced enough not to be afraid, as I was crying inside, "That's my dad! Stop it! That's my dad!"

On another occasion, when he turned up at the family home and wasn't allowed in, my dad picked up stones and broke every single downstairs window of the house out of sheer frustration. His behaviour now was so out of character. Before the illness took hold he was a gentle and non-aggressive man. As the windows shattered downstairs, I curled up on my bed upstairs, covered my ears with my hands and screamed – silently.

I can totally understand both his frustration and mum's, and maybe even then as a child I understood, but it was just so heart-breaking to witness.

The strain was getting too much for my mum. When she was out of the house, she started to worry about going home. One day, she was so stressed out about the thought of going home, that she stopped at the phone box and rang her friend next door.

"Is he there?" she asked Isa. "I can't face coming home if he's there. Is it safe to come home?"

Pulling back the net curtain, Isa looked out of the window. "No, he's not here," she said. "It's okay, you can come home."

Mum spoke to the hospital about my father's visits to the house and, in an attempt to prevent him from leaving the hospital grounds again, the hospital took away his clothes. Unfortunately, this didn't stop him and one snowy winter's day he walked out of the hospital grounds wearing nothing but a dressing gown. His feet were bare and frozen stiff and he made it half-way home before someone stopped him and asked if he was alright.

Mum was at her wits' end. She went to court in order to get dad's impromptu visits to stop and the court agreed that he should be moved to another hospital. On 23 July 1975, when I was almost a teenager, my father was moved to a psychiatric hospital in Surrey. His visits to us stopped and things at home finally got better.

Chapter 6

A family curse

The only thing we know about the future is that it will be different – Peter Ferdinand Drucker

My father was one of three children; he had one brother and one sister. I have vivid memories of my dad's sister Babs when she was a healthy young woman and, if she was still alive now, I just know that we would be the greatest of friends. A dancer and a teacher of modern ballet, I remember my aunty Babs as an elegant lady, a woman whose world was always wonderful and beautiful. Even as she battled with the illness that robbed her of her own father and was destroying her brother, she was still full of grace and love for everyone and everything. I've never in my life known anyone with such a joy in their heart under such terrible circumstances as she did. As far as I am aware, the illness didn't give her aggressive outbursts like it does with many people and amazingly she never seemed depressed at all.

My dad and his sister were now living in the same psychiatric hospital, which pleased me, because it meant that I could visit both of them together – one visit instead of two.

My auntie Babs was always so delighted to see us when we visited her at the hospital and it was guaranteed that she would always have a smile on her face. She took great pleasure in showing us that she could still do the splits, until eventually she became chair and bed-bound. Even when living got extremely difficult for her in the latter stages of her illness, I could see that her eyes were still smiling and dancing, when her body could no longer manage to react to her feelings.

Aunty Babs had a young child, a son. He was only two or three years old when she went into hospital and was unable to look after him anymore. Thankfully, my young cousin was adopted by our uncle Harry. Uncle Harry was the one lucky sibling in Dad's family not to inherit the faulty gene that causes Huntington's disease.

And so it came to be that my aunt's only son was brought up in my uncle's family, where his cousins became his new siblings and he became their brother. Of course, by then, the whole family understood the implications of the genetic illness, but although he now had a brother and two sisters to share his life with, he was alone in the fact that he was the only child in that immediate family to be at risk of the illness and of potentially inheriting the family curse.

In a way, I was lucky to be able to share my burden and my risk with four siblings. I was never alone in my nightmare and I was extremely thankful for that.

Chapter 7

The black cloud of doubt

My younger years took me on a thunderous roller-coaster ride of emotions. I was equally as troubled and terrified in my life as I was fun-loving and extrovert.

Everyone in the family was trying to cope in their own way with the effects of the illness. To the outside world it looked as though I was coping as best I could but underneath I wasn't actually doing very well. Each visit to the hospital brought my fear to the surface as I was reminded of my potential fate. The feeling I tried to push as far down into my boots as I possibly could, bubbled up to the forefront of my being and brought with it an ocean of sadness and tears.

That sadness became a part of my natural state and stayed with me for many, many years, underlying everything I felt and constantly interrupting my otherwise playful life.

Whenever I tripped, or dropped something, I worried that this could be the start of it. Any slight clumsy movement would trigger an instant panic within me – was this a normal gesture or was it a sign of the onset of HD?

My friends and my social life made me happy but when the partying stopped and I allowed my thoughts and feelings to creep back to the surface, the sadness welled up inside me again. I was sad about so many things; sad that I didn't remember much about my dad before he became unwell, sad that my lovely auntie was sick too and that they were both slowly dying and sad that I didn't have a 'normal' family like my friends had. I was sad about all the other people in the hospital, too. There were so many people with so many problems. Yes, I was sad and I was scared. I was scared about going to the hospital and I was scared when I thought about the future. I couldn't help but wonder if I would end up there myself.

I don't really know how a kid is supposed to cope in a situation like this, but somehow I got through, one year after another, with an underlying dread of the future.

I've no idea what my life would have been like if this genetic disorder wasn't in my family. I imagine that most little girls grew up wanting to be like their mothers: playing house, imagining their fairy-tale wedding and dreaming of one day having a family of their own to love and nurture.

I knew that the only way to stamp out the disease was by not having children. There was no predictive test back then and there was no cure, therefore it was considered by some people to be the only viable option.

Maybe if it wasn't for the Huntington's gene, I would have had more hobbies when I was a child or done better at school. Who knows? I know that my life would certainly have been very different, but it wouldn't help me to dwell on that now. I felt that to dream of a happy and healthy future would have just been building castles in the air. As a school kid, I accepted what I was told and each day and year came and went, without a dream of the future growing in my heart.

I continued to go to the support meetings in London with my mum and my sister, discovering more about the illness and the devastating affect it can have on complete families. I met other families with HD, but it was mostly partners of affected adults who attended the meetings. There were not many younger people there to talk to and I didn't particularly like going that much. It always brought the negative thoughts to the front of my mind.

After one of my visits to see my father, I spoke to my brother Nigel about my feelings.

"I hate seeing Dad like that," I told him. "I can't bear it, it makes me feel so miserable."

Nigel looked at my sad, young face for a while, struggling to put his own thoughts into words as I continued to talk.

"I'm scared about ending up like that myself, aren't you, Nigel? I don't think that I'd be able to cope with it. I can't even cope with the thought of it." I paused and looked at him. "Are you scared, Nigel? What would you do if you got it?"

"I'd shoot myself," my brother said, without any hesitation. "I couldn't live like that."

I wasn't shocked at all.

"No," I said, as sure as I could possibly be. "I couldn't either."

After seeing the devastating physical effect that the disease had on our father and auntie, we both knew categorically that this was not the way we wanted to live the final years of our lives. Nigel was quite adamant about it, and I didn't blame him one bit. I never got as far as deciding how I'd do it myself and I figured that I'd cross that bridge if I came to it. But Nigel knew - even back then - what he thought he would do.

Hummingbird

Despite my underlying worries and family problems, I actually had a great time growing up in Essex. I had fabulous friends, went to lots of parties, clubs and pubs and met loads of really nice people. Was it a wasted youth? I wouldn't say so. I thought that the University of Life was the best university in the world and if I only had just over 30 years of healthy living to do, why waste it on boring stuff like staying in and studying? That was for people who had a future ahead of them.

With each passing birthday, I was aware of growing ever closer to the big, black cloud looming above me, casting a shadow over the path that lead to my future and my ultimate destiny.

~ * ~

When my eldest brother, Stephen, was 22 years old, he moved out of the family home and got married.

Nigel moved out shortly after that, when he was about 20. After getting into an argument with mum about playing his music late at night, he moved into a flat with a friend and finally had his own room, where he could play his music to his heart's content. He was really into reggae music by then and he'd listen to it while he was indulging in his other passion – drawing. He was a sign-writer by trade and had an extremely steady hand. At home, he would take every opportunity he could to sit and draw. Mostly he loved drawing cartoons and he was really good at them. He would make us birthday and Christmas cards with funny cartoons on them. Nigel was a kind and caring man with a big, big heart, but the drawings on the cards he made for us usually had a violent theme to them, which I only now see was probably his way of expressing his anger. But they were always so funny and I admired his talent.

With a large bedroom all to himself now, Philip was in no hurry to leave home. He was a troubled young man who was very unsettled in his life. He used to be a panel beater - which I think he quite liked - and he also did small building jobs, but he found it difficult to hold down a job for very long.

My sister had a boyfriend and was doing well in her job at the bank.

I was enjoying life with my friends to the full, but at the same time was dreading the future. I didn't concentrate much in school and left with very few qualifications. At 16, I started my first job as an office clerical assistant, making tea and filing, that kind of thing. I used to smoke cigarettes in those days. It's almost impossible to believe it now, but back then we could smoke in the office at our desks!

One of the things I liked about my first job was that I had a good social life. The company was full of young employees and Friday lunchtimes were always spent in the pub. It's not surprising that usually the most productive thing we did on a Friday afternoon was the crossword. Oh, how times have changed.

The other thing I liked about this company was that they had a nurse in situ. My dad had been ill for more than eight years by the time I started work and by then the disease had really got its hooks into him.

It wasn't uncommon for my troubled heart to get the better of me at work. When thoughts of the illness pushed their way to the surface of my mind, I felt the sadness well up within me and I was unable to fight back the tears which, let's face it, is never a good look in the office. My thoughts evoked my feelings which then triggered a physical, tearful response.

Collecting myself as best I could, I would get up from my desk and go into my manager's office, which was a small wooden construction in the centre of the department.

"I don't feel very well," I'd tell her, not wanting her to know how upset I was or why. "Is it okay if I go and see the nurse, please?"

Whenever I went to see the nurse, she was always kind and understanding. She knew about the family illness and was very sympathetic towards me.

"I'm feeling really bad again, nurse," I'd tell her, as she greeted me. I never knew her real name, everyone just called her nurse. Embarrassed at what I thought was a weakness, I would mop my eyes with my handkerchief as I desperately tried to push down my feelings. "I've been trying not to cry, but I just can't seem to stop it once the feeling starts…"

Nurse looked after me.

"Come and sit down and take this," she would say as she handed me half of a tablet and a glass of water. After swallowing the Valium, she led me gently by the shoulder towards the bed in the room.

"Come and lay down for a while until you feel better."

The pill and a little sleep usually did the trick.

These were the times when I felt extremely low, but at other times I found life almost unbearable. I just couldn't cope with all the negative thoughts going around in my mind and it scared me.

"It would be better if I wasn't here at all," I'd think to myself in my darkest moments. "If I was dead, then I wouldn't have to cope with any of this anymore."

I never thought beyond that. I never thought about what I'd actually do, but I sometimes wished that I could just cease to exist. One day, realising that I needed help, I went to the doctors. It took a lot of courage for me to enter the doctor's surgery that day. I was feeling vulnerable and scared as I walked up to the reception and asked to see the doctor.

"Why do you want to see the doctor?" the receptionist asked, abruptly and coldly. "What's wrong?"

The energy I felt from this lady was not loving and compassionate like the nurse at work, but stern and bullish. It took me by surprise.

I found it difficult to speak.

"I'm feeling really down," I told her. "I'm not coping very well."

"Well, the doctor's not just going to give you pills, if that's what you think," she informed me harshly, knowing nothing at all about my situation or indeed what I really did think.

Her words felt like a slap in the face and I didn't have the strength to deal with her attitude, I could barely hold myself together as it was. Feeling rejected, I turned on my heels, walked out and I didn't go back.

Thankfully, I didn't do anything stupid afterwards, but it angers me that some people just don't seem to care. Maybe people who work in the so-called caring professions dealing with vulnerable and sick people, should be vetted for their level of genuine care or at least trained to learn how to deal with people with love and compassion. Some people just don't seem to understand that sick people just get sicker if they're not treated with kindness.

Chapter 8

The cycle of life

I was 17 years old when my father died. I remember it well, as it was a very challenging weekend for me. A few days before the phone call which told us that my father had passed away, I'd gone into hospital and had a termination of an accidental pregnancy. I didn't agonise over my decision, I just knew that it was what I had to do. I knew that I could pass on the faulty HD gene – if I had it – and I didn't want to be responsible for that. I was a few months into the pregnancy when I finally managed to get the courage to go to the doctors and, reminding the GP that I had Huntington's disease in my family, I was booked in for the operation without question.

I was young and I was scared. I remember waking up after the operation, bursting into tears and feeling devastated that I'd aborted the only child I knew that I would ever conceive. I felt alone, but relieved in a way that the worry of the past few months was over. I went home the following day feeling fragile from the physical and emotional effects of the whole experience. I made up a story to tell my mum so that she never knew about the pregnancy or the termination. I kept it to myself, my secret baby.

Two days later, on the 22 July 1979, I was woken up by the sound of the telephone ringing. We had finally had one installed after the connection charge was paid for by a charity. Mum was out of her bed quickly and I followed her down the stairs. She picked up the receiver and I stood beside her as she spoke on the phone.

"Hello," she said, wondering who could be phoning at three o'clock in the morning.

"Is that Mrs Goodman?" the voice on the other end of the line enquired.

"Yes."

"Mrs Goodman, it's Doctor Hughes at Brookwood Hospital. I'm sorry to wake you up, I have some bad news for you, I'm afraid."

"What's wrong?" she asked, wondering what might be so urgent that it couldn't wait until the morning.

Hummingbird

"It's your husband," Dr Hughes said. "He had a heart attack. I'm sorry to have to tell you, but he's passed away... I'm sorry."

"Oh."

It took a moment for the shock to wear off a bit and the information to sink in. I stood patiently beside my mum, wondering what was wrong.

"I need to ask you a question, Mrs Goodman," the doctor continued. "We would like to have your permission to take a sample of his brain for medical research, if that's okay?"

"Yes, that's okay," mum agreed. She didn't want to stand in the way of anything that might give hope to her children and others at risk of the terrible illness.

"Thank you, we appreciate that. Sorry to wake you up with this news, Mrs Goodman. I'll make sure that somebody calls you tomorrow morning."

"That's okay," said mum. "Thank you for letting me know."

She placed the receiver back down on the cradle. With watery eyes, she relayed the news to me. Four years after being admitted to Brookwood Hospital in Surrey, my father had died of a heart attack. Thankfully, he never suffered the final ravages of the disease and was still able to walk and talk (with difficulty) before he died.

The heart attack was probably due to a combination of things: medication, electric shock treatment and the stress of being separated from his family. The effects of the disease had finally taken my father's life, as it had taken his father's life before him.

I felt the sorrow of his passing and at the same time was relieved that it was over. I was pleased that there would be no more suffering for him and I was glad that I wouldn't have to witness his distress any more.

The arrangements were made and my father's body was cremated in Surrey. I'm sad to say that I barely remember that day.

Three months after my dad passed away, my sister fell pregnant.

I was totally confused when my mum announced that my sister was having a baby. I had a lot of questions going around in my head that, for some reason, I didn't voice. I don't really know why. All I know is that I didn't speak about how I felt at the time.

The news of my sister's pregnancy triggered many questions in my mind. Surely we weren't supposed to have babies, were we? Had I got it wrong all these years? Did we have a choice after all? Wasn't it the only way to stamp out the disease?

That's what they'd told me and that's what I'd believed. I never knew I had a choice. I didn't even think to question it, I'd just accepted it as a fact. I'd grown up believing that I'd never be a mum and it was so ingrained into me by then, that I couldn't imagine it any other way.

Not having children had seemed the right thing to do. It had been easier to accept when I'd thought about the possibility that my children could grow up as I had, under the HD cloud of uncertainty – the 50/50 chance of watching their own mother suffering as I had watched my own father suffer. My children may have the same sadness in their lives that I had in mine. No, it was best not to have children. I had agreed to it wholeheartedly.

I thought that we had all felt the same but I didn't discuss it with my sister. We were not close siblings and she didn't tell me that she was pregnant.

When she was 18 years old, my sister gave birth to a beautiful baby girl. Her boyfriend moved in with us and they had a temporary bedroom downstairs in the dining room until they moved into their own home.

Then, six years after my father died, my auntie Babs passed away. At 50 years old, the disease had really taken control of her body and she was completely bedbound. Unable to move, speak or do anything for herself, she had suffered the full ravages of the illness to the bitter end.

Chapter 9

Love hurts

I stayed working with my first company for seven years and was given the job of accounts assistant. It's strange remembering back to those days when we were manually inputting figures into huge ledgers and using calculators to find the missing pennies or pounds in order to balance the books. The typists used manual typewriters and no-one in the company had a personal computer.

I had started to have a few boyfriends by the time I was 15 and they were all lovely guys, but I got bored easily and the relationships never lasted longer than about six to eight months. Then, at 18 years old, I fell in love. It was a nice secure feeling and I had a wonderful couple of years with my boyfriend. I was open and honest about Huntington's disease and the 50 per cent possibility of developing it myself, but it never seemed to matter to him and we had a normal relationship. We never talked about the future and I took it for granted that we'd stay together. Why wouldn't we? We had a really enjoyable time and I was happy being with him.

My boyfriend's mum never really liked me (and I never really like her, either). She certainly didn't like the fact that I wasn't going to have any children. Not being able to accept the possibility that her beloved son wouldn't have kids, she jumped on any opportunity to mention her future grandchildren. To her mind, it was the given truth that we'd break up and he would marry someone else and have a family. She was tactless and hurtful, but I took no notice of her because I was in love with her son. And he was in love with me.

On weeknights, we'd go out together for the evening and he'd drop me at my home before going home to his parents' house. Every weekend he stayed with me at my mum's house and, for a couple of years, things between us were great. Then, one Saturday evening, something changed.

We were relaxing on the sofa after a night out, having a kiss and a cuddle.

"Let's go to bed," I suggested, getting up from the couch.

Jack hesitated.

"I'm going home tonight," he said, not being able to look me in the eye.

"What?" I wasn't expecting it. "Why are you going home?" I asked, worried and confused.

He never went home at the weekend, he always stayed with me.

"I just want to go home tonight. I'll call you tomorrow."

What kind of explanation was that?

"What's up?" I asked him, feeling the panic rising inside of me. I didn't understand why he was going. He hadn't said anything about going home that evening.

"I just need to go home."

"Please tell me what's up," I begged. "You have to tell me, I have to know. You can't just say that you need to go home. Tell me, PLEASE! What's wrong?"

And then the bombshell came.

"Debs, I want to have a family. I couldn't cope if you became sick with HD. I'm sorry, I need to go home."

"Oh… I see," I said.

And I did see. I understood exactly what Jack was saying. I could feel myself getting angry, but at the same time I tried not to allow the anger to surface because, in a way, I couldn't blame him.

"Well, there's no point in you calling me tomorrow, is there? We may as well break up here and now."

I was a hard-nosed, stubborn girl back then.

"We don't have to break up," Jack suggested. "We could still see each other… I still want to see you, Deb."

I didn't understand his thinking.

"What's the point?" I argued. "If you don't want to be with me and you want a family, then we have to break up. What's the point of seeing each other still?"

My barriers were well and truly up. God, I was so upset and hurting like hell. I wanted to punch him, to hold onto him and to push him away all at the same time. Then, suddenly I lost control and I allowed myself to cry and my crying turned into sobs – deep, hard convulsive sobs that wrenched through my body, making me gasp for my breath.

Jack tried to comfort me.

Hummingbird

"Get off of me!" I pulled away and turned my back on him. "Just leave me alone… please, just go home now."

He did as I asked and left.

I was absolutely devastated, but I understood his reasons. I'm sure his mother was putting pressure on him, but I don't know that for a fact. Completely heartbroken, I took myself to bed and stayed there for a week. I cried my heart out as I tried to come to terms with what this meant. I couldn't blame him. HD is a cruel disease and if I had been in his shoes – and I knew what I knew – I'd have run from it myself. I remember thinking at the time that there was no way I would have taken on anyone at risk of this destructive illness myself. And it was in this way that I justified my boyfriend breaking my heart.

Ouch, that really hurt!

Chapter 10

Doctors don't know everything

Being the fun-loving, social butterfly that I was, I picked myself up, dusted myself off and started to have fun again. Bearing and burying the emotional scar, I went out with other boys and got back into the business of living.

I was seeing my local GP every so often for a repeat prescription of my contraception pill. My GP was an Indian man. I only mention this because I was so shocked at what he said to me one day, that I can only imagine it was because of his culture that he said it.

"Isn't it about time you started a family?"

"What?" I said, bewildered.

"You should be starting a family now," he told me.

"No!" I said surprised and shocked that he had even suggested it. I didn't think that it was his place to tell me what to do – HD or no HD! But to save an argument I just reminded him that I had Huntington's disease in my family.

"That only affects men," he told me, very matter-of-factly.

"No, it doesn't," I answered back. "It affects both men and women alike."

"No, no, no," he continued, adamantly. "It's just the men that have it."

Back in those days I was much more vulnerable than I am now and I hated any form of confrontation. I felt extremely uneasy in the doctor's office, but I knew absolutely that he was wrong. I knew just about everything that was known about the disease at that time.

"My aunty had it," I told him.

"Oh," he said, writing out my prescription. I was totally stunned at his casualness and indifference to the fact that he had given me the wrong information.

I left the surgery feeling extremely upset. People trust their doctors. They think that the doctor, being a health professional, will give them the correct information about their health. What if I hadn't known the facts? What if I had believed the doctor and gone ahead and had children, then

36

developed HD? The episode left me feeling many things — disappointed, angry, upset and hoping that he wouldn't ruin anyone's life with his false information.

I'm guessing that he probably never gave the incident a second thought.

Chapter 11

A happy reprieve

My mum started to create a social life for herself. After spending so many years looking after her children, the house and working hard to keep everything going, she finally started to do something for herself. Getting an extra evening job at The Robert Beard youth club in Hornchurch (yes, it was still work, but in a more sociable way), she started to make new friends and get out and about. Mum began to enjoy her life again.

A vacancy came up at the club for someone to work in the snack bar and I took the job. I worked two evenings a week and I really enjoyed it there. I signed up for a youth workers course and it was on this course that I made a new and dear friend called Steve. After a while I obtained my part-time youth workers qualification and I joined my mum and her colleagues in the sometimes challenging but rewarding role of part-time youth worker.

Working alongside my mum helped us to become closer and form a new and different kind of friendship. While at the club I called her by her first name. It would have been weird and wrong to call her Mum in front of the youngsters. Some of them weren't that much younger than me. Most of the members of the Robert Beard didn't know that she was my mum. Not unless I told them.

Some of mum's new friends became my new friends and I made other new friends as well. We all went to the pub together after the club closed and we had a lot of fun – Mum with her tonic water and the rest of us with a proper drink!

Mum went on walking holidays and weekends away with her new friends and at last she had a social life again.

I was getting fed up with my day job and after seven years at my first company, I left. Without another job to go to, I helped out in my new friend Steve's shoe shop for a while. I enjoyed working in the shop with him and one evening a week I went to night school to learn how to type. My typing qualification enabled me to apply for a job as a copy typist and aged 25 I started work with my second employer, British Telecommunications plc.

Being a copy typist was the best job I could have had at that time. I loved it. I adored it. I did flexi-time so that I could lie in if I was tired and I went home early if the mood took me. I worked late some days to build up my hours. We had proper tea breaks and I worked mostly with young women like myself. I found the work quite therapeutic. No stress, no worries. It was a real dream job as far as I was concerned.

Now that my dad and auntie were no longer suffering, it was easier to put the illness to the back of my mind. For a while. Without the visits to the hospital, the continuous reminder was absent and I was able to enjoy my twenties without too many problems.

Chapter 12

A different kind of grief

At 25, I also began dating Alan. Alan was one of Philip's friends. They were the best of buddies and they had a lot in common. They liked the same music and were both interested in astrology.

Alan was four years younger than me, but I didn't mind that. I really liked him and we got on well.

He was a bit of a punk rocker and a free spirit. He played the guitar and was in a band called The Sticklebacks. I'd always lived with my mum and thought that Alan was adventurous when he told me that he'd left home once and lived in digs in London. His parents had been really worried about him when he left home, because they didn't always know where their teenage son was living.

When he returned from London and went back to his parents' house, he promised that he'd never leave them again without talking to them first.

After we'd been together for about six months, Alan broke up with me, saying that he wanted to concentrate on his music. He'd been accepted for a place at college, where he could study music properly and being with me was a 'distraction'. He wanted to spend all of his time playing guitar and therefore didn't want to be tied down in a relationship.

He surprised his parents by telling them that he wanted to live at home when he started college and drive into London every day. After their previous experience of him moving out and living in digs and not knowing where he was, they joked with him and told him that he *had* to leave home – that's what students did!

I really liked Alan and I didn't want to break up with him, but the stubborn girl in me put up her barriers again and simply accepted his decision. I didn't have the maturity or the know-how back then to work it all out. Alan was still a regular visitor to our home – he came to see Philip - and thankfully we remained good friends.

I remember seeing the article in the local paper. A young lad of 21 had been killed in a car crash. The article had a picture of the mangled wreck of the car and I remember wondering if the un-named boy had been anyone I might've known. It went through my mind that maybe it could have been someone I knew from the youth club. The lad's name hadn't been released as his mum was in hospital having just had a major operation.

~ * ~

Lying in a hospital bed, recovering from her operation, was Alan's mum, Eileen. Her stomach muscles had been cut and she couldn't turn over without assistance. Her heavily-sedated body had several drips attached to it.

After a few hazy days, she woke up feeling extraordinarily well.

When her mum and uncle came in that afternoon they remarked on the difference in her and when her husband and eldest son came to visit that evening, they were astonished to see her looking and feeling so well. They presumed that she had been taken off of the drugs that sedated her, but she was still being given them.

Eileen felt so well that, for the first time since the operation, she was helped out of bed and into a chair and when her visitors finally left, she even walked with them to the lift, drips hooked up onto a trolley, to bid them farewell.

When the surgeon came in to see her that evening, he was delighted with her progress, but was concerned that she was overdoing it. He prescribed her two sleeping tablets, telling her not to worry if she didn't wake up until late the next morning. Eileen understood what he was saying – the drugs were quite powerful and were expected to knock her out for many hours. Her body needed the rest. She took the tablets and fell asleep, unaware that her life was about to change forever.

That night – on Thursday 9 July 1987 – Alan was driving home from a night out. He lost control of his car and was killed. When the police arrived, there was no other car at the scene.

At exactly the same moment, Alan's mum Eileen woke up feeling very agitated, despite having taken the strong sleeping pills. Unaware of how she'd got herself out of bed, she found herself staring out of the hospital window at the night sky.

"I definitely didn't have a premonition – but I was very unsettled," she told me afterwards.

A nurse appeared at the door of her room. She had heard someone moving about and couldn't understand how Eileen had got out of the bed on her own.

"Who helped you up?" The nurse asked her, knowing that she wasn't even able to turn over by herself when she was lying down. "Come on, let's get you back to bed."

Alan's mum was distressed.

"I feel bothered," she told the nurse repeatedly. "I don't want to go back to bed. I want to be by the window."

It took two nurses to get her back into bed where, despite the sleeping pills, she couldn't sleep.

Then, unexpectedly, her stomach drip came out of its own accord. The nurse had a look at it and was so impressed at the very healthy looking wound that she decided to leave it out and let the surgeon have a look at it the next day.

Then her bladder drip came out and again, the nurse decided to leave it, as she couldn't get it back into the wound.

"It's as if your body is rejecting them," the nurse said to her patient.

In the office, the phone rang. It was the police.

"She's just had major surgery," they were informed. "She's too ill to be told at the moment."

An hour or so later Eileen had a visitor. Still awake, she heard her husband come into the room. He looked sad. Very sad indeed…

~ * ~

It was the week of my mum's 50th birthday and preparations were being made for a celebratory party in a hall that my mum had hired. Everyone was going to be there.

"Where's Alan?" I asked my mum when he didn't show up to the party. "He was supposed to be here." My mum pleaded ignorance. Later on that evening, when Alan still hadn't shown up, I asked Philip where he was.

"I don't know," he lied.

Despite his absence, the party was a big success and I was pleased that all my mum's efforts had paid off and that the evening had gone so well. I had quite a lot to drink that evening and was pretty drunk when we all got home after the party. Tired and ready for bed, I was about to make my way upstairs, when my mum interrupted me.

"Deb," she said softly, "before you go to bed, come and sit down in the front room a minute. I've got something to tell you."

Hummingbird

I followed her into the lounge. She looked as though she had something serious on her mind. It wasn't often that my mum sat me down for a chat like this.

She knew that I'd seen the article in the newspaper.

"It was Alan who was killed in that car crash," she told me. "Eileen rang me today and when she found out it was my birthday party tonight, she asked me not to tell you until afterwards, because she didn't want to spoil it for everyone. That was so thoughtful of her. You can call her tomorrow and she'll be happy to talk to you."

I was absolutely stunned. I didn't really have anything to say back to my mum at that moment.

"Can you just leave me alone, Mum?" I asked.

"Yes, of course... are you okay?"

"Yes," I lied. "I just want to be left alone."

I felt as though I wanted to run and run and run – as far away from the truth as I could get. Thank God I was drunk.

I didn't bother getting up from the sofa, I just lay there and cried myself into a deep sleep. I remember thinking: "There's no point in staying awake all night, I need to sleep so that I can deal with it properly in the morning."

I woke up the next morning on the sofa, looked down at the party clothes I was still wearing and instantly remembered mum's words from the night before.

"It was Alan who was killed in that car crash."

And that's the day I learned that grief feels very different depending on the circumstances.

Alan's sudden and untimely death hit me hard. The only place I wanted to be in the days following the accident was at his house with his family. They understood what I was feeling, they were feeling it too. I wasn't able to share my grief with Philip, even though my brother and Alan were best friends. He bottled it up and didn't show his emotions. I can't remember Philip ever speaking about it, to be honest.

Eileen welcomed me into her home with an open heart and we talked and cried together. We looked through photos and we shared stories about the young man who we both loved and grieved for.

After the operation, Alan's mum healed extraordinarily quickly. It's as if her body was getting itself healthy to cope with a much bigger challenge. If it hadn't have healed so rapidly, she wouldn't have be able to leave the hospital as soon as she did.

Alan's brother took me to see his body. It looked a lot like Alan, but my dear friend clearly wasn't there anymore.

"It's just the body his soul lived in," I thought to myself as I looked down at the empty shell, but the pain I felt was almost unbearable. It wasn't just a mental and emotional pain, but a physical pain, stabbing at my heart.

I touched his hand. I knew there would be no response, but still I wanted it, I longed for it – just to reassure me that it was all a cruel joke.

His hand felt cold and weird, not soft, warm and gentle like it used to feel. When his fingers didn't respond, again the tears came. I leant forward and touched his chest, his brother reaching out to stop me.

"No, be careful," he said. I turned and looked at him confused. "His chest was crushed by the steering wheel, they've padded it out, don't press on it, Deb."

It was too much to bear. I stood sobbing in silence, looking at the body of a man I loved. I didn't want to leave, but I knew I had to. I didn't want to walk away and let him go.

The day of the funeral inevitably came. The flowers I had sent were placed on the coffin and went into the ground with Alan's body. I sat with Alan's parents during the service, his mum and I holding hands.

"I never told him I loved him," his dad confided in me. "I wish I'd told him now."

I thought that was extremely sad. To lose a child at the tender age of 21 and to regret never telling him you loved him. It was a very significant moment for me. From that day on, I told everyone I loved, that I loved them. I still do, to this day. Maybe my friends and family think it's over the top, but I don't mind what they think. It's important to me that they know.

Six weeks after her surgery, Eileen went for her post-op checkup.

"It looks as though you had this operation months ago, not weeks ago," she was told when they looked at the scar on her tummy – the only evidence that she'd had major surgery only weeks before. It had healed incredibly fast.

"Someone is looking after me," she replied.

Alan's mum went home. She sat at the table and ran her hand over the

Hummingbird

cover of the book in front of her. It was a book about the stars that she had bought for Alan a few years before. Her mind went back to when he had come home from London and had promised her that he'd never leave again without talking to her first.

"You were saying your goodbyes to me that night," she whispered to her darling son. "That's what drew me to the window and compelled me to stay there, looking up at the night sky."

~ * ~

I carried on with my everyday life, but I visited Alan's grave most weekends. Just pulling into the graveyard car park sent the tears rolling down my cheeks, but it was comforting to be near his body. I felt that this was a place where I could talk to him and I knew that I had to feel the pain to release it. I grieved for exactly a year and then, for some reason, my subconscious flicked the grief switch off and I suddenly felt better.

Life has moved on, but Alan will never be forgotten. Both his two brothers got married and had children and his parents now live in France. I exchange emails and Christmas cards with Eileen and I thank her, with deepest love, for helping me with this chapter of my book.

Chapter 13

Something in common

My typing job at BT was going in the right direction. I worked my way up to assistant supervisor, then supervisor and was finally given my own office, with one member of staff to help me out. I spent half of my time typing and the other half on administration and management of the office. This is where I met my friend Sonya. The general manager of the group that I was typing for was impressed with me and offered me the job as his secretary. Thankfully, I turned it down. I say thankfully because otherwise I would never have met my best friend.

Sonya came to work for the general manager and we hit it off immediately. Half Italian and half Guyanese, her naturally tanned skin, small frame and long dark hair contributed to her elegance and beauty. She was smaller than me in height, but I soon discovered that her personality and presence were every bit as big as mine!

She is so unbelievably in tune with me. Sonya gets me one hundred per cent, all of the time. She is one of my blessings that I count every day. For more than 20 years we've been partying together, laughing, crying, and supporting each other through life.

Luckily, the general manager didn't hold the rejection of his offer against me and I was later approached by a member of his team and offered a job as a desktop-publisher, which I accepted.

I'd never done desktop publishing before and I soon found out that it was very different to word processing. It was far more complicated and much, much harder. I really had to think about what I was doing, all of the time.

"This is Brian," my new boss told me, as he introduced me to my work colleague. "He's an expert on all of this stuff. If you need any help, just ask him and he'll show you what to do. He knows the software inside and out. Okay?" he concluded, when the introductions were over. "I'll leave you two to it then."

Even though I was sent on a course, I still found the application really difficult to get to grips with and initially I was extremely frustrated with it. I kept asking Brian to show me how to do things. Brian was helpful, but I felt as though I was constantly bothering him. I felt stupid and uncomfortable with him and I didn't feel that there was a good bond between us. We never talked about personal stuff – it was all work-related – and I felt awkward because I was struggling so much with getting used to the desktop publishing package.

After a while, our relationship improved. I'd been given some raffle tickets to sell for the Huntington's Disease Association and I took them into work.

"Want to buy some raffle tickets, Brian?" I asked him, when he came over to help me (yet again).

"I don't know, maybe," he said. "What's it for?"

I didn't really want to go into any detail with him, but I did want to sell as many tickets as I could for my cause, so I casually brushed over it.

"Oh, it's just something you've probably never heard of," I explained. "It's for Huntington's disease. The prizes are really good – you could win five hundred pounds! Go on, you know you want to buy some... how many do you want?"

Preparing to tear some off for him, I was surprised when he showed an interest in the charity.

"Why are you selling tickets for the Huntington's Disease Association?" he asked me.

"It's something my dad had," I said. "Look, the second prize is three hundred quid and the third is a hundred pounds – in cash."

Brian continued probing and I was absolutely gobsmacked when he revealed to me that his father had Huntington's disease.

I couldn't believe it. I had no idea. We started to talk about it and I finally opened up to Brian and told him all about my father and my life and how I was so scared of my future.

"My family never talks about it," he told me. "It's a taboo subject in my family."

"Why is that, Brian?" I asked. "I don't get it?"

"It's like they are ashamed of it or something," he said "I've never met anyone else with it in their family. I've never spoken to anyone else about it before. I can't believe how open and honest you and your family are, Deborah. My parents didn't even want to tell my cousin, who is also at risk, like I am."

Brian was totally surprised at my frankness about the illness, but I didn't know any different. From the day we had found out about HD, it had never been suggested that it was a secret or something to be ashamed of. It wasn't our fault, it wasn't dad's fault and I didn't understand why a family would keep it a secret. It wasn't as if anyone could help it – it was the illness and it was in the genes.

Brian was the first friend I had met with HD in their family and talking to him made me realise just how different someone else's experience of Huntington's could be.

It was refreshing and comforting to have someone at work who really understood where I had come from in my life.

While my father was in his forties when he died, Brian's family tended to have a later onset of the illness and his father was still alive in his sixties. Some people can develop mild symptoms as late as in their seventies and – on the other end of the scale – it has been known for small children as young as two to develop symptoms. Juvenile Huntington's disease progresses more quickly than the adult form, but less than 10 per cent of people with HD develop symptoms before the age of 20.

When I asked Brian if he'd mind being named in my book, he said: "I would be very proud to be in your book, Deborah. I don't think I will ever forget that day we both found out about each other. It still fills me with utter wonder at the improbability of the situation.

"You've been a great inspiration to me when I've had those black days and you and your mum (I'll explain about my mum later) have helped me in ways you don't even know. If I have learned anything, it's that honesty and truthfulness are the best ways to deal with HD."

I'm so pleased that Brian and I were able to open up to each other; we both gained a great deal from it.

Chapter 14

Star struck

When I was 27, I had a boyfriend called Ian. Ian was a sound engineer and toured around the world with various bands. When I met him, he was working with the British punk rock band, Siouxsie and the Banshees.

Towering above me at six foot seven, I felt safe in his arms and by his side. I felt as though he was a man of the world, someone who was used to travelling and knew how to take care of himself.

A month into our relationship, Ian flew off to California for a few months to tour with the Banshees. He rang me every day from America.

"I miss you, Ian," I told him when he rang.

I'd only just got together with him and already he had gone away.

"I tell you what, Deb," he said. "Why don't you come out here and meet me?"

"Really? Are you serious?" I asked him, hardly believing my ears.

"Yes, of course I am," he reassured me. "We have a week off in LA coming up. I could get you a flight and meet you at the airport. We could stay in Hollywood for a week. What do you say?"

"That would be amazing!" I answered, all excited about the prospect of going to Hollywood. "I'm sure I could get some time off of work."

"Can you get three weeks off?" he asked. "I could meet you at LAX airport, we can have a week in Hollywood together and you could come on tour with us for a couple of weeks afterwards."

I was so excited. I couldn't believe my luck.

"Are you sure that would that be okay with the band?" I asked, hopefully.

"Yes, I'm sure it would," he told me.

True to his word and to my utter delight, Ian bought me my ticket to California and I flew out to meet him. He met me at the airport and carried my bag to the car. My mouth dropped open when I saw what he'd hired – a convertible Nissan 300ZX. It's true to say that I was suitably impressed. I was so excited.

I spent three amazing weeks in Los Angeles. Ian had the first week off work and we spent it together in Hollywood, staying at the luxurious Roosevelt Hotel on Hollywood Boulevard. It was truly magnificent and he spoilt me rotten.

I was completely starstruck for the whole three weeks. Seeing someone familiar being interviewed in the lobby, I asked Ian who it was.

"It's Arnold Schwarzenegger," he answered. "Don't you recognise him?"

"Yes, of course I do," I lied. "I just wasn't 100 per cent sure from here, that's all."

I felt a million dollars driving around Hollywood with him in the sporty black convertible. Back at the hotel, we pulled up at the entrance and gave the keys to the valet, who parked the car for us. Oh, what luxury. I loved it, every minute of it!

When we went out again in the evening, we stood waiting for the valet to bring us back the car. Seeing someone else who looked familiar, I asked Ian who it was.

Ian turned his head to the side and leaned forward slightly to see passed me.

"Oh, that's Charlton Heston," he casually replied.

It was obvious that he was used to seeing famous people and was taking it all in his stride, but I was having some trouble containing my excitement with all the adrenaline that was whizzing around in my body that week.

After an incredible seven days in Hollywood, we boarded the tour bus and the luxury was over. Everyone had a bunk bed on the bus and I paired up with Ian in his bunk. Being in the narrow bunk bed with a six foot seven, well-built guy was a bit of a squeeze, to say the least. But I didn't complain. It was a great adventure.

We travelled to different venues and it was interesting to watch the daily soundchecks and see how the business of gigging and touring worked. The catering was great. I had lots of really tasty food to eat and it was fun to go backstage and experience the show from the performers' side. I felt important with my Backstage All Areas pass hanging around my neck.

I tried not to get in the way when everyone was working. The members of the support band, Tom Tom Club, were really friendly and at one gig I even got on stage with them (along with a few other people) and sang along, which was rather exciting!

After a while though, the novelty wore off and I began to get a bit bored. Ian was working a lot of the time and without a job to do, I was trying to find ways to amuse myself. One day, I was watching TV alone on the tour bus – avoiding hanging around like a spare part during the soundcheck again – when suddenly I felt the bus moving back and forth.

"Oh no, the fans outside are rocking the bus!" I thought alarmingly, as I wondered what on earth to do. I was really unnerved and glad that I'd locked the door of the bus behind me. Then a newsflash came up on TV. There had been an earthquake and what I was feeling was a distant tremor.

"I think I'm just about ready to go home now," I said to myself, a little frightened.

Safely back in the UK, I reflected on the trip. What an amazing adventure I'd had and what a lucky girl I was to have had such a fabulous experience. I was so happy.

Ian continued to ring me every day and things went well for a while.

~ * ~

It was while I was with Ian that my mum re-married. It had been over 20 years since my dad was diagnosed with HD and 12 years since he had died.

Like my mum, my stepdad also had five children – four girls and a boy. We were all adults by the time my mum and stepdad got married and I was happy that mum now had someone to share her life with.

Prior to the wedding, Philip moved in with a friend of his and I decided to rent a flat with Ian. My step-brother-to-be had an empty flat and was looking for tenants, so I arranged to go and have a look at it. I hadn't met him before and I was looking forward to seeing the flat and meeting a member of my new family.

It was the morning of the viewing and, as I got into my car, I could feel the excitement mounting at the thought of having my own place. Driving along my road, wondering what my new step-brother was going to be like, I suddenly saw a car reversing straight into me. It came out of nowhere. I slammed on the breaks, but it was too late to stop it and BANG it hit the front of my car.

Time stopped still for a moment. I was so shocked. I couldn't believe it, my neighbour had reversed off of his drive and hadn't seen me.

He didn't do too much damage, but the accident shook me up quite a bit. After a brief conversation with the driver of the other car, I got back into mine and drove off to my destination, about 15 minutes away. I got to the flat, parked my dented vehicle and walked up the stairs to the entrance. I was feeling really shaky and tearful, but I wanted to keep my appointment, so I knocked on the front door.

As I expected, a man opened the door. He had a friendly face and, with a warm and happy smile, he extended his hand to shake mine.

"I'm Spencer," he said. "You must be Deb."

"Yes, hello," I managed to reply before bursting into tears.

It makes me laugh when I look back and think about the first time I met Spencer. Poor bloke, I really don't think he knew what to do with me. What an introduction to his new family. I'm sure it was the last thing he was expecting to happen.

"Blimey, are you okay?" he asked me, with a horrified look on his face.

He invited me into the apartment and then realised that there wasn't anywhere to sit down. He was still waiting for the furniture to be delivered.

"What's up?" he asked me, extremely concerned.

I felt so embarrassed.

"I had an accident in my car on the way here," I told him. "I'm okay, it just shook me up a bit. Sorry."

Spencer took me around the corner to the café, bought me a cup of tea and we had a chat until I calmed down. He was such a lovely guy. I felt really embarrassed, but thankfully he put me at my ease. I'm happy to say that the incident didn't have a negative effect on our relationship and we've got along extremely well ever since.

Ian and I moved into the flat and our relationship lasted for a couple of years.

When he was touring in America with a band called The Fixx, I flew to Fort Lauderdale and spent another wonderful week with him, this time in Florida. It was amazing.

Ian became a tour manager, which involved a lot more responsibility and hard work and I travelled to New York and France with him when he was working with a Scottish band called The Soup Dragons. I went to plenty of gigs in those days and had backstage passes to the concerts of stars like Culture Club and Prince. I met John Lydon (AKA Johnny Rotten) and Jools Holland. The Soup Dragons came to our flat a few times and I also met some members of other famous bands.

It was a fun two years, but our relationship was strained as Ian was often away for weeks on end and sometimes months.

While he was away, I fell into my own routine, going out with my friends, going to bed at a reasonable time during the week and getting up early for work. When Ian came home from tour, my routine was interrupted. He was still on 'tour time' and usually American time as well. He stayed up really late at night and got up late in the mornings. Living in different time zones meant that our relationship suffered.

After trying to make it work, but not being able to find a compromise, sadly it came to an end. I bought a little two-bedroom maisonette for myself and I moved in on my own. Mum and Nigel helped me to shift my stuff on what must have been the hottest day of the year. I was thankful for two things that day: that I didn't have much furniture and that Ian and I were still on friendly terms.

Chapter 15

Like father, like son

Meanwhile, my brother Philip was feeling the strain of living away from home. He wasn't coping well at all and he had a breakdown. He was admitted to Warley psychiatric hospital when he was about 30 years old and continued to have problems coping with life.

I went to visit him with my family, but never on my own. Philip had an aggressive side to him that scared me. When we saw him at the hospital, we would often take him out of the hospital grounds and walk around a nearby nature reserve with him. Philip enjoyed the nature reserve, but sometimes he didn't want to go back to the hospital. He was a strong and determined man and it was sometimes difficult to get him to come back with us. I was always grateful that either Mum, my brother Steve or my brother-in-law was with me as I was frightened of my brother when his anger surfaced. I never enjoyed visiting him at the hospital, but I went because he was my brother.

One day, Philip spoke to a doctor at the hospital and asked him straight up if he thought he had HD. The doctor told my brother that it was highly likely that he did have the illness.

When my mum next went to see him, the nurses told her that there was something wrong with Philip.

"We don't know what's up with him," they said. "He's stopped talking to us and he doesn't want to eat anything. He's just sitting there on his own."

Mum sat down with Philip and put her arm around him. She asked him to tell her what the matter was and he relayed to her what the doctor had said to him. His fears had been confirmed and he was struggling to deal with the devastating truth.

Chapter 16

A happy home

I loved my new home and I was happy there. My two-bedroom downstairs maisonette was in a block of four and it had both a front and back door leading out onto my very own garden. It felt more like a little house than a flat. The building was the first on the left in the cul-de-sac and only a five-minute walk from the tube station.

My neighbours were delightful. I couldn't have wanted better people around me at that time and I was thankful for that. I enjoyed working in the garden at the weekends and never felt alone there. The fences dividing the gardens were low and open and so it was easy to get to know my neighbours. Mary next door was like a second mum to me, giving me advice on my garden and teaching me about the plants that were growing in it. She was happy and fun and a perfect person to have living next door. I had an elderly lady living above me who was pleasant enough and I used to cut her grass for her sometimes, for which she was extremely grateful. It pleased me to help her in this way. I was eager and happy to get on with everyone and it wasn't difficult because everyone living around me was so nice.

When I was out in the front garden weeding or watering, people would always have a friendly or witty comment for me as they walked by.

A sweet elderly couple lived across the road, directly opposite to me. As regular as clockwork, on my way to work each morning, I'd pass the gentleman coming back from the shops with the daily newspaper.

"Morning, love," he'd say in his cockney accent. "How are you today?"

"Great thanks, Ken," I'd reply. "How are you?"

"Oh, you know, can't complain."

It was our daily ritual.

His wife, Molly, stood at the garden gate each morning and greeted me as I came out of my front door. If I had the time, I'd stop for a moment to exchange a few words with her. They were such a darling couple.

"How old are you, love?" she asked me one day.

"I'm nearly 30, Molly," I answered her, truthfully.

"Are you really?" she said, surprised. "I was just saying to Ken the other day, I wonder how old that little girl is over the road."

Oh, how I laughed! I must have seemed so young to them. Sometime though, I really did feel like a little girl.

"Oh, bless you, Molly," I said to her, laughing and gently touching her arm. "Have a good day now, won't you." And off I went to work, feeling great.

Living two doors down was a lady called Sarah. Sarah and I came from very different backgrounds, but we got on really well. She was about my age, but much more refined than I was and liked the good things in life. She worked in the City and knew lots of well-off and well-spoken people. Sarah regularly drank Champagne and ate out in the best restaurants.

Her sense of humour was right up my street and our words and lines bounced off of each other as we joked around. We laughed so much when we were together – you know that real belly laugh you get when your sense of humour blends with someone else's so perfectly. In the evenings and at weekends, we'd often get together with a bottle of wine and try to put the world to rights. Sometimes we'd laugh until we had tears running down our cheeks.

I loved living in my maisonette in Hornchurch. I was content there and – if it wasn't for the black cloud hovering above my head and having to visit Philip at the hospital which I found so upsetting – life would have been quite wonderful indeed.

I still had my other friends, of course. Childhood friends from my schooldays, friends at work and at the youth club and I spent a lot of time with my cousin Jo back then. I have always been blessed to have so many wonderful people in my life.

Chapter 17

Rollercoaster

It was 1992. I was still working for BT when I was moved into the Project Management Group.

I didn't give up dating, but I never allowed myself to think that any relationship would be a forever thing. That was until I met Richard. Even then, at the start, I didn't dare to dream about the future.

Richard was my new line manager. He was kind and caring and a sympathetic listener and it was my good fortune that he had recently broken up with his girlfriend.

The trend in my family is that the symptoms of HD start to appear when a person is in their early thirties. As my 30th birthday drew closer, it was not surprising that the fear within me became much louder and stronger.

I don't know if you can imagine the feelings of despair that were coming up for me. Feelings of utter dread of what could be imminent. I will try to explain it for you.

I felt as though I was on a very steep roller coaster, in a carriage that had been slowly cranking its way up to the top of the hill for the past 29 years. At the top, I could see my 30th birthday and as I looked down over the side and behind me, I could see the ground below – the safe and healthy years – inching away from me as I had made my way towards the sky, and the big black cloud that was looming above me. In the carriages in front of me were my three brothers and my sister. They had already gone over the hill before me. As I now reached the top, the thoughts in my head were a jumbled mess of fear, anxiety and utter dread. I was now at the peak of the hill: my 30th birthday. The train had come to a sudden stop and my heart was in my throat. I was looking down the steep track into the uncertain future, trying to prepare myself for the stomach-churning descent into the unknown. Part way down the track below me there was a junction where the track divided into two. Which path would my carriage take? One had the HD gene and the other one didn't. My solar plexus was in knots, and I was gripping on tight, not wanting to leave the top of the hill. Not wanting to cross the line into the black abyss of what might be.

That's how I felt. Only it wasn't a roller coaster, it was my life and the fast, thrilling descent could be a possible slow, relentless decline towards my death.

Richard offered to take me out on my 30th birthday to cheer me up and he drove 53 miles from where he lived in Luton to take me out for dinner. It was our first date.

As we ate our meal I talked about my fears.

"I wonder how people usually feel when they turn 30," I said to my dinner date. "Maybe it's the time when their biological clock is ticking away and they start thinking about having a family."

Most of my friends already had their kids by then and were starting to get their second wind.

Or their second husbands.

"Yeah, I guess so," he said. "I'm not sure I have that urge to have a family myself. It all seems like a lot of hard work if you ask me."

Our conversation was dominated by my concerns about my age though.

"I don't want to be 30, Richard," I protested. "That's when the symptoms of Huntington's disease usually start to show up in my family, in our early thirties."

As long as I was in my twenties, I felt safe.

"I'm scared, Richard," I admitted. "What if I start showing signs of it? I couldn't cope with it… I just know I couldn't cope with it."

Richard was absolutely lovely. He listened to all my worries and feelings of despair and I found him so easy to talk to.

"You'll be okay, Deb," he reassured me. "I'm sure you will. I understand how you must feel though. You must be so worried."

Worried? I was bloody petrified.

"I wish I could hold back time." I told him, trying to steady my quivering voice.

We finished our dinner and he dropped me back home. Hovering on my doorstep, hesitant about leaving me, he politely said goodbye with a hug.

"You okay, Deb?" he asked me.

"Yeah, thanks for dinner, it was so nice. Talking to you is easy. You've made me feel much better, thanks Rich. Have a safe journey back and I'll see you at work tomorrow."

I closed the door, smiled and thought about how lovely the evening had been. But, oh God, how scared I was too. After a while, my phone rang. It was Richard.

"Are you really okay, Deb?" he asked me. "I didn't want to leave you."

"I could tell that," I said, smiling.

"I wanted to kiss you."

I was pleased.

"Well, you'll have to take me out again then, won't you?"

"Yeah, that'll be nice. I'll do that. I just wanted to check that you were okay. See you at work tomorrow. Goodnight, Deb."

"'Night, Richard. Thanks for calling. Drive safely back."

That was the start of a fabulous relationship. Richard always said and did the right thing at the right time. He became my rock at a time when I was at my most fragile and – thank God for him – he supported me all through my thirties. It couldn't have been an easy job for him by any stretch of the imagination.

After dating for a year, Richard rented out his flat and moved in with me. He paid me rent every month and we shared the cost of the bills. For the first time in my life, I really felt well off. All of a sudden we both had extra money and each month I treated myself to something new, like a lawnmower or a set of saucepans or a new duvet cover. I gradually got rid of all the second-hand stuff I'd acquired and we went out to eat regularly, had fabulous holidays and bought new clothes. It was lovely.

Five years after buying my maisonette, Richard and I decided that the time was right for us to buy a house together.

Chapter 18

From Essex to Kent

I'm often asked why I moved to Kent when I meet new people who find out I grew up in Essex.

"Well, I'd never lived anywhere but in the Hornchurch area and at 35 years old I thought that that was boring – not the area, honestly, but the fact that I'd never lived anywhere else. So, I decided I wanted to live somewhere else."

"But why Orpington?" they'd inevitably ask. "What made you move there?"

When Richard and I were looking around at different areas in Essex, we couldn't find a house we liked. Then Richard was sent on a residential course at Sundridge Park Manor in Bromley, Kent. He'd booked a hire car for the Sunday evening, but for some reason it didn't turn up, so I offered to drive him over to Bromley and drop him at his destination. Neither of us had been to the area before, although one of my step-sisters was renting a flat there with her friend. As I drove through Bickley, I was impressed with what I saw.

"This is a lovely area, Richard. Perhaps we should look around here for a place," I suggested.

Richard liked the look of it as well.

"Yes," he agreed. "Let's come back here next weekend and have a look at the estate agents in the area."

So, that's what we did. We didn't see anything nice within our price range at first, but then we were sent the details of a house in Orpington.

"Where's Orpington?" I asked him, as I opened up the post and looked at the house details.

"I've no idea," he replied. "Let's get the map out."

After studying the map and finding out that Orpington was just next to Bromley, we arranged to have a look at the house and decided that it would be perfect for us. It was a 15-minute walk from the train station with fantastic links into London. It wasn't far from the M25 and we really liked the neighbourhood. So, we bought the house, moved in and spent the next seven years decorating it and furnishing it to our taste.

To my delight, I soon discovered that Richard was a dab hand at DIY and what he didn't know how to do, he found out how to do. He laid tiles, decking and sanded and stained the oak flooring. He turned his hand to carpentry, painting and together we transformed our house one room at a time. We had so much fun looking through home magazines, collecting pictures and designing our new home together. We were lucky that we had the same taste in decor and if we didn't agree on something, we'd keep looking until we found the thing that we both loved. We worked together as a team. We shared the chores and I never had to nag him to do anything. Living with Richard was the easiest and nicest existence I could have ever asked for.

~ * ~

At this point of my life, I was coming across many new faces – people who didn't know my history. I was often introduced to friends of friends, people at parties, pubs, clubs, work and just generally everywhere I went. I'm a very sociable person, I always have been, and I quite like the fact that women are exceptionally good at small talk, but there was one particular topic that I didn't always want to discuss with someone I'd only just met. It tended to shift the mood from light-hearted chit-chat to a more serious conversation. I didn't feel that it was always an appropriate subject.

"Do you have children, Deborah?"

It was a perfectly normal question, really.

"No, I don't have any kids," I'd casually reply, probably smiling far too obviously and hoping that they would change the subject.

"Oh well, plenty of time for that," I got used to hearing.

"Yeah, maybe."

I tried not to get drawn in on this subject, but I found it difficult to lie. I've always been such an open person.

"Don't you want a family, then?" I'd be pressed.

Oh, God, here we go again... My mind would quickly try to figure out how I was going to play it this time. Sometimes I would just lie and say "maybe" and other times I'd just say that I didn't want children. Occasionally, if I felt that it was appropriate, I'd tell the truth.

"I have a genetic illness in my family and was told when I was young that the only way to stamp it out was not to have children. There's no test and no cure, so I've never really thought about having children."

Sometimes it was enough to change the topic of conversation and sometimes it left an awkward silence. On the odd occasion, it actually led to a meaningful and genuinely caring discussion which usually meant that I made a new friend.

It did get a bit wearing though and so, when I moved to Orpington, I took the decision to be sterilised. I had no problem with persuading the doctor to refer me.

"I have Huntington's disease in my family," I told the lady doctor. "My father and my auntie both died of it."

"Okay," she said straight away without any further questions. "I'll send a letter to the hospital for you, Deborah."

It was as simple as that. Job done!

"It's like a weight off my shoulders," I told Richard after the operation. It's the best thing I could have done." I had absolutely no regrets whatsoever.

After that, when people asked me if I had any kids, I just told them: "No – I've been sterilised."

It usually did the trick.

Chapter 19

Discovery of the HD gene

I was 31 when the faulty gene responsible for Huntington's disease was discovered. It was an amazing and magnificent breakthrough, which enabled a predictive test to be developed.

Of course it's not compulsory to take the test – it's each individual's personal choice.

For some people at risk of HD, making the decision to take the test must be the hardest decision of their lives. The outcome determines their future and impacts on the choices they make in their lives – not only choices about having children, but choices about work, money, how they live their lives and so on.

A positive result affects insurances and mortgages and could well affect someone's chances of gaining employment, if disclosed.

On the other hand, receiving a good test result can cause a person to feel guilty (especially if a sibling has the HD gene) and they may suppress their happiness and not live their life to the full, because of the feelings of guilt and the sadness they feel for their brother or sister.

Understandably, before taking a predictive test for Huntington's disease, an individual is given counselling to talk through the options and the consequences of those options.

Personally, I didn't have to think about it. I couldn't face being tested. I knew that testing positive for the gene would have completely destroyed me. I just knew I wouldn't be able to bear it and I couldn't take that chance. At least without the test, I still had a 50 per cent chance of being okay. I wasn't going to have that taken away from me.

After a few years in psychiatric care, my brother Philip was eventually tested and his blood sample showed what the doctor had long suspected – that he did indeed have the Huntington's gene. My mum wasn't surprised. I think she knew it all along.

Chapter 20

A shop-bought card

My mum woke up on her 55th birthday with eager anticipation of what the day ahead would bring. She was looking forward to opening the pile of cards that had been growing in size over the past few days. Going through the pile, one by one, she took her time to read the wonderful birthday messages written inside each card. She had so much love and support from her friends, her family and from her colleagues at the local HD support group that she helped to run.

As she finished looking at each card in turn, she placed them on the coffee table in front of her and selected the next card from the pile.

Mum suddenly stopped in her tracks. There in front of her, in the pile of cards she had yet to open, was a card from her middle son. She knew it was from Nigel, because she recognised his writing but the writing wasn't as smooth as it used to be. It was larger and a bit shaky.

As she opened it up and looked at the shop-bought card she held in her hand, a sickening black feeling came over her.

"Nigel never buys birthday cards," she whispered gently to herself. And then the words repeated louder in her mind: "HE NEVER BUYS BIRTHDAY CARDS. NEVER!"

When I rang my mum that morning to wish her a happy birthday she sounded upset. She told me about the shop bought card.

"That's unusual for him," I said. "He always makes his own cards."

"Exactly. And his writing is different, too. He can't draw me a card anymore, because his hands are too shaky. He's finding it too difficult. It's the start of HD I just know it," Mum stated. Her happy mood was now fading away. "I'm going to ring him after breakfast. He won't be up yet."

An hour later, mum picked up the phone and dialled Nigel's number. The phone rang and rang and no-one answered. Later on she tried again. Still there was no answer.

Sitting in his armchair at home, Nigel stared at the phone. He could hear it ringing, but he didn't pick it up. Nigel didn't want to talk to anyone, he didn't know what to say to people any more. After letting it ring for a while,

Hummingbird

he got up and pulled the phone wire out of the socket. He picked his drawing pad up off of the floor next to him and selected a coloured pencil. His hand was unsteady and the lines he was making on the paper were shaky. He tried to go slower, but it didn't make any difference; he couldn't steady his shaking hand and he could no longer draw a smooth line. After a while he gave up and reached for a can of beer instead. At 35, Nigel had started to experience the symptoms of HD.

Although in denial of having the disease, he began to drink more alcohol and shut himself away from his friends and family. When we did manage to visit him, we could see that his flat was becoming dirtier, messier and smellier each time we went. My lovely placid brother was experiencing increasing episodes of anger and frustration and wouldn't let us clean or tidy his place for him. He'd insist that everything was fine and would get angry if we persisted in trying to persuade him, so we had no choice but to leave him for a while to cope the best way he could. I was heartbroken. I hated seeing him living like this.

Chapter 21

My busy life

My life was busy. With Brian's help, I had finally got to grips with my job and with a combination of sheer hard graft and a natural ability to get on with people, I worked my way up the ladder to become a manager at BT. How it happened, I'm not really sure. With Nigel and Philip suffering so much, I spent a lot of time crying – even at work – but because I was a team player, a peacemaker and a good diplomat I got on with most people and I managed to keep my job somehow.

Thankfully, I wasn't always sad. The gloom came and went. I used to laugh a lot too and try to stay as upbeat as I could whenever possible. I'm extremely grateful that my managers and colleagues were all very supportive of my underlying sorrow. I was very open about what was going on in my family and in my mind, and this helped them to understand me better. To my thinking, it was the only way to be. I certainly couldn't pretend I was okay when I wasn't and so I figured that the best way forward was to just be up front about it. Anyway, the tears were always a big giveaway.

Mum was still busy too. She held car boot sales and quiz nights and did what she could to raise money and awareness for the HDA.

After 12 years at BT, I resigned to take an opportunity to work for an American telecoms company, MCI WorldCom, taking on what was a new and extremely challenging role. It was a big step up for me in terms of status and responsibility – a *very* big step.

As bid production executive I worked within a team of bid managers. It was my job to produce proposal documentation and graphics for potential telecoms networks.

When I joined the team, there was no proper system in place for producing the proposals, so it was my job to track down and collate all existing proposal text from each group: finance, sales, project management, technical, bid management, etc. I had to work with the head of every department to re-write the text and ensure that it read properly when it all came together in one big document. I'd never worked directly with such senior people before and I found it a bit scary, to be honest, but I just pretended that I was used to it and got on with the job. And, yes, actually, it was okay.

Hummingbird

We had no central library of information before then and no automated means of producing standard proposals, which were being re-invented over and again. It also fell on my shoulders to find the most suitable system available for the job, then upload the re-worked documents and train the sales guys on how to use the system.

"How about running a workshop for them?" my manager Liz suggested.

I gulped.

"Yeah, that's a good idea," I agreed, adding the word 'not!' in my mind as I spoke.

Now my new job was really getting scary.

Knowing that I had little choice in the matter if I wanted to keep my job, I went away, wrote a training workshop (with no previous experience of training) and had the bright idea of including a section on bid management in it.

"That way I don't have to do it on my own," I cleverly thought to myself.

"We may as well kill two birds with one stone," I suggested to Liz at our next meeting, crossing my fingers under the table. Thankfully, she agreed. Phew!

My colleague added his bit on bid management to my workshop and we ran the first one together in London for the UK sales team. It went surprisingly well and I really enjoyed it. After that, we had to train the European team.

We booked the flights, hotels and travelled to the European offices to run the workshops. It was actually really good fun and we had a great time. What an amazing opportunity Liz gave me to really push my boundaries and see what I was capable of. I would never have thought that I could achieve so much and I was really proud of myself for the work I did for MCI WorldCom. Liz was a great role model and fantastic manager and I was extremely lucky to be working for her.

With the help of my colleague Paul, I created and implemented a corporate style for the European bids and I worked with the sales team to collate monthly statistics on the success rate of the proposals and the value of the business that we won. Each month, I presented this information to the bid director at our monthly meetings. It was a far cry from my previous job, where I had managed to merge into the background and keep my head down behind my PC screen.

The job was stressful and extremely busy, but the upside was that I had a fantastic manager in Liz. She believed in me and allowed me to fly, and that made all the difference. There were lots of social events going on and I earned a decent wage with good yearly bonuses. I believe I was the only one in that office who had never been to college or university. I was more proud of myself than ever for what I was achieving in my working life.

Chapter 22

Another devastating diagnosis

We continued to keep an eye on Nigel as much as he allowed us to. None of my family lived close enough to him to be able to just look in on him from time to time, so our visiting opportunities were limited and depended on whether he would physically answer the phone to make an arrangement with us.

Nigel became increasingly reclusive. Drinking was his substitute for drawing. It helped him to forget his problems. He liked to sit in the front room of his flat in his comfortable armchair and watch his TV and videos. As his movements became harder to control, he found it harder to adapt himself.

I can picture him now reaching for a video cassette and trying to insert it into the player. I can see him fumbling as he attempts to get the cassette into the slot. He tries and tries to line it up, but just can't steady his hand and eventually he gives up. Typically by now, he would inevitably reach down to the floor and pick up another can of beer.

Maybe he looks up and notices the pictures on the wall in his lounge, his mind free of the distraction of videos or music. Unable to draw any more, he cut images out of magazines and bought bits of patterned material and arranged them to make pictures on paper. He continued to find ways to express himself artistically, but now he was fighting a losing battle.

Thankfully, Nigel had a really good social worker who he liked and trusted – a young lady. I never met her myself, but my mum has told me that she was extremely helpful and did over and above what the job required of her because she liked my brother. Nigel thought it was cool that she wore leathers and rode a motorbike and he would always let her into his flat when she came to visit.

She had a good relationship with my brother. Even when he lost his temper with her, she was patient and kind and I'm so thankful for how much she helped Nigel in his darkest days.

One day, Nigel told my mum that he was going to Scotland for six weeks to see his friend, John. We didn't have mobile phones back then, so we had no way of keeping in touch with him. My mum wasn't sure if he was telling the truth or whether it was just a ploy to shut himself off from us, so she continued to phone him at home. His phone rang unanswered for weeks, but she persevered. Then, one day, he picked it up.

"Help me," the voice on the other end of the line begged. That's all he said, just those two words: "Help me."

Mum knew something was seriously wrong. Nigel never asked anyone for help, he was so independent. She got into her car and drove the 30 miles to his flat, not knowing what situation she would be faced with when she arrived.

Desperately knocking on Nigel's front door, she called out to him.

"Nigel, open the door, it's Mum… Come on, Nigel, *please*. Open the door."

The door opened and there, standing in front of her, was her son. He was barely recognisable. As he stood in the doorway, she looked at him with such deep sadness in her heart.

He had hardly any flesh on his body and his skeletal frame was covered from head to toe in cuts and bruises. His eyes were sallow and desperate. He had clearly not eaten for days and it was also obvious that he had been drinking heavily.

"I need more vodka," he said to her. "I want you to get me more vodka."

Mum knew that Nigel needed professional help and she used his phone to call an ambulance. He was taken to hospital and sectioned for his own safety.

Mum got back into her car and followed the ambulance to the hospital. When Nigel saw her, he was angry.

"Why did you do that?" he asked her, furiously. "I wanted you to get me some vodka. I wanted to sleep."

"I couldn't do that, Nigel," she told him. "I couldn't watch you starve and drink yourself to death like that. I'm sorry."

"If you ever do that again," he told her, "I'll never speak to you again… *ever.*"

He was adamant that he wanted to die.

To see my poor brother in such mental agony wasn't an easy thing for any of us to witness. He was dehydrated and malnourished. The cuts and bruises that covered his body were testament to the unsteadiness brought on by the illness and the alcohol. He was deeply and darkly depressed and desperate for a way out.

At the hospital, Nigel was bathed, fed and medicated and he began to look much healthier. After a while, he was deemed well enough to be sent home.

At home, his drinking continued and the downward spiral began again. When he was sent back into hospital, they fed and medicated him once more and he was forced to stop drinking, as he had no access to alcohol there. His condition improved, but his mission was still the same – to escape from his mental agony.

"Why did you have me sectioned?" he asked me, after I called for an ambulance one day.

On arrival at his flat, I had been greeted with the sight of my gaunt brother, walking naked in the street outside his home, being pointed at and talked about by the neighbours.

"It's the worst thing that you could've done," he said. "You should have left me to suffer, Deb. I just want to die."

"I couldn't just sit back and watch you suffer, Nigel," I told him. "Could you have done that if it was me? Really?"

But his troubled mind couldn't see it from any other point of view but his own.

"Why are the doctors asking me about Dad?" Nigel asked me one day when I was visiting him at the hospital.

I was confused and I didn't know how to answer. I thought he realised that he had Huntington's disease and that that was why he was trying to kill himself. He obviously knew that there was something wrong with him, otherwise he wouldn't be doing this to himself.

It seems that, even though we consciously know the truth, our unconscious mind still has a remarkable way of protecting us from facing our worse fears, particularly when the consequences are so devastating.

Mum made frequent visits to Nigel at the hospital. And when the time came around to find out the medical truth, she spoke to him gently and lovingly.

"They want you to have a blood test to see if you have the Huntington's gene," she said. "I'll come with you for the result. Don't worry, I'll be there with you."

In her heart, she knew for certain that when he got the results, he would need her support.

Nigel agreed to have the predictive test and he had a sample of his blood taken. The hospital assured my mum that they would let her know when the result of the test came through so that she could go to the doctors with her son to receive whatever news they had to give him. However, the hospital neglected to contact my mum and they sent my brother to receive the results of his predictive test without her. As luck would have it, my mum was visiting Nigel that day, totally unaware that the results had come through. It was just coincidence that she there. Thank God she was.

She walked through the double doors leading onto the ward and expected to see him, as usual, sitting in a chair in the lounge. But he wasn't there. She looked around for him but she couldn't find him anywhere. He wasn't in the lounge and he wasn't in his room.

"Maybe he's in the toilet," she thought, hopefully. She caught sight of a nurse. "Excuse me," she said to the nurse. "Where's Nigel?"

"He's gone to the doctors to get his test results," the nurse answered, matter-of-factly.

"What!" My mum was stunned. "But I was supposed to go with him," she said anxiously. "Nobody told me about this. I promised him that he wouldn't have to go on his own. I said I'd go with him… When did he go?"

"He should be back soon," the nurse casually informed my mum, without apology. "It's okay, don't worry, he isn't on his own. He has a nurse with him. You can sit and wait for him."

My mum felt utterly deflated. The staff had really let them down and they obviously didn't appreciate the importance of the appointment. Why didn't they understand the implications for my brother of getting a positive test result for Huntington's disease? This was supposed to be a psychiatric hospital after all – where were the bloody psychiatrists?

Mum could do nothing but wait. When Nigel came back to the ward he looked at his mum with a face that had been drained of all colour and tone. He was completely floored by what the doctor had told him and any spark of hope that he had left in his unconscious mind had been extinguished forever. It was a face that looked as though it would never smile again.

He threw his arms around her and clung on to her for ages, not moving and not saying a word.

Hummingbird

"I'm so sorry I wasn't here with you, Nigel." Mum's voice was soft and soothing. "I can't believe they took you there without telling me."

As she hugged her son she wiped the tears away from her eyes. It was as much as she could do to stop herself from breaking down and sobbing.

~ * ~

After Nigel's positive diagnosis, his relationship with Mum became a lot closer and they began to go out together once a week. At first they went to London to visit the museums, but after a while Nigel became anxious about getting on the Tube because of the crowds. My extremely sociable brother now couldn't cope with so many people around him.

They went to the seaside and walked along the promenade. Sometimes they'd go to the shopping centre to look around the shops. They'd have lunch there in the store restaurant and then go to the cinema to watch a film.

Despite knowing what was happening to him, Nigel was finding it increasingly difficult to control his behaviour.

If you're interested in the science, Doctor Jane S. Paulsen, Ph.D describes how and why Huntington's Disease can change a person's behaviour in her book *Understanding Behaviour in Huntington's Disease*:

> There are a number of behavior problems that can accompany HD. Specific behaviours vary significantly from person to person and can change throughout the progression of the disease. There are many reasons why a difficult behaviour may be occurring. Typically, the behaviour is related to changes taking place in the brain… The frontal lobes make up the largest area of the brain and contain the highest levels of our behaviours. The frontal lobe area of the brain is often considered the boss, or chief executive officer (CEO), of the rest of the brain.
>
> The following list includes executive functions of the frontal lobes:
>
> Organising, establishing the priority of various events, controlling impulses, monitoring self-awareness, beginning and ending activities, creative thinking (and) problem-solving.
>
> Although the effects of the HD gene are not fully understood, the primary site of known pathology is the

caudate nucleus in the brain, where the greatest number of brain cells die because of HD… The caudate has been found to be a very important brain gate because it has the most connections with the frontal lobes and it influences mood and cognition as well as motor skill… The caudate is necessary to regulate information in the brain (and) when the caudate breaks down, the person with HD cannot control the feelings, thoughts, or movements that are experienced or expressed. An additional function of the caudate gate is to assist with the organisation of information that travels to and from the boss of the brain, or the frontal lobes.

The information needs to be organised and prioritised. The caudate is thought to assist with the organisation and transfer of information from the frontal lobes and their circuitry. A problem arises when certain circuits aren't functioning, because neurons or brain cells have died, interrupting the flow of messages through the brain.'

This explains the changing behaviour of people with HD – why they have outbursts and sometimes act differently to the way they usually behave.

Whilst out one day at the shopping centre, Mum took Nigel for lunch at the store restaurant. She took a tray from the stack and they queued up at the hot food counter. Unfortunately, the food had run out and was being replenished and the queue was quite long. Nigel became agitated as he stood and waited in line. His fuse at this time was becoming shorter and shorter and in a rather loud voice he piped up, "It's those old ladies, why don't they move along? They're holding us up!" Everybody looked around at Nigel and my mum. It wasn't like Nigel to be rude to anyone; it just wasn't in his nature. The staff behind the counter quickly replenished the meals and the queue began to move forward. Suddenly, Nigel realised what he'd done and he was ashamed.

The effect of the disease on Nigel's brain was clearly having an impact on his conduct and mum had to find ways to adjust and to cope with it. His outbursts were sporadic, due to the interrupted flow of messages, and Nigel was embarrassed by the things he was saying and doing.

"Oh, no," he exclaimed, as he realised how bad his behaviour had been. "I was so rude, wasn't I Mum? I was awful to those ladies. I'm so sorry I've shown you up, but I couldn't seem to stop myself."

Nigel hated what was happening to him. His personality seemed to be changing and at times he didn't even recognise himself. He was increasingly impatient. On the way back to the hospital they usually stopped in the same roadside café for ice cream. The girl who worked there knew that my brother was unwell and that he didn't like to wait for his ice cream and so she always tried to serve them quickly. His brain was playing tricks on him and after already consuming three ice creams, my brother was insistent that he wanted more.

"I really want another one," he said, "but I know that I'll be sick… but I must have another one… I don't want it, but I must!"

He found it difficult to understand himself.

"I'll tell you what," mum suggested, plotting to get him out of the café before he made himself sick. "Let's wait until it's all clear and then we'll be Bonnie and Clyde – we'll plonk down the money at the till and get out of the shop quickly so that the waitress doesn't catch us to buy another ice cream!"

"Okay," he agreed, but as they got to the till, Nigel couldn't go through with it. "I must have another ice cream," he said, agitated, and went back to sit at the table.

A customer at the till was annoyed by my brother's strangeness and voiced her opinion.

"I wouldn't let him get away with that," she said to my mum, who just ignored her.

The lady didn't understand that it was the brain disorder that was causing him to behave in this way.

Mum was getting worried that she might not be able to get her son out of the building and back to the hospital. She ordered another scoop. Two spoons this time, so that she could share it with him and so he wouldn't eat as much. Mum tried to think up an alternative tactic to get Nigel back in the car.

"Let's be *Mission: Impossible* this time," she suggested. "You take the car keys and unlock the car so that I can pay and then we can quickly make our getaway."

She wasn't worried about him driving the car away because she knew that it would be impossible for him to get the key into the lock because of his unsteady hands.

"Good idea," he said. "I'm sorry about costing you so much on ice-creams mum," he told her. "I can't help it and I feel really bad about it."

"It's okay. It doesn't matter… don't worry."

Nigel took the keys and left the café and mum was relieved that her little game had worked this time.

During this short period of Nigel's life, they had a lot of laughs together as they grew closer and got to know each other better. Each time they went out together Nigel would eventually bring the conversation around to the subject of dying and more specifically, ways in which he could die.

Mum started to make plans for her son's future by arranging funding for his care and trying to find the best care home that she could for him. But she was just going through the motions, because she knew that Nigel had other plans. He was hugely independent and he hated the thought of having to be looked after. He loved his flat and couldn't bear the thought of living in a care home.

When I visited him at the hospital, Nigel wasn't very happy with me. I hadn't brought him any beer as he'd asked me to. I felt mean, but I didn't want him to be drinking again and I didn't want to be responsible for making him sick or hindering his progress.

"Look, Nigel," I told him. "It doesn't have to be the end of the world. Mum will find you a really nice place to go live. A place where you can have your own room, with your own TV and listen to your music whenever you like. You'll get all your meals cooked for you and we'll come and see you regularly, I promise, Nigel. I promise we will visit you all the time."

Nigel wouldn't even consider looking at any care homes.

"I don't want to live like that!" he insisted, agitated that I wasn't hearing him. "Listen to me!" He stressed the words, slowly and precisely. "*I… just… want… to… die.*"

It was no use. I couldn't get him to think about living.

I couldn't disagree with his decision. I understood it perfectly. However, that didn't mean that I was happy about it. I didn't want my beloved brother to die – either slowly from HD or quickly from suicide. I had to accept it, but I didn't want to accept it.

I was sad. So very, very sad.

"Can you go now?" he asked me.

I didn't know what else to do or say. As I was walking out the room, he called my name. I looked back at my poor brother.

"Can you bring me in some beer and some spliffs next time you come,

Hummingbird

Deb?"

"Yes, I will Nigel. I'll do that for you."

I hurried back to my car, hoping to get there before losing my composure. I opened the car door, got in and burst into tears. I gently rested my head on the steering wheel between my shaking hands. 'Oh, God help us,' I pleaded. 'Help *me* – I can't take much more of this.'

Next time I went in to visit Nigel, I took six joints with me. I'd heard that smoking pot can be beneficial for Parkinson's disease sufferers and so I thought that it could help to calm my brother's agitation.

A friend got them for me and I gave them to Nigel as soon as I arrived. "Have one a day," I told him. "And don't let the staff find them, for God's sake!"

"Okay, I won't. Thanks, Deb."

It seemed that this was all he wanted from me at this time and it wasn't long before he was asking me to leave him alone again. The next time I visited, he told me that he'd smoked them all, one after the other and had been really, really sick. Oh, no! It was so hard to know what was the right thing to do.

~ * ~

Mum continued to take my brother out once a week regardless of where he was – at his flat or at the hospital. She'd always give my brother a shave before they went out and he didn't like that – no, he didn't like that at all! But, under great protest, he allowed his mum to shave him. Interestingly, Nigel never drank alcohol when he was out with mum and they'd usually have a nice day out together.

At the same time mum was also driving a 200-mile round trip each month to visit my other brother Philip at the hospital in Northampton. Unlike Nigel, Philip was very settled and he liked it where he was. The nurses were fantastic with him and treated him like one of their own family, with love and kindness, cuddles and laughter.

My stepfather was supportive and didn't complain about mum being away from home so much. He understood that she needed to visit her children on a regular basis and be there for them.

At the hospital, Nigel wasn't being helped with the cause of his problems. He was being treated for his alcohol problem and malnutrition and when he seemed physically better, they sent him home and the downward cycle started again.

One day, my brother Nigel told me that he wanted to commit suicide.

"I don't want to be on my own when I die," he told me.

I tried to swallow the knot that was rising in my throat but without much success.

I didn't even ask what he had in mind. I didn't really want to know, to be honest.

"I went to the train station," Nigel continued. "I was going to throw myself under the train, but I couldn't do it."

"Oh God, Nigel," I whispered as I sandwiched his hand between my own hands and squeezed it gently.

"I thought about the people on the train," he said, "and how it would affect them and the driver and I couldn't do it. It wouldn't have been fair to them. It would have been horrible for them."

I squeezed tighter. Even in his despair and desperation to end his life, he was unselfishly putting other people's feelings before his own.

Every time I left my brother, I cried all the way home in the car.

Chapter 23

Hummingbird

And so we come to the story of the little hummingbird.

It was just after Nigel told me that he wanted to commit suicide that I went to Costa Rica with Richard and our friends, Tim and Louise. I was so excited about going on such an amazing holiday and I really felt that I needed to get away from it all for a couple of weeks. Mum was visiting Nigel regularly and she encouraged me to get away. I was emotionally exhausted and finding life hard to cope with again.

When we had initially thought about going away that year, none of us could decide where to go. For months the four of us had been looking for a holiday we would all enjoy and just couldn't find the right destination. Then I saw Costa Rica in a brochure and in an instant I knew that this was where I wanted to go. It jumped out of the brochure at me, screaming – like Donkey in *Shrek*: "Pick me, pick me!"

Tim and Louise came over to discuss the holiday. They were barely over the threshold when I blurted out the words that were on the tip of my tongue: "I'm so excited. I know exactly where I want to go!"

"So do I," replied Louise and then, in unison, we both chanted, "Costa Rica!"

We had independently decided on the same destination. How funny! The decision was made and the die was cast.

And so it was that we came to be in Costa Rica. And I met Larry. And Larry found the hummingbird. And I had a breakdown. And my breakdown led to my breakthrough.

Let me explain in more detail for you.

~ * ~

Costa Rica truly is a tropical paradise. Situated in Central America and bordered by Nicaragua to the north, Panama to the east and south, the Pacific Ocean to the west and south and the Caribbean Sea to the east. It had everything I could have ever wanted from a holiday. Stunning beaches, coral reefs, volcanoes, rain forests, jungle and giant turtles. There were endless possibilities to explore the wonders of nature in this fabulous country and the joy of it was that we could do it all in just two weeks.

Our holiday consisted of a week's tour with a guide, followed by a 45 minute flight on an extremely small plane to our beach resort at Tamarindo, where we would stay for another week.

I was so relieved to get away and was really looking forward to two weeks of relaxation and adventure.

What I didn't know then was that my holiday to Costa Rica was to be the turning point in my life. That the heavy black cloud that had been hanging over me for so many years, depressing my soul and dampening my spirit, would begin to lift and that the misty fog that clouded my life would start to clear. After so many years of sadness, I was finally to see the sunshine again in all its glory.

On arrival at the hotel, we were met by Larry M Perara. Larry was our tour guide, a slender and very handsome Costa Rican guy with a wonderful romantic Spanish accent. Larry was an expert naturalist and birding professional who had a passion for his work that permeated into your bones and your soul. It was a passion that carried you along with it, merging with you until suddenly it was not only his, but yours as well.

I was excited about being in Costa Rica and I was having a fantastic time. The rest of the group were friendly and likeable and we were having so much fun. The tour was proving to be a great adventure.

Larry introduced us to Confucius, a little baby hummingbird that he'd found in the forest, and showed us how to feed the bird with a tiny syringe.

As I mentioned in chapter one, Confucius became sick and I watched as Larry squeezed his little lungs until the tiny bird was no longer suffering.

Most people choose to do the exact same thing with their beloved pets and there is no law or lawful debate about it. It's socially acceptable and humane to put our pets to sleep.

Once the hummingbird was gone and I started to cry, I couldn't stop. Although I'd cried so many times in recent years, this time it felt different. It was as if everything that I'd been holding down for the past 37 years came up from the pit of my being and poured out of me like a volcano.

Larry couldn't understand why I was crying so much over the little hummingbird. But of course, I wasn't crying for Confucius. I was crying for my sick brothers, for my dad, my auntie and for me. I was crying for my mum, for Stephen, for my sister and for everyone whose life was affected by Huntington's disease. For the years we'd all suffered and for the loss of my normal life. At that moment, I felt like I was crying for the whole flipping world. The grief was overwhelming as the banks of my sorrow finally burst and the pressure was released.

Larry came over and sat next to me.

"What's wrong?" he asked. "It's not just about the hummingbird, is it? It can't be just about the bird. What's troubling you, Deborah?"

So, I told him.

And just like Confucius, he took me under his wing and looked after me.

~ * ~

Larry was the first person to talk to me about my spiritual self. I didn't know what he meant at first. To be honest, I thought that he was talking about religion or the spirits of dead people or something. Nobody had ever spoken to me about my spirituality before.

In those two monumental weeks, Larry Marin Perara became my guru. He explained to me that my spirituality wasn't necessarily about a religion or dead people, but about the essence of my own being, my spiritual self, my inner life. Me.

He helped me to understand that the suffering came from within me and that, whatever happened around me or to me, my spiritual strength could hold me together and keep me grounded. He taught me about meditation and suggested some books for me to read.

Larry also introduced me to the *I Ching Symphony* CD.

The *I Ching* (or Book of Changes) is an ancient book of Chinese wisdom and philosophy. As the world's oldest oracle, the *I Ching* has offered people help and guidance for generations. Some of the greatest sages in history consulted the book to formulate their own answers to life's great questions, while others have consulted it to regain inner balance.

The composer of the *I Ching Symphony*, Frank Steiner, studied classical piano, trumpet and music theory. He learned the backgrounds of Far Eastern religions, cultural roots and music and was fascinated with his newfound knowledge, especially that of Indian and Chinese music. He began to compose works based upon these ethnic influences. Steiner was able to absorb the wisdom of the 5,000-year-old text of the *I Ching* and he composed the amazing interpretation of the ancient oracle.

Listening to the eight tracks on the album helped me create change within myself by focusing my thoughts on what it was that I wanted to alter. Each track is based on one of the eight building blocks of the I *Ching*. These are Heaven, Earth, Thunder, Wind, Fire, Water, Lake and Mountain. Each track has a unique sound and feel to go with the element it represents. It's a truly beautiful collection of music.

I listened to these enchanting compositions and focused on change. I meditated, I talked and I listened to the wisdom of my guru, Larry.

All the while, the emotion was flowing out of me.

As each day came and went, my heartache deepened, as I re-lived every moment of my life that had brought me to this point of surrender.

Despite the minor inconvenience of my breakdown, we somehow managed to have the most amazing two weeks in Costa Rica. We trekked to the crater of Poás Volcano and saw its incredible steamy green sulphurous lake and we hiked down to the bottom of a La Fortuna Waterfall and played in the turbulent waters below. It was so much fun.

Swinging through the rain forest canopy on zip wires got our adrenaline pumping and we explored the relaxing waterways in a boat from our jungle lodge at Tortuguera. I'm aware that I'm beginning to sound like a holiday brochure, but I make no apologies about this because it *was* just like the brochure said it would be. There were so many fascinating things to see and do in Costa Rica. I loved it.

We spent a day and a night at a place called the Tabacon Hot Springs, a stunning landscape of exotic gardens situated at the foot of the Arenal Volcano.

As we walked around the picturesque gardens, I took Richard's hand in mine and my fingers found their way between his.

"This is truly a beautiful piece of heaven," I sighed, squeezing his hand firmly. "I feel so lucky to be here."

Richard stopped still and the resistance in his hand gently commanded me to do the same. He looked into my watery eyes and watched as the tears escaped, one by one, with each blink of an eyelid.

He looked sad.

"I'm really glad we're here," he told me, "but I'm so worried about you, Deborah."

"I feel really bad, Richard," I said, as I tried to gain control of my quivering jaw. "I just don't know why it's all coming up now. Everything is coming up for me, even things I haven't thought about in years. I feel so depressed, but I know that Larry is helping me."

"Being around Larry just seems to be making you worse," Richard pointed out. "I'm not sure it's a good idea to spend so much time with him, you know."

I knew exactly what he meant and why he said it and he was right.

"In a weird way, Richard," I answered, "I feel as though I have to do this. I have to face up to the pain of the past and Larry is helping me to understand myself better. I can't explain it properly, but I know that I have to listen and learn from him. I know that it's time to face it now."

"Well, do whatever you need to do," he said. "I'm here for you, you know that."

"Thanks, Rich. *Thank you.*"

I was crying again and he hugged me closely.

A river of naturally hot geothermal water flowed through the lush gardens and into a swimming pool. The pool was our preferred location that evening for watching the distant active volcano spew out its glowing red rocks, silhouetted against the blackness of the night sky. And to add to the magic Richard, Tim, Louise and I sat in the warm water drinking cocktails as we watched the volcanic glow and listened to the sounds of the eruptions.

"It's so surreal," remarked Tim and we all agreed. I couldn't believe I was in this place, feeling, seeing and experiencing this magic.

"Can you pinch me, Richard?" I asked in all seriousness. "I want to make sure that I'm not in a dream, that my mind isn't just playing a trick on me, trying to escape from the reality of my life."

"OUCH!"

"Well, you did ask me to," Richard chuckled mischievously. "Sorry, Deb."

I smiled.

When we retired for the evening, reluctantly leaving the stars and the cocktails behind, we still had a magnificent view of the erupting volcano through large glass windows at the foot of our bed, as it lulled us to sleep with its distant but constant rumbling.

The next morning, Louise reported that she was scared of the volcano and that its rumbling hadn't soothed her at all, but had kept her awake half the night. It turned out that one person's lullaby was another's nightmare.

The holiday continued and the magic never stopped. We felt highly privileged to be escorted to the beach one night to watch giant leatherback turtles laying their eggs.

In the blackness of the night, we sat silently as a huge adult female – six foot round and weighing one ton – dug her nest and laid her eggs in the sand. I'm not kidding you, we were so close to her that we could almost feel her breath as she panted and squeezed each egg, the size of a golf ball, out of her body and into her sandy nest.

Then, finally, when she had emptied around sixty eggs out of her body, we watched in silent fascination as she covered them over and made her weary way, slowly down to the water's edge and back into the sea. Wow!

The whole incredible Costa Rican experience was enhanced by my heightened emotions. I was wide open to every bit of wonderment that this beautiful country was sending my way and I was soaking it up like a sponge. In my hypersensitive state, it seemed that each and every amazing experience was intensified a hundred times, overwhelming me more and more with its magic and beauty. The intensity was almost unbearable at times.

In the midst of my release of tension and emotion, everything felt so surreal. I was so open and hyper-vigilant as I began to let go of the vast black cloud that had been hovering above my head for so many years that I could not have failed to touch the very core of myself in such an awesome place.

I was finally allowing myself to feel the unbearable grief that had been pushed down inside of me and just like the Central American volcano, it was now bubbling over.

Cleansing myself of years of sadness, depression and fear, I woke up each morning crying and I cried myself to sleep each night. And during the day, whilst I was having such a fantastic adventure in Costa Rica, I cried some more.

I lost my appetite, I was depressed and grieving, and yet I had the most amazing experience of my life. It was a bittersweet fortnight.

~ * ~

Hummingbird

Healing crisis

I didn't realise it at the time, but I now understand that what I was experiencing was exactly right and perfect in its own way. It was a healing crisis.

A healing crisis occurs when the body tries to eliminate toxins at a faster rate than they can be properly disposed of. It works in just the same way on the emotional self, as it does with the physical body. A crisis is usually brought about by past conditions (physical and emotional) in whatever order we are capable of handling them. We may often forget the illnesses and issues we've had in the past, but are usually reminded of them during this time of crisis.

The more toxic a person is, the more severe the detoxification is. I had a lot of deep-rooted issues and many years of sorrow, grief and pain to deal with. My emotional symptoms intensified during the cleansing process and I had to get much worse before I could begin to get better.

Think of it this way: When we first have a facial we may get a few spots afterwards. We don't like the spots, but we still have the facial because we know that it's good for us. We know that the spots are the result of the toxins coming out. This is an example of a healing reaction. When the spots disappear, we will most likely have better skin than we had before.

The bird Confucius was the catalyst, Larry was the teacher and the breakdown was the sign that the process was working and that cleansing was taking place.

~ * ~

After a week of touring and sightseeing, we flew to the other side of the island to stay in a hotel for the second week of the holiday. As we arrived at the 'airport' (a landing strip with a wheelie bin to rest the paperwork on) and saw the plane, Louise's face dropped.

"Oh my God! We haven't got to get in that, have we?" she asked nervously.

Sitting on the tarmac was a tiny eight-seater plane which had seen far better days.

"You'll be fine, Louise," I assured her, sending out a silent prayer to the Universe. "They do this all the time."

The overweight, unhealthy-looking pilot dropped his cigarette butt on the tarmac and stubbed it out with his foot. He beckoned us onto the aircraft. Richard was chosen to sit up front next to the pilot and the rest of us took our seats behind them. Usually Richard and I have no problem with flying, in fact, we both love flying, but I must admit that I did feel a bit apprehensive that day. I gritted my teeth as Louise's fingernails sank deep into the flesh on my arm and stayed there for most of the short journey.

Everyone on the plane sighed with relief as we touched down at Tamarindo. If it had been at all possible for us to have held our breath for 45 minutes, I think that we would have.

"Bloody hell, that was a bit harrowing!" remarked Tim as his feet finally made contact with the earth again.

Tim was the most adventurous one of all of us. Not much fazed him. Louise was whiter than a ghost, my arm was redder than a tomato and Richard just looked completely dazed.

"You okay, mate?" Tim asked him as we alighted.

"I was watching everything the pilot did," said a rather pale-faced Richard. "If he'd had a heart attack, I would have had to have flown the plane myself, so I thought I'd better concentrate really hard on everything he was doing. What a stressful flight that was!"

We were all laughing, but we were all so relieved to be off the plane and back on solid ground.

The accommodation at the hotel was gorgeous. We stayed in luxurious bungalows dotted around the lush gardens, with a large bed and a separate lounge area. The bungalows all faced towards the tropical beach, which was white and beautiful.

It was soon evident that my emotional cleansing wasn't going to stop for anything – not even for paradise.

The next day, we were looking through the hotel information folder.

"Why don't you have a massage, Deborah?" Richard suggested after seeing it listed. "It might do you good."

"D'you think so? I've never had a massage. I could try it, I suppose. I'll try anything to make me feel better."

"Let's go and book it up now," he said. "Before you change your mind."

We booked the massage for the next day and for some reason I was a bit apprehensive. I suppose it's just that I didn't know what to expect, but I was pleasantly surprised at how therapeutic the massage felt.

Hummingbird

I found that the movement of the therapist's hands kneading and stroking my body made me feel supported and comforted. It felt reassuring and it gave me the sanctuary I needed to calm my mind for a while. It felt like a bubble of silence in my otherwise turbulent and crazy head.

Throughout the treatment I felt the release of even more tension, both emotional and physical, as my mind and body relaxed further into a calmer place.

When the therapist left my room, I rested for a while, allowing the full effect of the treatment to penetrate into the core of my being.

"Oh wow, that was amazing!" I reported back to my friends. "I can't believe I've never had a massage before. I didn't know what I was missing!"

Richard looked up at me from his sun lounger and smiled.

"You look a bit better, Deb. Calmer and more rested. I'm glad you enjoyed it."

The next day, as the boys were kayaking in the sea, Louise and I saw the massage lady walking along the beach, looking as though she didn't have a care in the world.

"What a wonderful job that lady has, Louise," I said to my friend. "I wouldn't mind her job, you know."

I booked a second massage. When the therapist came back to my room, I told her more about how I was feeling.

"I haven't been good," I confessed. "I'm in a bit of a bad way. I broke down and cried when I got to Costa Rica and now I can't stop crying. It's as if the sadness of my whole life is coming up to the surface. It reminds me of the volcano we saw last week. It's been bubbling away for years and now it's exploded. I just can't stop crying."

"It's okay," she reassured me. "This will help you to get your balance back."

When the second massage was over, the therapist reached into her bag and took out a small rolled-up bundle. She placed it on the table and unravelled it to reveal a set of tuning forks, which she proceeded to use on me. She carefully selected each fork and tapped it on a surface to start the vibration, before placing it onto a specific point on my body.

I'd never seen or heard about this type of therapy before, but I was happy to go with it and to trust her. I was in such a bad place at the time that I was just pleased that she was giving me some attention, to be honest.

As she worked on me with the tuning forks, I wasn't really aware of any different feelings. I just laid there relaxing and allowed her to do her job.

When she finished the tuning work, she laid her hands on me and something amazing happened. I felt what I can only describe as a rush of energy, surging through my body. It was as though she'd plugged me into a power socket.

With my eyes closed, I had a clear picture of the network of blood vessels in my body and the river of energy flowing through them. I instinctively knew that blockages within me were being released. I could literally feel them releasing.

As I laid there, breathless and trying to figure out what had just happened, the young woman went over to the sink to wash her hands.

"Did you feel that?" I asked her curiously.

"Yes, I did," she replied. "Just rest for a while."

She smiled as she packed up her things and left me to recover.

Before my massage treatment in Costa Rica, I thought that tuning forks were used to tune musical instruments and of course this is true. However, I have subsequently learned that the tuning forks she used that day were another type of tuning fork, specifically designed to tune the human body.

To understand how it works, we first have to understand that everything in the Universe is made up of energy and that this energy is vibrating at different frequencies or notes. Science tells us that everything in nature vibrates. The cells in our bodies vibrate to sound, colour and light. Everything that exists in the physical, mental, emotional and spiritual realms vibrates.

This is my understanding of it. Each organ, gland and cell in our body vibrates at its own specific frequency. These frequencies correspond with musical notes.

When we are in perfect health and all the different parts of us are vibrating to the correct note, our body is in harmony and we are in balance. But when we are under stress and we have physical and emotional problems, it has an effect on our flow of energy, causing blockages and resulting in parts of the body playing the wrong notes.

Eventually the body will tell us, one way or another, that something is wrong with our personal melody and this is when we need re-tuning.

When the correct tuning fork is placed in relation to the organ or body part that is out of harmony, that area will align its vibration and synchronise with the fork, returning us to health and harmony.

The amazing response I had to the tuning fork session seemed a bit crazy to me at the time, because I knew very little about how my body actually worked and absolutely nothing of my vital or spiritual energy. I'd never heard of chakras, meridians or auras. And I didn't know that we could hold onto emotions like this, pushing them down into our bodies over the years, obstructing our pathways and causing blockages both physically and emotionally.

I can't tell you how, but I just knew that this was only the start of my healing. It was as though my inner voice was telling me and, at last, I was listening.

By the time I came home from holiday, I'd cried an ocean of tears and I'd lost four kilograms.

Chapter 24

What now?

I was 37 years old when I went to Costa Rica. I was almost out of my thirties at last. I could see the big Four-O looming in the distance and I was eager to rush towards it. As far as I knew, I hadn't started to show any concrete signs of Huntington's disease. I say 'as far as I knew', because it's easy to be in denial. I say concrete because with every clumsy gesture or absent-minded action came the big and logical question, 'could this be the beginning of the end for me?'

Although my relatives developed symptoms of HD in their early thirties, there was no guarantee that this timescale was set in stone and that I still wouldn't develop the disease. My risk decreased with every passing year, but according to standardised figures I still had a risk factor of 42 per cent.

As the black cloud started to lift and I considered my own family history, I came to realise that most likely I was going to be okay.

So, I finally let go of my fear and was reborn as someone who was planning to live, not die. And with that awakening, came a second big question….

What now?

Chapter 25

The healing power of touch

When I came home from holiday I did three things: I went to see the doctor and was diagnosed with depression (no surprises there); I booked onto a course to learn Swedish massage; and I bought some books about healing and meditation.

The doctor prescribed antidepressants, but I didn't want to take them. I struggled with the depression for a while, not really knowing which way to turn for help. The crying wasn't stopping. I cried myself to sleep every night and the minute I woke up, I burst into tears again.

I took up yoga and I went swimming and walking in the countryside as often as I could. A few weeks went by and the crying and depression continued. So, I took the tablets.

After a while, the medication started to help and I stayed on the tablets for a few months, before slowly weaning myself off. *Slowly.* I've never been a big fan of pharmaceuticals and I hated taking them, but I had to acknowledge that I needed them for a while to help me to climb out of the depression. I knew in my heart that, if I didn't rely on them and did other things to help myself, I would be able to gradually come off of them.

Meditation brought me an inner peace that I'd never experienced before. It also brought up feelings and realisations that were sometimes very painful, but by facing them and dealing with them, I was able to let them go and move forward.

Once I started to feel a little better, my journey of self-healing really took off. From my breakdown came my spiritual breakthrough. I started to see things differently. It was as though my eyes had been opened and the blinkers removed. I started to really notice nature, the flowers, the trees, colours and smells. I loved to be outdoors in the fresh air.

I visited Nigel at the hospital. "I'm doing a massage course, Nigel," I told him. "Would you like me to massage your shoulders for you? I could do with the practice..."

"Yeah, if you like," he agreed and with his permission I laid my hands upon him and started to work gently on his shoulders and back.

"Ooh, that feels good," he said. "Can you do it over to the left a bit?"

Thirty minutes later I was still massaging him. An hour passed and I'd worked gently all over his back and on both of his hands.

"I'd better be going now," I told him. "I wasn't expecting to be here this long. I thought you'd have asked me to leave by now."

"Oh, don't go yet," he begged me. "It's really nice what you're doing."

I felt rotten leaving him. I guessed I'd only be there for a short time as per usual, so I'd made other plans. Besides, my hands were aching.

"I have to go now, sorry, Nigel. But I'll come back soon and we'll do it again, okay?"

"Okay. See ya then," he said and reluctantly he watched me leave.

All the way home, I smiled and sang happy songs.

Before I started my massage course, I didn't have the confidence to massage my brother, but now it made the world of difference to my visits. Nigel was a proud man and he didn't like to complain about his situation. He didn't have anything to talk about apart from the fact that he didn't want to die the same way as his father and he used to get agitated after a short visit from me. Massage became our means of communication. The value it added to our time together was priceless.

That night I spoke to Richard about my visit to the hospital.

"If I never do anything else with my massage qualification, Rich, it won't matter because every penny and hour I've already spent on the course has been worth it for the difference it made to my time with Nigel today."

Chapter 26

Choosing to be happy

My new knowledge and spiritual awareness helped me to cope in a much better way. I was able to visit Nigel and Philip with a happier heart. I no longer came away from their hospitals in floods of tears, but with a smile on my face, knowing that I was doing the best and only thing that I could do. I began to look at things from a totally different perspective.

Richard noticed the change in me.

"You seem to be much better now," he said. "It's so nice to see you smiling again."

"Yeah, I am feeling much happier now. I've finally realised that I don't have to be so sad about things. I can't do anything about the situation. I can't change anything, Richard. All I can do is change myself and change the way I look at my world and what's happening in it. Now that I understand that – properly understand it in my heart and my unconscious self I feel **so** much better. I'm the lucky one. It's not me who has the illness, so I shouldn't be suffering as well. Actually, there's no need for me to be suffering as well. I should be thankful and happy. If I'm not, then I guess it may just as well be me with HD."

"Yeah, you have a point. But you can't help the way you feel, Deb. You've been through a lot. It's not surprising you've been so sad."

"Ah well, that's where you're wrong, Richard," I pointed out. "I *can* help the way I feel. How we feel is a choice. I can choose to feel miserable and sad or I can choose not to. Okay, so it's not always easy, but from now on I'm going to choose to be happy. I'm not going to waste any more of my precious life feeling sad. What's the point of that?"

"There is no point, Deb. You're right," he agreed. "If you can be that way, then it has to be better doesn't it? Tell you what, I'll take you out for dinner tonight and we'll celebrate your life and the new you."

"Yeah! Great. Let's make the most of every day if we can. Thanks, Richard. Thank you for putting up with me and supporting me all these years. I don't know what I would have done without you, I really don't."

I continued to visit Nigel at the hospital and each time I gave him a simple massage over his clothes. It had a calming and soothing effect on him. Sometimes I just sat and watched TV with him, not talking but holding and stroking his hand. We communicated through touch.

He was eating properly again and his condition had greatly improved, so the psychiatric hospital discharged him and he went back to his flat. The hospital was treating him as though he was an alcoholic. They didn't take into consideration the cause of the alcohol abuse. There seemed to be no comprehension of the bigger picture. When I spoke to some of the staff, they didn't seem aware that Nigel even had Huntington's disease. I don't think that most of them even bothered to read his notes.

Predictably he re-established his drinking habit, stopped eating and got himself into a bad space again.

Christmas 1999 and New Year were very difficult for my family because of Nigel's illness and mental state, but somehow we managed to get through it, as we did the next few months.

For his own safety, my darling brother was sectioned again and sent back to the hospital. He was extremely agitated as he withdrew from the drink and he became increasingly focused on wanting to die. He absolutely hated being at the hospital.

Chapter 27

Choosing to be free

I now saw my life as a precious gift and I wanted to make the most of it. I loved my holidays and in March 2000, I went to the Red Sea with three girlfriends. I had a wonderful time and arrived home a week later with my friend Emma who was staying over at our house that night.

It was getting quite late and Richard was in bed.

"We're home," I called as I opened the front door and stepped over the threshold.

Richard came down the stairs to greet us.

"Hiya. Did you have a good time?" he asked.

"Yeah, it was great," I told him, putting my case down to give him a hug. Something about him didn't seem quite right, but I thought it was probably because he was sleepy.

Richard put the kettle on and excitedly we told him about our holiday. It had been quite an eventful week and we had a lot to report back.

"Are you okay, Richard?" I asked him, sensing that something was up.

"Yeah, I'm just tired that's all."

We finished our tea and I made up the spare bed for Emma before Richard and I retired for the night. When we were finally alone, he told me what was on his mind.

"I've got something to tell you," he whispered, not wanting our guest to overhear him. I could see that he felt awkward and I wondered what on earth he was going to say. He must have gone over it in his mind a hundred times that day.

"Your mum rang me today," he said.

Richard looked pale. Something was seriously wrong, I could tell. I sat silently on the bed as I waited for him to compose himself and give me the bad news.

"Nigel's dead."

"Oh God."

I was stunned at the news, even though I knew that it would happen sometime. I don't know what I was expecting him to tell me, but I wasn't expecting it to be that.

"Your mum was with him," he said.

"What happened?" I asked him, quietly and surprisingly calmly. "Did she tell you? Is mum alright?"

"He took an overdose of heroin and your mum stayed with him until he died. I think she's okay. She's been to the police station."

"Oh God, I hope she's alright, Richard. Shall I call her?" I was starting to worry about my mum. "Maybe it's a bit late to call her now, I'll have to wait until the morning. I'm sure she'll be asleep. Where were they, do you know?"

"At his flat," he told me.

I wasn't sorry that Nigel had died. He had been suffering so much of late, but I was a bit numb, not really knowing how I felt or what I thought. I was sorry that I'd been away when it happened. Richard and I talked a little bit more before our weary eyes closed and we drifted off into a restless sleep.

The next morning we didn't talk about it until Emma had gone home. I was surprisingly calm, but I was eager for her to leave the house so that I could phone my mum. Unfortunately Emma's car wouldn't start after being on my driveway for a week. Borrowing some jump leads from my neighbours, I didn't let on to them that my brother had died. I just wanted to speak to my mum before I discussed it with anyone else.

Eventually, we got the car started and my friend drove off, smiling and waving goodbye and thanking me for a wonderful holiday.

I picked up the phone and dialled mum's number. She answered the phone.

"Mum," I said. "It's Deb. Richard told me what happened yesterday. I'm sorry I wasn't here. I just got back late last night."

"Oh, Deb," she said, sounding exhausted and deflated. "The police have been here and have gone through the house with a fine tooth comb. They've charged me with murder."

"They what?" I couldn't believe it! "Mum, what happened? Are you okay?"

"Nigel had some heroin. He wanted me to stay with him while he took

Hummingbird

it. Oh, Deb, he wanted it so badly I couldn't say no to him."

I listened attentively whilst my exhausted mother relayed the events of the day before.

~ * ~

She'd collected Nigel from the hospital. It was his birthday and she had arranged to take him out for the day.

"Hi Nigel," she said as she opened the door of his room. She gave him a kiss on the cheek and hugged him. "Happy birthday. Are you ready to go out for your birthday? I'll take you to the park and we can go for something to eat," she suggested.

Nigel wasn't in the mood to go out though. He had other things on his mind.

"Can we go back to the flat and have dinner there?" he asked. "I want chicken, sweetcorn and rice."

It seems like a simple request, but it was his favourite meal.

"OK then," she agreed. "We'll go back for a while, if that's what you want."

Mum drove Nigel home and parked her car outside the house, which had been converted into two separate flats. Nigel lived in the top half of the house. Mum took her keys, opened the front door and followed her son up the narrow stairs and into the flat. They entered the untidy lounge. Nigel had taken to sleeping in this room and in the middle of the floor was a mattress which he had dragged from his bed.

"Let's put your birthday cards up, Nigel," she said as she took them from her bag.

"It's okay," he answered. "Don't bother with them mum."

"Come on, Nigel," she persisted. "Let's sit on the sofa and look at them."

She opened the cards in front of him, one by one, and read them out.

"Happy Birthday to you…"

Mum sang…

"Happy Birthday to you. Happy Birthday dear Nigel, Happy Birthday to you!"

Nigel looked at his mother.

"Mum," he said, as he got up and left the room. "I have to show you something. It's in the bedroom. I'll go and get it. Wait there a minute."

She waited.

Nigel was soon back and was eager to show her what he had in his hand.

"I've got this, Mum." He held out a small packet and a syringe for her to see.

"What is it?" she asked, looking down at the packet.

"It's heroin," he said. "My friends got it for me. This will be a good day for me Mum."

My mum knew that this was truly what her son wanted for his birthday. He'd already attempted to end his life by starving himself, but we'd rescued him and had him sent to hospital under section. He'd been to the train station to throw himself under the train, but hadn't carried it through because he hadn't wanted a violent death. He'd spoken to my mum about hanging himself and she knew that he would end his life in some way, at some point very soon. She also knew that he didn't really want to die alone because he had told her as much on more than one occasion.

"I don't want to live like this, Mum. I'll get worse and worse and eventually I won't be able to do anything for myself. I'll have years of this and I can't bear it. I hate it at the hospital and I'd hate it in a care home. It's the best present I could have."

Mum knew that he was adamant and that this would be a better death for Nigel and so she accepted his decision and she didn't try to stop him or dissuade him.

"You don't have to stay with me," he told her. "You can go if you want to." But he knew that his mother wouldn't leave him to end his life alone.

"No," she said. "I'll stay with you."

"Will you be alright, Mum?" he asked her, worried that she might get into trouble for staying with him.

"Yes, of course, I will, Nigel. Don't worry about me. I'll be okay."

"I love you, Mum," he said as he hugged her. "Thanks for staying with me."

"I love you too, Nigel," she simply replied.

"You have to promise me something, Mum," he continued, with

urgency in his voice.

"What is it?"

"You must promise me that you won't let me leave this flat alive," he said. "I'll never speak to you again if you let me live."

"Nigel, you won't be able to speak to me again if you die," she reminded him and seeing the irony in his comment, they both laughed a little as they hugged each other again.

"My friends told me what to do," he pointed out as he put some of the powder on to the spoon.

Once again Nigel left the room and this time my mum followed him into the kitchen. He added some water to the powder, reached for the button on the cooker and turned on a gas ring. Nigel heated up the mixture and picked up the syringe. He sucked the substance up into it. His hand was unsteady and he dropped the syringe.

As my brother tried again and again to inject himself with the heroin, his uncontrollable movements prevented him from succeeding with his task. Repeatedly he dropped the syringe. After several unsuccessful attempts which left numerous marks on his arm, his frustration got the better of him. Nigel grabbed the spoon and swallowed what was left on it.

"Oh, that's horrible," he said, making a face as the powder went down.

"Let's lay down," mum suggested as she gently guided him to the mattress on the floor.

They laid down together and waited for the effects of the drug to work. As they rested, they talked about Nigel's life and his friends.

"I really enjoyed my life before I had Huntington's," he told her.

"You have so many friends, Nigel," mum reminded him. "You've always been such a popular lad."

"Yeah, I have some great friends," he agreed. "I've been lucky. But I can't face seeing them now. Not like this. I don't know what to say to them, Mum."

The day was warm and the curtains to the room were closed to keep the sun out. After talking for a while, the pair of them cuddled and drifted off to sleep.

Mum woke up and looked at her watch. Four hours had passed. She looked at her son – barely alive – lying next to her on the mattress. She knew that he was close to death. His lips were very blue, his skin was white and his breathing was extremely intermittent – he was only taking the occasional breath.

"Nigel," she whispered. There was no response.

It was unbearable to witness. My loving mother had watched her son suffering for many, many months and now she wanted to grant him his final wish.

"This has got to end," she thought as she lifted her head off her pillow. "I promised you I wouldn't fail you," she whispered as she picked up the pillow and placed it over his face. "Goodbye, my darling," she said. "I love you so much."

She didn't hold it there for very long, just a few moments.

My wonderful brother was gone.

He was free again and out of his pain.

Like the hummingbird.

For thirty minutes my mum stayed with my brother. She knew that the arrival of the police and ambulance would be the end of her precious time with him. She knew that there was a hectic situation ahead of her. She never felt scared but she did feel alone.

In the quiet moments that followed my brother's death, my mum started to wish that she herself didn't have to be on her own, facing this situation. She needed a hand to hold, a hug to embrace her and some reassuring words of comfort. Her actions started to hit home to her. She couldn't quite believe what she had done but she had no regrets. She was not concerned for one moment about the consequences but was relieved and happy that Nigel had found a peaceful and loving way to end his suffering.

She asked herself why it had to be this way. Why her son could not have asked for medical assistance to end the suffering of his incurable illness and his mental torture. Why was it that she had to endure this plight on her own, without any support for either her or her son?

Mum picked up the phone and dialled the number. 999.

"Police and ambulance, please."

She waited to be connected.

"Hello," she said to the call handler.

"My son has taken an overdose of heroin."

Chapter 28

A mother's love

I'll never know myself what a mother's love feels like or how powerful it is, but I think that its essence is captured extremely well in a beautiful poem by Helen Steiner Rice, entitled *A Mother's Love*.

My mother's love for my brother was strong, devoted, endless and unselfish. She spared no thought for herself and did what he asked of her. She did what she thought was right. It was what Nigel wanted.

Mum went to the police station where she was interviewed. She told them everything that had happened. She couldn't keep the truth to herself and she confessed that she had used the pillow.

The post-mortem on Nigel's body revealed no evidence of suffocation because he was so close to death at the time the pillow was placed on his face. If mum hadn't told the police about the pillow, they would never have known. The charge of murder was reduced to aiding and abetting a suicide, which carries a maximum sentence of 14 years in prison.

The on-going investigation and the stress of having to build up a case for her defence, took its toll on my mum and her husband. Their friends were extremely supportive, as were my stepfamily. I'm pleased to say that mum had a lot of love and positivity around her during this time and thankfully she had a fantastic lawyer who did everything he could to help her.

A lady detective came to my house and questioned me for three hours. She asked me about my life and about my family. I told her that I was one hundred per cent certain that this was Nigel's decision and that he had always insisted that he would commit suicide if he developed HD. It was a long and emotional meeting. By the time the detective left my house, I was totally exhausted.

I'd talked to Nigel about living with HD, but I could totally relate to how he felt because I knew that I would have felt exactly the same after being given a positive diagnosis. I'd had plenty of years to come to that decision, and so had he. It was not a choice he'd just made in the last year, or two, or even three. It was something that he'd known for many, many years.

Mum recognised Nigel's reasons for wanting to end his life and she understood them totally. They'd talked a lot about it over the past months and so when he produced the heroin, she knew that this would be the best way for him to go.

With her there beside him.

~ * ~

Six to ten thousand people in the UK suffer with Huntington's disease and many live a long and meaningful life, cared for and supported by their loved ones and carers, in a happy and loving environment. It's never an easy existence for anyone involved, but with good support and love, it is possible for a sufferer to enjoy some level of well-being.

Through the HD support groups, I have known some amazing people, who have done an outstanding job of caring for their loved ones, making their lives as comfortable as possible and giving the sufferer the best quality of life that they could possibly have.

The creation of internet chat rooms has given people much more support than ever before from other people at risk and from sufferers like themselves. People can easily connect with each other to talk about their concerns, fears and their struggles. They can now share positive stories and find the latest research in a matter of minutes over the internet. Anyone with access to the internet can find all the information they need these days.

Unfortunately we didn't have that technology available to us back then. We felt much more isolated and alone.

Chapter 29

The funeral

On the day of the funeral, as we pulled into the crematorium in Upminster, I noticed a lot of faces that I hadn't seen for many years. It warmed my heart to see that so many people had turned out to say goodbye to their friend.

I stepped out of the car and bit down on my lip. I didn't want to cry before I'd even made it into the chapel.

Nigel's coffin was lifted out of the car and on to the shoulders of the pallbearers. Slowly and rhythmically they walked his body into the chapel and I followed behind with my family by my side. The other mourners entered the chapel in procession behind us and we quietly took our places as the burgundy coffin was placed on the catafalque in front of us.

The vicar stood at the lectern and waited patiently for the congregation to settle down. Being a long-standing member of the church, my sister had asked a friend of hers to conduct the service on our behalf and it was comforting that the vicar was able to deliver a very personal and sympathetic service.

When it was my turn to speak, I composed myself and picked up my paper. Walking carefully up to the lectern, I was aware that everyone had their eyes turned towards me. I stepped up to the desk and opened my paper.

I didn't look up.

I couldn't look up.

Swallowing hard I sent out a silent prayer to anyone who might be listening – God, my guardian angels, spirit guides, my dad, Nigel – anyone at all who's essence might be around me – for the strength that I needed.

I took a deep breath and as clearly and as loudly as I could manage, I started to read the words I had composed.

"I heard talk about the end.

"I saw pain, suffering and fear.

"I felt exhaustion and there is no exhaustion where there is much to be hoped for and something to work towards."

Feeling the emotion rising inside of me, I swallowed hard again.

"When you can still visualise a better life for those who suffer."

My voice starting to quiver, but I continued.

"Exhaustion is when you can no longer dream; no longer see possibilities and alternatives.

"When you can only see limitation, decline and despair.

"The exhausted are those who believe that they have come to the end of their road, with no new dreams to hold on to.

"The exhausted are those who have come to the end of their ability to cope."

I paused for a moment and swallowed hard.

"The exhausted will clear the way for others to live."

My voice was shaking and the tears were coming. But I went on, determined to finish.

"The death of a loved one can fill us with despair and emptiness. In others it releases enlightenment and a sense of the limited time we have to be as happy as we can: to explore our potential to the fullest and to lose our fear of death.

"Let us join together, celebrate the life of Nigel and remember this moment and the beginning of our greater love and reverence for life.

"Let us gather ourselves together, clear our minds, concentrate, listen and be focused and awake. Let go of the troubles from our past and look into our future with a fresh and open mind.

"Nigel does not want us to suffer. He never did want us to suffer.

"We owe it to his memory to unite as his family and friends and ensure that we *do not* suffer."

Saying these positive words out loud settled my emotions a little and I felt a bit calmer. I briefly glanced up at the sea of faces in the congregation. At that moment, I don't think there was a dry eye in the church. I continued to read an excerpt from a letter that my cousin had written to my mum after Nigel's death:

"Life was certainly never dull in Nigel's company. I never saw Nigel ever be mean to anyone. He was always really kind to me and his friends. He could infuriate me sometimes, but I found it hard to be cross with him for long as he had that ability to let you accept him for being him.

"He was very intelligent and apart from larking and joking around, we would have some serious conversations. A few times he said to me that if he got Huntington's, he would take his life. I knew then that he was serious and that he meant it. Nigel couldn't bear the thought of having a life in limbo. Nigel, to me, was always such a free spirit and his being ill for a long while would be terrible for him.

"Whenever I think of Nigel, I always remember some funny incident and it makes me smile."

I had to pause again to compose myself.

"I don't know what Nigel would say if he were here with us now, but on his behalf, I'd like to read the following:

"Weep not for me though I am gone, for now I am at peace. Grieve if you will, but not for long, then let your sorrow cease."

I continued to the end of the poem, asking people not to dwell on Nigel's death, but to celebrate my brother's life.

And with the concluding verse, the tears came and I stepped back down and made my way, gently sobbing, back to my seat.

With my contribution to the service over, I spent the rest of the time trying not to fall completely apart. When the music played and the curtains closed around the coffin it was just about too much to bear. The music was familiar to me, as it was to many of the congregation. It was a Terry Callier track that Nigel had played often. Disco in the sky.

His friends were mouthing the familiar words, smiling and crying at the same time, as they said a final farewell to their beloved friend.

We stepped outside the chapel and into the sunshine to greet the mourners.

I'd ordered a cheerful wreath made of sunflowers and I could see it lying amongst the many other floral tributes. As I looked at the flowers that had been laid in Nigel's memory, I was amused and touched to see that one of his friends had organised a tribute in the shape of one of Nigel's favourite cartoon characters, Noddy.

Nigel absolutely loved this character because, as he had always said, Noddy never had to grow up and get older. Noddy was forever young.

I smiled as I looked at the Enid Blyton figure, made up entirely of red, yellow and blue flowers. It was an amazing piece of floristry.

Oh yes, with the HD cloud looming over our heads, I could understand why Nigel loved Noddy.

Chapter 30

You have suffered enough

In October 2000, at the age of 63, my darling mum pleaded guilty to aiding and abetting a suicide at London's Central Criminal Court, The Old Bailey.

Sitting in the public gallery with my family, I listened intensely as I heard it said that my mum was a doting mother who had a 'deep love for all her children'.

It was comforting to hear the defence lawyer state in court that my mum did all she could to give Nigel great support.

As the court case went on, I silently wept as I looked at the familiar face of the white-haired lady re-living every moment of the final birthday of her second son. She looked so alone to me.

'That's my mum,' I reminded myself.

It all seemed so surreal.

Watching the tears run down her face and hearing mum's barrister recount the events of that day was enough to break my heart.

Again.

I seem to remember that the journalists were not allowed back into the public gallery whilst the sentence was announced. I held on to my elder brother's hand as I prayed for a miracle. And then it came.

I listened intensely to the judge's words. Summing up, he said:

"Human life is precious, many regard it as sacred. It follows that only in the rarest and most exceptional cases can those who contribute to the death of another be sentenced to other than immediate imprisonment.

"But your case is indeed exceptional. Your story is one that would move the hardest of hearts. You committed the offence when confronted by one of the most distressing situations that can be imagined."

And he continued: "I believe you have suffered enough," and we knew she would be a free woman.

The judge sentenced my mum to a one-year conditional discharge.

After sentencing, Judge Graham Boal, QC warned the court that the unusual course he had taken was not to be regarded as a precedent. In other words, if someone thinks that they can take the same action, he couldn't guarantee that they would be allowed to walk free from the courtroom.

"Let no one who hears of this case misinterpret my decision," he said.

Addressing my mum again he continued:

"I would add – in view of your plea and frankness to police – that I would regard you as a very brave woman."

As we left the Old Bailey, emotionally exhausted, but delighted at the outcome, we were surrounded by photographers and journalists. With cameras and microphones in front of our faces, questions were being fired at my mum from all angles.

My mum and stepfather made their way home, along with my uncle who had flown over from Australia to be with his sister for the court hearing.

I went to find a bar with Richard and my brother, Steve. "Ring me when you get home, Mum," I told her. "I love you."

A few hours later my mobile phone rang. It was a friend of mine, ringing to tell me that my mum's case had been reported on the BBC news website already.

Then my mum rang.

"We're home, Deb," she reported as promised. "You want to see what it's like out there! The house is surrounded by reporters. They're putting notes through the letterbox, they all want an exclusive. It's overwhelming."

"Oh, blimey." I was shocked. I didn't expect that level of attention and neither did my mum. "What you gonna do?" I asked her.

"I don't know what to do," she said.

"Well, just ignore them and eventually they'll get fed up and go away," I suggested, hopefully.

~ * ~

The next morning, on the way to work, Richard and I bought a copy of every newspaper. We wondered if the story had been reported in any of them – we guessed that it probably had – but we certainly weren't expecting what we saw.

The case had been reported in nearly every paper. I took the *Daily Mirror* in my hands and looked at the words, in very large print, across the width of the front page: **'You've suffered enough'**.

Hummingbird

We couldn't believe our eyes. We spent the train journey that morning flicking through the papers, reading all the articles, from one paper to the next.

By the time I got to work, I thought that the whole world knew exactly what had happened in my life. As I walked into the office that day, I was expecting everyone I passed to stop and comfort me with their words and actions, but strangely they didn't. It seemed to be a normal day at the office. I was expecting people to make a fuss of me – I wanted their comfort and attention. I felt that everything I'd gone through in my life so far had broken out into the world and yet nobody in my world had seemed to even notice.

I arrived at my desk. My team members greeted me as usual.

"Morning," they said as I sat down and turned on my PC.

"Have you seen the papers this morning?" I asked them, dumbfounded.

Of course, they'd seen them, they just didn't know what to say to me. I couldn't ignore it, push it down and get on with my day without even the tiniest acknowledgement or mention of it. This was my life. This was a big issue for me. Didn't they understand that?

They nodded.

"Yes, of course we've seen them," they said.

I waited… was that it?

My desk phone rang.

"Debs, it's Louise," the familiar voice of my friend said. "Oh, my God! We're all reading the papers here at the office and we can't believe it!"

"Oh, Louise, I'm so pleased you've rung," I replied with relief. "I can't believe it either. It's surreal."

"It's so sad, we're all crying," she told me.

Her colleagues didn't even know me and they were showing more interest in my life than my own work buddies.

"I wish I was there Louise, in your office with you. No-one here's saying anything. It's mad, I feel as though I can't talk about it to anyone. I've got all of this stuff – I don't even know what it is or how to describe it – but it's all going around in me, and in my head, and it's as though it's just another normal day here. No-one's saying anything."

"How strange. Well, babe, we're all crying here," she said, laughing. I can't believe it's been reported so widely… Are you okay, babe?"

"Yeah, I think so. It's just so weird, that's all Louise. Seeing it all in print like this. Thanks for calling honey, I can't tell you how much I appreciate it. I'd better go, I'll give you a call later." And with that, I felt that my situation had at least been acknowledged by someone. One of my friends at least had some idea of how I might be feeling and had wanted to connect with me.

It was a long and unproductive day as far as my job was concerned. I couldn't concentrate on work and I spent quite a bit of time on the phone to my friends. I was pleased to see the end of the day and go home to Richard.

Chapter 31

A positive way forward

Relieved that my mother's court case was now over and that my mum had not been sent to prison, I looked forward to moving on to a new stage in my life.

Although mum's case had been extensively reported in the national papers, I certainly wasn't expecting the level of media attention that the case attracted for months and even years afterwards.

After some deliberation, mum decided to sell her story to *The Daily Mail* for £8,000, recouping a fraction of the £20,000 it had cost her for the legal fees of the court case. At first, she didn't want to do the interview for money because it seemed wrong to her to gain from what had happened, but we persuaded her to see that Nigel would have wanted her to get some of the money back.

Taking the opportunities that the court case had opened up for her, my mum took advantage of the chance to raise awareness of the illness and to continue to tell her story. After years of quietly caring, fundraising and supporting others with the disease, she was finding her own voice and using it to the good effect of her cause.

Mum became an active member of Dignity in Dying, an organisation that demands greater choice and control to alleviate suffering at the end of life. It's such a prominent and popular issue that the organisation has more than 25,000 active supporters.

My mum took part in many TV and radio interviews and it was difficult for me to lay my past to rest and to concentrate on other things. Each repeated account of her story brought back the sadness and the tears flowed freely again.

Although I was working through my issues, the sorrow was stuck in my cell memory and I was desperate to find a way to fully release it once and for all.

When Nigel died, I already had my first massage qualification and I was studying reflexology. My busy and demanding job made me tired and stressed, but I was now working four days-a-week instead of five. I was the only one in the company working reduced hours and this was made possible with the backing of my line manager, Liz. Without Liz's support and understanding I would have left my job behind and been absolutely broke as I studied. I was adamant that this was what I was going to do – there was no doubt in my mind.

I thank her wholeheartedly for believing in me when I started at the company and for supporting me at this difficult time.

I was much happier and I was learning so much more about myself and about a different way of looking at life.

I decided that I wasn't going to spend any more unnecessary time feeling sad because being sad would be a waste of the precious life I had been given. I was the lucky one after all and I didn't want to waste one more day of that gift of a healthy life. It so easily could have been me that had drawn the short straw. I'd had as much chance as any of my siblings of inheriting the disease. Fifty-fifty.

I knew how fortunate I was. Oh boy, how I knew it.

I was determined to remember my loved ones in a positive way and be happy that I had them in my life for the time that I did. Of course, sometimes I'd feel sad, it's only natural and I'm only human, but once I realised that my way of thinking was a choice, I actively changed my negative thoughts to more positive ones. Practicing positive thinking made a world of difference to me.

If we allow ourselves to dwell on a negative thought, it leads to another negative thought, which leads to another and we can get swept along into a downward spiral of unhealthy emotions which can bring us down even more. Sometimes people get so familiar with their negative thoughts and feelings that they can't imagine themselves being any other way. They wouldn't recognise themselves if they were positive and happy and that can frighten them into not wanting to change.

It didn't happen overnight for me. It took some effort and time to perfect my new skill, but with practice, it gradually became easier and easier to change my negative patterns.

I came to realise that I had been getting something out of being a victim. I got attention – usually in the form of sympathy or cuddles – and that was what I had needed to make me feel safe, secure and loved.

I didn't want to have this need any more. I didn't want to lean on Richard and my friends and to have to count on them to prop me up emotionally. I wanted the crying to stop. I wanted to find my own strength – strength that emanated from the core of my own being. Strength that enabled me to stand upright on my own, whatever challenges life had to throw at me. I could totally imagine the person that I wanted to be.

Studying reflexology taught me more about complimentary therapy. I learned about the energy pathways called meridians and our energy centres known as our chakras. I found the subject completely fascinating and when I started working with reflexology, I realised just how powerful it could be.

My plan was to leave my office job and work as a therapist, but something was holding me back. I found it difficult to make the transition because I was earning such a good wage. I was in the money-trap, living according to my means with a mortgage, a car and the lifestyle that went with the wages. And I liked the perks of a well-paid job. So, I stayed in my job, not quite ready to make the leap. I gave a few treatments at the weekends, but I didn't have the time and energy to properly devote to my work as a therapist.

Chapter 32

A new life

At the end of 2001, my company re-located out of London to Reading, Berkshire and this was my perfect opportunity. It was as though the Universe had intervened and was telling me that it was time to make the change. Even so, I did try working in Reading for a month, staying in a hotel during the week and coming home on Thursday nights. It was okay, but not ideal. It couldn't last. Unless I wanted to do a two-hour commute each day or I wanted to move house, I had no choice but to take redundancy.

In January 2002, I took the plunge and left my job, with a small redundancy pay-out of three months wages. As redundancy packages went back then, it was nothing at all, but it was a very welcome and much needed little boost to my bank account.

It was extremely significant to me that I was entering this new phase in my life at 39 years old. Now in my 40th year, not only was I leaving my old life behind me, but I was also leaving my thirties behind.

Heading towards my big Four-O brought a totally different feeling with it. When I turned 30 I was petrified, but now, as I looked forward to being 40 and was entering this unknown new world, I felt excited and happy.

"Would you take the test now?" my dear friend Sonya asked me. "Now that you're sure you're gonna be okay?"

I didn't even have to think about it.

"No" I told her. "I'm still not ready for that."

"Why d'you think that is, Debs?" Richard asked me, when I was discussing it with him one evening.

"I don't know really, Rich. I obviously still have a tiny doubt somewhere in my subconscious that's stopping me from taking it."

"I wonder why though? You're so certain now that you'll be okay and you're much older than your dad and brothers were when they became ill."

I thought about it for a while.

"Maybe I just know I'll be okay because I'm incapable of even contemplating any other option," I said. "Yes… I think that's it, you know. I just can't believe that I could have HD because the thought itself would be too much for me to bear. But as you say, I'm much older now and the odds are stacked in my favour."

"You're gonna be fine, Deb, I'm absolutely certain," Richard assured me. "You don't have to take the test. It doesn't matter now."

So, I still wasn't tested and I carried on believing what I desperately wanted to be true, that I'd had a very lucky escape.

I wanted to start taking control of my life. Now that the black cloud had lifted and I realised that I was going to live, there were suddenly so many things that I wanted to do.

Chapter 33

Making plans

Before I left my job, I went out for dinner with Sonya to discuss my future plans.

"I've worked in London for corporate companies since I was 16 years old," I told her. "It's all I've known for 22 years."

"Yeah, me too," she said. "How boring is that? Pass the wine list…"

"I've been on holiday abroad every year since I was 18, but I've never been away for more than two weeks at a time. I want to have a longer break, Sonya. I think this could be a good opportunity for me to do something meaningful and spend some proper time away before I start working for myself."

"Wow, that sounds great," she said, impressed. "What do you have in mind, then?"

"Well, I don't just want to go on another holiday, I'd quite like to spend some time alone and experience things that I haven't experienced before. I don't want to lean on Richard like I always do when I go away. I need to do something by myself. I want to prove to myself that I can."

I looked at the wine list in her hand.

"What d'you fancy? A bottle of white?"

"Yeah, a dry crisp one."

Sonya caught the attention of the waitress. "A bottle of No 6, please," she said. "Thanks."

Putting down the wine list, she turned her attention back to me.

"Where are you gonna go then, babe?"

"I'm not sure yet. I'm thinking about doing some voluntary work somewhere. Africa maybe?"

"Oh wow, that would be amazing. I'm so jealous."

"Yeah, it's a bit scary though. I've never been away completely on my own before and I'd have to rough it, I'm sure. I've never backpacked or anything like that."

Hummingbird

"Oh, you'll be fine," she said laughing. "I'm sure you can fit a pair of heels and a hairdryer into your rucksack, hun!"

The wine arrived with two glasses. After a little taster, the waitress poured it out.

"Cheers, Debs," my friend said, holding up her glass for a toast. "Here's to your adventure."

The glasses met with a ching and we drank the cold white wine as we chose our meal.

"They might not have any of this in Africa, babe!" she said, referring to the wine and rubbing it in a little.

"Well, it'll do me good to have a detox," I told her, knowing that this was true.

Our corporate London lives were pretty boozy in those days. As we ate our meal, we talked more about my prospective adventure.

"How long are you going away for then?" Sonya asked.

"I'd like to go away for a few months, if I can. I'll have to go on a tight budget though, if I want to do that. I need to save as much money as I can, because I have no idea how my business is going to take off when I get back home. I only have a few clients at the moment, so I need some money in the bank to tide me over until I get busier."

"Yeah, I see what you mean," Sonya nodded. "What's your budget?"

I told her what I thought I could afford to spend.

"About a thousand pounds, I reckon. More wine?"

"Of course!" She held out her glass. "Where are you gonna go, then? Do you know what you're going to do yet?"

"I haven't got that far yet, Sonya. I need to start looking on the internet."

"Roughing it isn't really your style, is it, babe?" she laughed. "You're more used to expensive holidays and posh hotels. How you gonna cope?"

We were laughing so much that I had to wipe the tears from my eyes.

Then we drank more wine.

"Oh, God, I don't know," I said, trying to compose myself. "But I do want to do it. I want to see what it feels like. I've always been a bit jealous of people who do things like that – you know, backpack and do voluntary work and stuff – even though I do really love my nice holidays and luxury hotels."

I looked at the empty bottle of wine on the table.

"Another bottle?" I asked.

"Of course!"

Sonya was an awesome drinking buddy!

"Here's a toast to roughin' it," she said, when the next bottle arrived and had been poured.

"And nice holidays and luxury hotels," I replied, raising my glass and laughing again.

With the meal over and the second bottle of wine polished off, we made our merry way home.

~ * ~

I began to look at my options. Surfing the internet I found plenty of information about voluntary projects abroad, but the idea of donating my time and manpower to help a good cause in a faraway country (wherever that turned out to be) was soon quashed. My research showed that it would cost me at least double what I had budgeted for. I was gobsmacked. I didn't realise that it would cost so much to give my free-of-charge help on these projects.

I had to have a re-think. If I couldn't do voluntary work, then what could I do that would help me to grow as a person and give me what I needed at this time in my life? Acknowledging to myself how important this trip was to me, I wanted to get it right. After all, it was the bridge between my old life and my new life.

Googling some more, I came across 'a spiritual journey to India' trip, which I thought looked amazing. But at £2,000 it was way out of my price range. However, it got me thinking about two things: spiritual journeys and India. I searched a bit more on spiritual and India and an ashram in Kerala in south-west India caught my attention.

An ashram is a place where you go to practice all aspects of yoga without the distractions of daily life. These being: *asana* (proper exercise), *pranayama* (proper breathing), *savasana* (proper relaxation), vegetarianism (proper diet), *vedanta* (positive thinking) and *dhyana* (meditation).

At the same time as I was researching my adventure, I was also looking for a new yoga class. I'd asked my reflexology teacher if she could let me know where her son did his yoga. I knew that he was really into the proper spiritual yoga that I wanted to practice, as opposed to the more Westernised classes that focus mainly on the stretching.

On exactly the same day as I discovered the Sivananda ashram in Kerala, I received an email from my teacher with the information that her son attended the Sivananda Yoga Centre in London.

Some may call it a coincidence, but I believe that the Universe has a way of organising things for us. I took this as a good sign.

Then the second sign came. Talking to an acquaintance at work who was also taking the redundancy option, I asked her, "What are you planning to do when you leave in a few weeks' time?"

"I'm going to go travelling for a bit," she replied. "For a couple of months."

"Oh, how exciting," I said. "I want to do the same. I've never been away on my own before. I'm a bit nervous, but I really want to do it. Where are you going?"

"I'm going to India with a friend," she told me.

"That's what I'm looking at, as well," I replied, astonished that, of all the places in the world she could be going, she was going to India!

"Whereabouts?" I asked.

"Well, first of all," she said, "we're going to an ashram in Kerala, down south. Then, we're going to work our way up to the north."

"Which ashram are you going to?" I asked and was again astonished when she told me she was going to the Sivananda ashram that I'd been looking at!

There are so many ashrams in India she could have been visiting. I don't know how many, but there are certainly a lot. After all, India is the home of the ashram. It was my second sign.

The third defining factor for me was that it wasn't expensive. The flights would cost me £600 and the ashram charged only £7 a day. That was well within my budget.

~ * ~

"So, what are you going to do exactly?" Richard asked me when I told him I'd decided on my destination.

"Well, if I'm really careful with my money, I think I can afford to spend a total of six weeks in India. I'll spend three of them at the ashram and then, hopefully, I'll meet some people there to travel with afterwards. If I don't meet anyone there, I'll book into a hotel for a week at the beach and then maybe come home."

I looked at Richard's face and detected a look that I couldn't quite fathom out.

"How do you feel about me being away for so long, Richard?"

"I'll miss you of course," he said. "But I think it's a great opportunity for you, Deb, and I think you should go for it. It's really brave of you."

Richard was always so supportive and was always 100 per cent behind me in whatever I wanted to do.

I bought a travel book on India and made a list of the places that I wanted to visit whilst I was there.

"I want to go to Cochin (now known as Kochi)," I told him. "I'd *love* to see the wild dolphins there and they have these amazing big fishing nets, look!" I turned the book towards him and showed him the photo. "And this place looks good…"

His eyes followed my finger as it pointed to the entry for Varkala.

"It's a beach resort. I definitely want to go to the beach while I'm there."

It was no use, I simply couldn't imagine a holiday without a beach.

"I don't think I could stand the heat there," Richard said. "With my pale skin, I'd be burned to a crisp after six weeks in India."

It was the Irish blood in him. Whenever we went away he would tell people, "Yes, I do get a tan. I go from blue to white!"

"Seriously though, Deb," he said hugging me. "Just be careful, okay?"

"I didn't think I'd ever be brave enough, or experienced enough come to that, to travel around on my own," I admitted. "I really hope that I meet some people to travel with at the ashram. I should do, shouldn't I? Loads of people travel in India."

"Well, if you don't, you can always just get a taxi from the ashram to a hotel at Varkala for a week and then come home."

I had a Plan B. I liked that.

And so, in January 2002, I embarked on my journey to India.

Chapter 34

Off to India

If we don't change, we don't grow. If we don't grow, we are not really living. Growth demands a temporary surrender of security – The Daily Love.com

Richard drove me to Heathrow airport. I was full of excitement, but also really pleased that he was with me.

At the departure gate, my excitement was replaced by a strong feeling of nervousness. I hugged him tightly.

"I'm really gonna miss you, Richard."

"I'm gonna miss you, too," he said, hugging me back.

We both had a few tears in our eyes.

"Let me know that you got there safely."

"I will, I'll email you from the ashram. Bye, babe. I love you."

"I love you, too. Be safe. Have a great time. I'll be thinking of you… Bye."

Both waving until out of sight, Richard turned to make his journey home alone and I went forward as I started my spiritual journey to India.

As I went through security, I gathered myself and focused on boarding the right plane. For years I'd relied on Richard to sort out the practicalities of travelling.

"This is going to be good for me," I said to myself, trying hard to sound convincing.

I successfully found my way to the departure lounge of Gate 25 at Heathrow airport. It wasn't difficult at all. As I waited to board my flight to Bahrain, the first stop of my three leg journey to Kerala, I dug deep to find the courage to overcome the fear that had started to rise within me.

As I sat there waiting, my thoughts turned to my mum. I thought of how scared she must have been when Nigel died and wondered how afraid she had felt when being interrogated by the police. I was trying to imagine being in her position. She must have felt a sickness in her stomach as she was standing in court, not knowing if she would walk out that day a free woman or not.

I thought about how miserable and painful Nigel's life had become and how he had faced his decision with courage and strength and how powerless Philip's existence was now, trapped inside a body that was not allowing him to communicate with anyone or even participate in his life in any way.

Thoughts of my family gave me the strength and courage I searched for. I had to do this for myself. I wanted to make the most of my life, to do things with it, to make it count.

I boarded the plane and found my seat. I put my luggage in the space above the seat and sat down, saying hello to the man sitting next to me. The man smiled and in an Australian accent said hello back and introduced himself as Tony. He was quite a chatty Aussie.

"I'm on my way to my brother-in-law's funeral," Tony told me. "He had cancer. It's been awful for my sister, having to watch him suffering like that. The whole family has suffered. In a way, I'm glad I wasn't there to be honest, poor bloke."

"Yeah, I can understand that," I answered, wishing he would stop telling me all this.

Of all the seats on the plane, I had to sit next to someone who was going to a flippin' funeral!

He needed to talk and I was a captive audience. Not that I would usually mind. I'm usually a very compassionate person and a good listener. It just wasn't what I needed right then, that's all. A comedian would have been a good companion for me or a traveller with interesting stories of places they had been to and people they had met along the way.

"Universe," I asked silently. "What's going on?"

"Why do people have to suffer like that?" Tony continued. "They don't let animals suffer like that, do they?"

I agreed with a shake of the head, as he hardly stopped for breath.

"I'm glad he's not suffering anymore."

I let him talk, filling any gaps with the odd sympathetic phrase and nod of the head. When he'd got it off his chest, I went to sleep for a while.

Arriving at Bahrain airport I said my goodbyes to Tony and disembarked.

Hummingbird

My first flight transfer was a success. Having to rush to the gate meant that I didn't have any time to think about what was happening. I don't remember seeing any other single women at that airport, just either couples or lone men fitted out in their traditional long cotton thobes. It was all very unfamiliar to me.

I sat on the plane, waiting to feel its movement as it taxied to the runway for takeoff.

And I waited.

"We're sorry for the delay," the voice on the PA announced. "We are just waiting for the luggage from the late arrival of the London plane."

I swear that I could feel all eyes on me and I tried to sink inconspicuously into my seat, but with no success I'm sure. I was sticking out like a sore thumb, with my white skin and my Western clothes.

As I waited for takeoff, I looked out of the window and had to double take.

"Blimey", I thought. "There's a KFC!"

As we finally took off, I found myself smiling. The familiar sight was strangely comforting.

Sitting next to me on this flight to Muscat in Oman was a middle-aged Arabic woman. She didn't look too happy to me.

"I'm afraid of flying," she confessed.

"Would you like me to hold your hand?" I asked her, happy to be helping someone who, at that moment, was feeling more vulnerable than I was.

She gratefully took me up on my offer.

"Thank you," she said and slipped her hand into mine.

Then she prayed.

"Deep breaths," I suggested. "Take nice deep breaths and you'll be fine."

Needless to say, she survived the takeoff and letting go of her grasp, I shook the feeling back into my hand.

"Wow, that's quite a grip you have there, lady," I thought to myself as the blood rushed back in.

Sitting the other side of the woman was a man dressed in a thobe.

Making conversation in quite good English, he was really friendly and I began to feel less anxious and alone.

Muscat airport was fairly quiet and easy to navigate. With a two-hour wait ahead of me, I had another chance to think about my trip. I wrote in my journal and reflected on my reasons for travelling to India. I asked myself what I wanted to get out of this? I hadn't quite left the corporate world behind me, I was still looking for a mission and a clear idea of what my future would look like.

As I made my way to India, I decided that my mission was to find out who I am and I wrote down my vision statement: "A better me and a better life. To become more disciplined, focused, passionate, positive, courageous, alert, confident, fit and healthy. To be stronger in both mind and body."

So, that was sorted.

My third flight to India was also delayed. I was feeling quite tired, but was afraid to close my eyes and rest in case I fell asleep and missed the flight. I decided to wander about for a while and came across a couple of Europeans guys.

"May I sit with you?" I bravely asked them and was thankful when they agreed.

One of the men was English, the other German.

"It looks like we're the only Westerners here," I said as I sat down. "What are you going to India for, business or pleasure?"

"A bit of both, actually," the friendly Englishman informed me, in his terribly posh accent. "How about you?"

"I'm going to an ashram," I answered. "I've never been away on my own like this before and I'm a bit nervous, to tell the truth. Do you know anyone in India?"

"We're being met by a friend who's a priest. He's been doing some work in India."

"Oh, that sounds interesting. Will you be doing some voluntary work with him?" I asked, hoping that I wasn't coming across as too nosey.

"We'll be looking at some of his projects," the young English gent said. We never actually introduced ourselves by name.

A bit more probing led me to discover that the German guy did some kind of teaching and was to be giving some talks in India, but I didn't really understand their story properly and I didn't want to pry. Whilst the English guy was very friendly, the German fellow was extremely staid.

Talking to the men about the ashram and meditation however, I discovered that the German man had once spent two whole weeks in a monastery in total silence.

"Now that's what I would call a real challenge," I thought. I was suitably impressed.

Eventually, it was time to board the final plane to Thiruvananthapuram and I managed to sleep for a while on the flight to India. I was so tired, but my mind was still really active.

I have a strange feeling that this plane journey is going to be the easy part, I wrote in my journal. The closer I get to my destination, the more nervous I'm starting to feel.

When we arrived at Trivandrum airport I followed the other commuters like a sheep. I hoped that they'd lead me to the point where I could collect my backpack and thankfully they did. It was here that I met up with the two Europeans again and we soon realised that there was a problem with the luggage.

Luckily, my bag had arrived safely in India, but the two guys were not as fortunate. Their luggage had somehow been left at Muscat airport. I couldn't begin to imagine how I would have felt if that had been my bag. I was so relieved that I had my stuff safely in my arms and didn't know what I would have done out there on my own without my things. Looked up at the ceiling, I whispered, "Thank you."

Leaving the airport, I was immediately approached by several taxi drivers offering me their services. I got into one of the taxis and showed the driver the address of the ashram.

"Yes, yes, okay," he said, with a nod and a shake of the head.

Speeding off, the kamikaze driver negotiated the traffic like a madman, as he tore through the dusty hot streets. He continuously sniffed in, coughed up and spat out of the window all the way there and I can honestly say that it was the scariest and most unpleasant car journey I have ever encountered. I was really beginning to fret as I felt the anxiety rising up from my solar plexus again.

I was so busy trying to focus on staying calm that I can't recall all the details of the taxi ride to the Ashram. I remember that it was extremely hot in India and everything there was so unfamiliar.

I had been to a lot of different countries before and so I kept telling myself that I only felt anxious because I was there on my own. As the panic gripped me, I started to wonder what on earth I was doing there, all alone in this foreign land.

Chapter 35

The ashram

After a couple of hours of hair-raising driving, I arrived at the ashram alive and in one piece, no thanks to my driver. I was shown to the office.

Taking off my heavy backpack I placed it on the ground beside me. My back and my forehead were damp with sweat. I was so relieved to finally be there and was looking forward to a nice cool shower.

"I have a booking with you," I told them. "Deborah Goodman."

Most people at the ashram stayed in the dormitory. There were two on site, one for the men and one for the women. I hadn't fancied that, so I had booked a two-person room at a cost of one pound extra per night. I figured it would be worth it and I was looking forward to meeting my roommate.

I waited as the lady looked for my name, following her finger with my eyes as it went from one name to another down the page in front of her.

I was relieved when she found me on her list.

"Your room isn't ready yet," she told me. "You can leave your bags here for now. I'll show you where to go for dinner."

I was disappointed. I was definitely hungry, but I was eager to freshen up after the long journey from England. I was desperate to have a wash and to change into some fresh clothes.

The woman showed me where to wash my hands and then I followed her to the hall, looking forward to meeting some other people and hoping that talking to someone would make me feel a bit calmer.

As I entered the large hall where dinner was being served, I soon realised that I wouldn't be chatting to anyone just yet.

There was total silence.

About 200 people were sitting on the floor of the hall. They were eating their meals with one hand, using the Indian bread to scoop the food up with. No-one spoke a word.

Contrary to how I was feeling, everyone else looked so at ease. I nervously sat myself down at the end of a row of people and waited to be served my meal. The silence felt very spiritual. It was obviously forbidden to speak during meals and with tears burning at the back of my eyes, I felt scared and alone.

I remembered what my colleague who had already been to the ashram had said in her email to me: "I found it really strange at first. It takes a few days to adjust." At that moment, I couldn't see me staying there even for three days, let alone three weeks!

I knew that I felt this way because it was all so unfamiliar and because I was on my own.

After the meal, desperate to connect with someone and without my room to retreat to, I hung around the office for a while. I was able to use the email there and I wrote to Richard, letting him know I had arrived safely, but also how I was feeling.

I kept on telling myself not to be so stupid, but unfortunately I wasn't listening. I had a quick look around the site but, still feeling vulnerable, I went back to the reception. For some misguided reason, I felt that I wouldn't have anything in common with anyone else there, so I made a £7.50 phone call home. It may not seem a lot, but to put it into perspective, it cost more than a whole day's stay at the ashram, including food.

"Richard, it's me." I was so glad that he was at home.

"Hello, you," he said, excited to hear from me. "I just got your email. Are you okay?"

"I'm here, but I'm not feeling very good," I told him.

"I'm so sorry, Deb." He sounded worried about me.

"I just feel so out of place here," I tried to explain. "It's so different to anything I've ever known before. So spiritual and weird. I don't think I have anything in common with anyone. I'm feeling scared and alone." Through my tears I told him, "I miss you. I can't believe I've done this. What was I thinking of?"

"What's your room like?" he asked me.

"I haven't even got it yet. It's not ready for me. I'm just hanging around."

I told him about eating my meal in silence.

"You wanted a spiritual experience though, Deb," he reminded me.

"I know, but I'm so far out of my comfort zone, Rich. I don't think I can cope."

Hummingbird

"It's okay," he reassured me. "I'll look on the internet for a hotel you can go to. I'll email you the details. Just get a taxi and check into it. Would that be better?"

"Thanks, Rich. It's such a shame I feel like this. I wish I was back at home with you in Orpington. I'll email you when I can use the computer again."

There was only one computer on site.

"I'm missing you, Deb," he told me as we hung up.

~ * ~

The first person I met at the ashram, other than the lady in the office, was an English guy called Gary. He came to the office for something while I was still hanging around waiting for my room.

He was quite friendly and it was great to talk to someone. I found out that he'd been in India for four months and was travelling alone.

"Doesn't it bother you, travelling alone?" I asked him.

"No, not at all. I'm used to it."

He seemed to be incredibly confident, which was a total contrast to how I was feeling.

After spending three hours in the stifling heat at the ashram, desperate for a wash after my long journey and something to drink, my room still wasn't ready. I was really tired, but thankfully feeling a bit calmer. I went to the on-site shop with Gary. I only had traveller's cheques and US dollars, so I couldn't even get any water or a yoga mat to sit on.

Gary was going to a lecture and not knowing what else to do with myself, I went with him. I sat for two hours on the hard wooden floor in the large rectangle room, barely paying attention to a word that was being said by the swami. I was far too busy listening to the negative thoughts in my head.

The ashram itself was situated on a large, self-contained site with everything that was needed to enable a person to practice the spiritual art of all aspects of yoga.

Here's a reminder for you of what these are: *asana* (proper exercise), *pranayama* (proper breathing), *savasana* (proper relaxation), vegetarianism (proper diet), *vedanta* (positive thinking) and *dhyana* (meditation).

It was expected that I participate in all these activities to enable me to get a fuller and more meaningful experience.

Each day, I was required to be up at 5.30am and ready for *satsung* at 6am. Satsung consisted of silent meditation, chanting of mantras and either a lecture or reading. This was always followed at 8am by two hours of yoga postures. At 10am we were more than ready for brunch. In the afternoon, there was another two-hour yoga class at 4pm, followed by dinner at six and satsung at eight. The lights went out at 10.30pm each night.

Is this what I had so happily signed up for back in the UK? I guess so. It seemed like such a good idea at the time.

When I was finally given the key to my room I was so thankful, but as I opened the door and looked inside it, my heart sank.

Don't get me wrong, I wasn't expecting the same standards as the luxury hotels I was used to (no, not at all – honestly I wasn't!) but the bare brick room I was faced with was far more basic than I had ever imagined.

"This is awful," I thought to myself.

The thought of spending three weeks in that room filled me with dread. Basic is definitely how I would describe it. I put my bag down on the bed and unzipped it. Slowly I unpacked everything and laid it on the bed in front of me as my already low spirits plummeted even further. To me, the bare brick walls felt cold and the two single beds were naked and uninviting.

"You must have a shower," the voice in my head was telling me. After many hours travelling I was hot and sticky and in desperate need of more than a little freshen up. I walked into the stark brick shower room and turned on the tap. As I felt the cool water splash over my body, I smiled for the first time since I left the airport. It was refreshing and I was thankful for it.

Feeling clean and refreshed at last, I placed my belongings back in my bag, laid out my sleeping bag liner on top of the bed and slipped into it. I fell asleep, emotionally and physically exhausted.

When I woke up, it was suppertime, so I got dressed and left the room. Almost instantly, feelings of panic started to rise and I felt the tears pricking at the back of my eyes. I felt so stupid for reacting this way and I didn't know what to do, so I turned on my heels and went back to the sanctuary of my bare brick room, which was suddenly looking a little more like a friend to me.

It was obvious that this was going to be one of the biggest challenges of my life so far. I sat down on the bed and I sobbed.

What on earth had I been thinking of, coming all this way on my own to a place that was so far removed from what I was used to?

"The main reason you feel so afraid, Deborah," the voice inside kept reminding me, "is because you are alone. You wouldn't feel as scared if you had a friend with you or if you were alone in more familiar surroundings."

The voice was right. The reason I was feeling so vulnerable was because the ashram was completely different to anything I'd ever known before and it had totally unbalanced me. I knew that I needed to make a connection with someone in order to get myself grounded again.

In addition to that, it was baking hot and I was thirsty. I still didn't have any rupees, water or a mat for yoga. I guess it wasn't surprising that my mood was so low.

I pulled myself together and gave myself a talking to.

"This is no good," I said. "You *have* to go out and get something to eat and drink. This is ridiculous. What are you going to do, stay in your room for three weeks? Come on, don't be an idiot. Try again."

I left my room for a second attempt at integration. Unfortunately, by then I'd missed the meal. I was hungry but thankful that I had some biscuits with me to eat. I found a quiet spot to sit and calm myself and as I was wondering what to do for the best, I saw Gary.

"Hello," he said as he sat down next to me.

I burst into tears.

"Whatever's the matter?" he asked, looking rather uncomfortable and surprised at my random outburst. After all, he'd only said hello, poor man.

"Oh, God, I'm sorry," I sniffed. "I just feel so out of place here, I'm completely out of my depth. I've never been away on my own before and this is so different to anything I've ever experienced."

I tried to catch my breath. Still sniffing and wiping my eyes with the backs of my hands I told him, "I just feel really vulnerable. I can't help it, I just keep crying. I shouldn't have come here on my own; I have no idea what I was thinking!"

"Well, you came here for a reason, Deborah," Gary pointed out. "And you might not even know what that reason is yet, but there's *definitely* a good and valid reason why you're here."

He watched as I tried to compose myself.

"Don't you have any water?"

"No," I told him. "I don't have any rupees yet and I can't change any until someone comes to the ashram in a few days to do the currency exchange."

"Here, have mine."

He handed over his bottle of water. I was so thirsty and was grateful for his kindness.

"Thanks. I'll buy you one back as soon as I can."

I felt so foolish.

Gary and I talked for a while and I calmed down a bit, but I still didn't feel at all comfortable. Gary seemed so confident and at ease with his surroundings that I couldn't imagine how he could understand what I was feeling.

Just then a young couple came and sat beside us.

"Hi, I'm Cassandra," said the attractive girl as she greeted us. "Or some people just call me Cass." Then seeing the tears in my eyes she asked, "Are you okay?"

"I think so," I told her. "I've only just got here and I'm on my own and I'm just feeling a bit lost."

Cassandra was a slender young woman in her late twenties, with short brown hair. She had recently arrived at the ashram with her boyfriend, Matthew. He was a tall, handsome young guy with a nice friendly way about him.

"That's how I felt when I got here," she said reassuringly. "We've only been here a few days and I'm getting a bit more used to it now. You'll be fine, don't worry."

She put her arm around my shoulder and gave me a much-needed hug.

"I wouldn't have come here on my own," Cass told me. "I think you're really brave."

I immediately knew that I liked Cass, she was friendly and open. She was so easy to talk to and our conversation flowed freely. We were soon sharing our worries and thoughts and I began to feel my spirits rising again.

I had an instant connection with her and although we soon discovered that our day-to-day lives back home were very different, I realised that she was just like me in many ways.

"We've been travelling together for months," she told me. "I'm used to roughing it now, but I don't like sleeping in the dormitory here. I wish I had a room like you do."

"I hate my room," I said. "It's awful."

"Well, it can't be as bad as the dorm, I'm sure!" said Cassandra, laughing.

"Do you want to come and have a look at it?" I offered. "There's not much else to do at the moment."

"Yeah, okay then." They all agreed and so Cass, Matthew and Gary came back with me to size up my accommodation.

"Wow, this is a good room," Matthew assured me as he looked around. "We've stayed in much worse than this. A lot worse. At least you have your own bathroom – and even a balcony."

To my surprise, he seemed really impressed.

"You're joking?" I said, astonished.

"No, honestly, this is nice. Who are you sharing with?"

"I don't know," I answered. "She hasn't arrived yet."

"I hope she doesn't come," said Cassandra. "Then I can share with you."

I hoped so, too. I really hoped so.

"Anyone want a Garibaldi?" I offered, sharing my biscuits around. "I missed supper 'cos I was hiding in my room."

At least now I was able to laugh at myself. That was a good sign. Definitely a good sign.

Cass and I talked some more, whilst the boys chatted together on the other bed. There were no chairs in the room.

"We've been thinking a lot about our relationship," Cass confided in me. "We're not sure what to do. We've come to the ashram to give each other a bit of space. It seemed an ideal place as we're in separate dorms here," she said.

They were obviously still great friends, but she told me that they needed some time to think and decide what to do for the best.

We sat and talked until the lights out curfew and beyond.

"We're already breaking the rules," I whispered, as my new friends finally crept out of my room into the quiet stillness of the night.

So, this was my first night in India. I had a headache and I was hungry, but I felt much better now that I had connected with Cass. I still didn't like my room and I still wished that I wasn't there alone. I unzipped my sleeping bag and got into it. After setting my alarm for 5:30am I instantly fell into a deep sleep.

Chapter 36

Stretch and grow

My alarm woke me up and I was soon aware that it was raining heavily outside. I got up and dressed and ran through the rain to the hall for my first session of meditation and chanting.

It wasn't easy to quiet my mind, but the meditation made me feel much calmer.

Lunch was at 10am in the large hall and I knew that it would take me a while to get used to sitting on the floor and eating in silence. I found Cass and Matthew and we joined the end of a row of cross-legged people and sat down, waiting to be served.

Carrying out their assigned karma yoga, the food monitors carried the food in large metal buckets, filling our trays with a healthy, fresh vegetarian meal.

"Make sure you eat the yoghurt stuff," Matthew whispered. "It has good bacteria in it that will help your tummy to stay healthy."

I held out my tray for the liquid to be poured over my rice. Thankfully, it tasted quite nice.

After lunch we poured tea from a large urn. The chi was milky and sweet and not at all to my taste, so I drank the herbal tea instead, which I found quite palatable.

Luckily, that day my scheduled roommate didn't arrive at the ashram and Cass was permitted to move into my room with me. The dormitory she was in was cold and noisy and it had a leak. She was pleased to get out of it.

"What a coincidence she didn't turn up," I said.

"It's not a coincidence," Cass told me, as she rolled out her sleeping bag on the spare bed. "That's how the Universe works. It was mean to be."

Cass was a wonderful person. I felt as though I'd known her forever and I loved her from the moment I met her.

I enjoyed the yoga classes. At first the classes were held in the main hall due to the heavy rain, but after a few days the rain dried up and it became hot and sticky again and we were able to perform our asanas down by the beautiful lake. The stunning views made it an idyllic place to practice.

In the afternoons, I went to the café with my new friends. The café was a basic outdoor hut, serving fruit salads, sweets and lassis, which are traditional yogurt-based drinks. When the rain stopped it provided us with shelter from the sweltering heat of the Indian sun.

"I still don't have any rupees," I told my friends. "And I can't exchange money until Tuesday. Could you lend me some please?"

I felt bad for asking. A lady overheard me.

"I'm leaving today," she said. "I'll exchange some money with you."

"Oh, that would be wonderful, thank you so much."

I was delighted that finally I had some cash to spend. I hated asking the others to buy me drinks or lend me money. With rupees now in my pocket, I went on a mad shopping spree, buying water, a yoga mat and a cushion for mediation. I felt positively rich!

Sometimes Matthew would come along to the café with us and occasionally Gary would join us there. I liked Gary but I never felt as comfortable with him as I did with Cass and Matthew.

"You know what?" I said to my new friends. "When I arrived here, I honestly thought I'd have nothing in common with anyone. Meeting you guys has been a lifesaver for me. I honestly don't know what I would have done if I hadn't met you both. I'm so pleased you're here, I really am."

"I'm really glad you're here too," said Cass. "I really wanted to get out of the dorm. To be honest, I didn't think I'd have much in common with anyone either. It was definitely meant to be."

She smiled at me and I gave her a hug.

I soon began to realise that the ashram would be a place of many discoveries and revelations.

"We should never judge a book by its cover, eh?" I remarked.

"No. It's a lesson learned," agreed Matthew.

During my first week at the ashram, I had some lows and some not-so-lows. Cass and Matthew were amazing, but they had a long history together and still needed their own time to talk and to sort out their issues. I had only just met them and I had to stand on my own two feet. I was still on my own quite a lot of the time.

At my lowest point, I rang Richard again and talked about coming home.

"I just feel so alone here," I told him, crying. "I miss meals sometimes because I don't want to sit alone in silence in the big hall. Am I the only one here who feels like this? What's wrong with me?" I sobbed.

Being brave enough to try new things and to step outside my comfort zone was all very well, but it certainly wasn't an easy thing to do. I had wanted to get away and have wonderful new experiences, however I was now more aware than ever that it was difficult for me to be by myself in such an unfamiliar place.

"There's nothing wrong with you, Deb," said Richard reassuringly. "You're just not used to it, that's all. I wouldn't go away on my own, not many people would. And it's nothing like you've ever done before. I'm so sorry you're so upset. Please try not to worry. Why don't you just get a taxi to a hotel by the beach?"

A heavy feeling of disappointment washed through me.

"I wanted to get so much out of this, Richard," I told my worried boyfriend. "I don't know if coming here has done me more harm than good."

A big part of me wanted to take his advice and run like crazy to more familiar surroundings.

"When I left home," I sniffed, "I honestly believed that I'd be able to deal with it here. I'm so disappointed at how I feel. I'm gutted that I'm finding it so difficult."

I began to wonder if following this spiritual path was really worth all the grief. I knew that there would be growing pains associated with my journey, but I had to question whether it was all in a good cause or whether I was just hurting myself more.

"I miss you so much. I miss everyone."

~ * ~

The real voyage of discovery consists not in seeking new lands but seeing with new eyes – *Marcel Proust*

I felt better for speaking to Richard, but I'd got myself into a right old state with my negative thinking. Upset and disappointed, I found Cass and Matthew.

"What's up?" Matthew asked me as soon as he saw my face.

I told him how I was feeling.

"Here, come and sit down, Deborah," he said.

I did as I was told. Matthew sat beside me and spoke kindly to me.

"Now calm down and don't worry. Everyone gets scared sometimes. You should confront your fears and persevere, otherwise how will you ever be able to do the things you want to do with your life?"

"I know, but I just feel so bad," I told him.

"Okay," he said firmly. "Why did you come here?"

I told him again all the reasons why I'd come to India.

"What do you want to achieve? Tell me exactly what you want to do and where you want to go." Matthew was certainly taking me in hand.

Again I told him of my vision and mission statements. I said that I'd like to become a stronger and better person, healthier and fitter in mind and body. I wanted see the dolphins at Cochin and to go to Varkala beach. I wanted to get a train and travel around a bit and see the other places I had marked down on my list.

"I can't imagine any of it now." I told him.

I had allowed my negative thoughts to escalate and to spiral my mind into a very low place.

Matthew was very wise.

"If you stay and make it through to the end of the six weeks in India and do all the things you plan to do on this trip, how do you think you'll feel, Debs?" he asked me.

"Oh, I'd be so pleased," I admitted. "So proud of myself."

"Imagine it. You will really have achieved something so great that you'll never have to be afraid of doing any of those things again. See, it's just like yoga. At first when we stretch, it hurts. Then the next time we stretch, it hurts a bit less and we can stretch a little further. We achieve more with every stretch and the more flexible we get, the more pleasurable it becomes and the more we can achieve."

I smiled at the thought of it. He was so right. I think it's one of the best pieces of advice I've ever heard.

Matthew told me a story about the first time he went away on his own.

Hummingbird

"I was petrified," he said. I phoned my mum in tears because I felt I was going crazy."

"Really?" I asked him. It surprised me but at the same time, it made me feel a whole lot better about myself.

For so many years I'd felt unable to cope well with the emotional challenges in my life and I yearned to become stronger. I wanted to make the most of my life now and I was eager to find out what India had in store for me. I really did want to see it through to the end, to do the things I'd planned to do when I left the ashram and I finally allowed myself to acknowledge just how big a challenge the whole trip was for me.

I didn't take a taxi to a hotel by the beach. I stuck with it and felt the pain – and pleasure – of the stretch.

Chapter 37

Everything is in divine order

I decided to stay for two weeks instead of three. That was the length of the yoga programme and the time when many others would be leaving the ashram.

I stopped fighting against my feelings. The yoga started to open me up and release deep-rooted problems. Issues that were pushed down inside me began to surface and now needed to be dealt with. The ashram was definitely the place to deal with them. For me, being there was like being in a non-stop, two-week therapy session. I found that the people there were generally very open, kind and easy to talk to. Many had their own issues to deal with and I found that sharing and discussing our thoughts, fears and feelings was not just beneficial for me but for others, too.

There was no more rain in India after that, only sunshine.

I had let go of the tension I was holding onto and I settled into my daily routine, focusing on the here and now rather than the past and the future. Yoga by the lake was glorious. As I teased my body gently into the different postures, the warmth of the sun felt nourishing and comforting. The spectacular view of the lake and the surrounding landscape brought with it a sense of tranquillity and freedom.

Every day we had a lecture. The lectures were informative and interesting and I really looked forward to them. The swami's voice was slow, soft and rhythmic and his words were comforting. It felt as though his voice was stroking me, like a mother's gentle touch.

The lecture one day was about following everything we do to completion, to enable us to gain satisfaction. The words were confirmation to me that I needed to stay in India and see my journey through to the end.

Cass and I spent many hours discussing our deepest thoughts and fears.

"Matthew and I have decided to break up and go our separate ways," she told me one day. She was clearly very upset about it. "It's the right thing to do, I just know it is," she told me.

I was upset for her but I was pleased to have the opportunity to return the support that she had so generously given to me. We propped each other up as and when was necessary.

"It's amazing how we've come to be together here, Cass. I'm sure we were sent here to support each other you know. I feel as though I've known you all my life."

"Oh, undoubtedly," she said. "We knew each other in a past life, I'm sure."

"I really thought that the Universe had sent you here to support me, but now I realise that it's a two-way thing."

Cass was also scared of being alone and needed to learn to be independent and strong in her own right. She had been with Matthew for a few years and had come to rely on him a bit too much.

"I'm certain that it was no coincidence that my roommate didn't turn up," I told her.

Now it was Cass's turn to need my support. It was difficult to know whether to let her cry it out for a while or to try to lift her spirits.

Now that she was single, I dared to hope that Cassandra would become my travelling companion when I left the ashram. I prayed with all my heart that this would be the case.

I'm not quite sure when I started to think of my room as a luxury, but somewhere along the line I did.

I became more comfortable about the eating arrangements and Cass started to let go of her worries and concentrate on the yoga and meditation more.

The swami explained how to sit properly for meditation and why we do the yoga postures which help to prepare our bodies for sitting meditation. He explained step-by-step how to meditate by firstly checking our body for tension and mentally focusing on it to release it. He explained how to relax the mind, how to breathe properly and the points of the body to focus on, such as the third eye or heart centre. He talked about using a mantra and how we can be a spectator of our thoughts instead of grasping onto them and allowing them to take control of our minds. I loved listening to the lectures and the scenery down by the lake was breathtaking. Finally, I began to feel blessed to be there.

Everyone at the ashram was assigned karma yoga or in other words, was given a job to do. My job was to lay down the mats for the daily lecture and take them up afterwards. This is how I met Debbie.

Debbie was a petite, spiritual, Earth Mother-type, reiki master. As we carried out our karma yoga, I told her about meeting Cassandra.

"God always sends you someone when you need them," Debbie said and I believe wholeheartedly that this is true.

Debbie was lovely. Being a seasoned traveller, she had many words of wisdom and, having suffered with depression herself in the past, was sympathetic to my plight.

That night at satsung, I closed my eyes and concentrated. I focused on my voice and on the individual sounds of the instruments. I had a completely different experience to the night before, when I allowed my mind to wander and wish that I was watching a show instead, with dancing girls and costumes, feathers and fans! I had been bored because I wasn't allowing myself to experience it properly and fully, purely and simply for what it was.

Satsung was followed by the swami reciting fables, which were not only interesting, but also quite amusing.

He told us: "Life is like a river, ebbing to and fro and going from side to side. We should not resist its flow, but allow ourselves to go with it. It's when we resist our fate that the pain comes in."

This reminded me of something that my guru, Larry, used to say to me: "It is what it is."

Which means that it isn't good and it isn't bad, it just *is*.

After another phone call to Richard, I decided that I needed to stop spending so much time on the phone to England. After all, the whole idea of the trip was to get away from home and to focus on myself and to become more independent, wasn't it?

One day, we had a lecture on the philosophy of yoga. The swami taught us that yoga is a spiritual science that brings the separate consciousness of the individual to oneness. He said that we have three bodies or vehicles: the physical, the astral and the causal.

The physical body is made up of food. The asanas or hatha yoga take care of our physical body. We are not our body. Our body is just the vehicle in which we travel. The body changes, but there is always the same I.

The astral body or subtle body is the engine of the car. It is made up of prana (vital energy), the mind and senses, the emotions, the intellect and the ego. The ego is our identification. It makes us who we are and it prevents us from becoming something else. If we want to grow and change, we have to change our ego.

The causal body is the spiritual body (the I).

There are five parts of yoga, which are:

Meditation
Exercise
Breathing
Proper diet
Proper relaxation

Practicing the five parts of yoga helps us to bring the three dimensions of the body together at the same time.

In addition to this, there is also:

Karma yoga (our deeds, or our selfless service)
Bakta yoga (love, devotion, and chanting)
Raja yoga (the control of our mind) and
Jnana yoga (yogic philosophy).

The lecture summed up and explained the things that we were doing each day at the ashram. Most people I know would think that yoga was simply the exercises that keep our bodies supple. I was fascinated by the holistic concept of yoga and yoga philosophy. It's so much more than physical movement. It's a way of life.

I realised that it was possible to incorporate these things into my life. It would certainly be possible to eat a proper diet, meditate and exercise and to incorporate proper relaxation into the exercise as I was being taught.

We can certainly all do karma yoga every day in some way or another and also bakta yoga by saying prayers.

It is also possible to practice a form of raja yoga in our everyday lives. Raja yoga focuses on bringing the mind and emotions into balance.

In its true nature, the mind is peaceful and enlightened. But for many of us, our minds are far from peaceful. They are constantly chattering away with meaningless thoughts and worries of our lives.

Take my mind for instance. Throughout my life it had been chattering away with unhelpful thoughts about what would happen to me if I got Huntington's disease, how it would affect my relationships, how my partner would cope, wondering how my dad felt, what my auntie was thinking, and why all this was this happening to us.

The list could go on and I could probably fill a page with the negative, unhelpful thoughts that were constantly running through my mind.

My heart would sink on the journey to the hospital, whether it was to visit my dad, my aunt or one of my brothers. It was my thoughts about seeing them suffering that would trigger the feelings of sadness that caused me to experience the event as a distressing encounter. When I learned about how our negative thoughts affect our feelings and cause us distress, and was taught how to still my mind and balance my energies, my mind became more passive and my visits became easier and certainly much less stressful and upsetting.

Being able to finally relax my mind gave me a very pleasant sense of velvety wellbeing.

The only way to master all aspects of yoga is to practice, practice and practice some more. We will never become experts unless we devote our whole lives to it, but we can become better at it throughout our lifetime if we incorporate it into our routine.

Chapter 38

Letting go

I already had my massage qualification when I went to India and I was eager to experience as many massages as I could afford. So, after a few days at the ashram I booked myself in for a treatment. The massages at the ashram were administered by the Indian women who, unfortunately for me, didn't speak a word of English.

I entered the treatment room and as I looked around, I noticed the large wooden table in the centre of the room. Using hand gestures, the petite therapist beckoned to me to take off my clothes. I did as she suggested, leaving only my knickers on, but as I stood in front of her in just my panties, I was surprised that she was indicating to me that I should take them off as well.

I pointed to them, just to make sure that this was what she meant. She nodded. I felt pretty uncomfortable with this, so pointing again, I mimed to her that I was taking them off, using a downward movement of my hands and a stepping-out-of-my-knickers mime, coupled with a questioning facial expression.

She nodded again.

"I was afraid that's what you meant," I muttered under my breath and reluctantly did as I was asked.

Her outstretched arm and hand invited me to sit on the chair provided.

Reluctantly and rather embarrassingly, I sat down. Feeling extremely self-conscious reminded me that nudity was something that just didn't happen in my family and I was far from comfortable with it. Even at the leisure centre I always felt embarrassed if anyone stripped off in front of me in the changing rooms. I was horrified the first time a woman took all of her clothes off, not knowing which way to look as I gingerly attempted to get dried and changed beneath my towel. Even showing off a nipple made me feel uncomfortable and I certainly never went topless on the beach.

I pressed my legs together so tightly that it hurt my knees. Seemingly oblivious to my embarrassment, the therapist started to massage my head, rubbing and kneading my scalp and her movements felt pleasing. As she worked the nourishing oils into my hair, I slowly began to relax and enjoy the massage a little more.

With the head massage over, she gestured to me to lie on the large wooden table, face down, and continued to work on my back, neck and shoulders. The warm oil felt soothing as her small strong hands worked on my body but with the bareness of the situation I found it rather difficult to let go and fully relax.

I tried to focus all of my attention on the massage, but unfortunately my thoughts were dominated by the anticipation of her asking me to turn over onto my back, face up. I was scared.

Inevitably, she finished working on my back and legs and it was now time. I turned over and there I was, laying face upwards, stark naked with the petite Indian masseuse now working on the front of my legs. After massaging one leg she moved it outward, further away from my second leg, which she then massaged and moved outwards the other way. Then she bent both legs to work on other muscles and I was fully exposed, butt naked, spread-eagled and totally embarrassed.

Oh, my God. I had to make a decision! I could either continue to feel uncomfortable or I could let go of my inhibitions, relax and enjoy it. I decided to let go of the tension in my mind and concentrate on the warmth of her hands and the pressure of the long, slow strokes as they glided over my body. I let down my barriers and opened my heart to receive the full benefits of the wonderful massage.

I was in heaven. I couldn't remember a time when I'd felt so utterly relaxed in mind, body and spirit. It was wonderful and I didn't want it to finish.

When the massage was over, I got dressed, thanked the lady and left the room. Outside, at the booking area, I booked myself in for another one and went back to my room. As I opened the door, I saw Cassandra was there.

"Well?" she asked. "How was it?"

"You have *got* to go and have one of those massages!" I told her, laughing a bit. "It was fabulous!"

~ * ~

I continued to practice yoga at the beautiful setting of the lakeside. As my body detoxed, I noticed that I wasn't actually missing my wine, chocolate, coffee, cakes and biscuits any more. I was enjoying my new healthy lifestyle and I realised just how powerful temptation is. I couldn't lay my hands on toxic foods and because I couldn't have any, I accepted my situation – and

Hummingbird

it felt good!

It's so easy to load our bodies up with toxins and sugar and many of us know only too well the internal argument that goes on in our heads along the lines of 'I know I shouldn't, but I really want to' otherwise known as 'Oh, what the hell, I deserve it. I'll be good tomorrow'.

As my mental and physical health improved, so did my level of concentration. Anyone who has ever meditated will tell you it's not an easy thing to do. Meditation doesn't always have to mean sitting still. Fully giving our minds to whatever we are doing at a particular moment in time is a form of meditation that is also extremely beneficial.

It was a challenge for me to fully focus on my yoga postures, particularly as my mind was processing so much emotional stuff that was coming up at the same time.

Gradually, as my body became more supple, my mind followed suit. I came to realise that the ashram was the ideal and perfect place for me to be. I was learning so many things that would be helpful to me, not only in my personal life, but in my working life as well.

My free time was either spent at the café or in the beautiful grounds of the ashram. I walked around, talked to people, read books, paddled in the lake or just sat and observed. I laughed a lot with Cassandra (it wasn't always tears) and all in all, it was a totally amazing experience.

One day, Debbie offered to give me some reiki. I lay down and closed my eyes to receive the healing energy. As her tiny hands hovered a few inches above me, I was aware of the powerful energy of the reiki. When I felt her hands pressing gently down on my abdomen, I opened my eyes and discovered that she wasn't actually touching me at all. I was astonished, it felt extremely powerful.

After the reiki session I slept deeply and I missed the early morning meditation.

The next day, we had a lecture about the breath and how it affects our vital energy. In the ancient Indian language of Sanskrit our vital energy is called our prana and the Sanskrit word for breath is ayama, hence, the practice of proper yogic breathing is known as pranayama. Learning how to breathe properly brings more oxygen to the blood and to the brain and increases our energy levels. Of course, we all know how to breathe, but when we learn to breathe properly, we can improve our health and wellbeing. Breathing is one of our most vital functions, so we may as well get it right and use it to our maximum advantage.

When our breath wanders, our mind becomes unsteady. Therefore, by steadying the breath we will, in turn, steady the mind.

We learned to use pranayama when practicing our yoga postures and uniting the two principles helped me to focus on myself more easily.

My development at the ashram wasn't a continuous uphill climb, it was unpredictable and variable.

Sometimes the yoga and meditation felt good and my mind was in a restful place, but at times my mood would drop and it was at these times that being at the ashram was more difficult for me. I was experiencing the release of emotions and past trauma that was now insisting on being dealt with. It was the perfect place for a healing crisis to occur.

As the days passed, my body moved into the postures more easily. The inverted postures, such as the headstand, shoulderstand and plough felt particularly good. One day, as I was holding the shoulderstand position, I suddenly found that I wanted to cry. It wasn't that crying felt weird to me, I'd gotten used to it by now. It was unexpected, because I was feeling in such a good place at the time, relaxed and focused on the postures, not thinking about anything else at all.

When the class was over, I found the teacher and explained to her what had happened.

"It was as though the emotion just came up from nowhere and burst its way out of me, without as much as an invitation or a warning," I told her. "How rude!" I joked.

"This posture is known to release the emotions," she said reassuringly. "It's good that they're coming up, Deborah. Go with it."

As I ate my lunch that day, I thought about reincarnation. It was something that we'd been discussing amongst ourselves in the café and I found it quite an interesting topic. I was pondering the idea that my soul may have been here before and had been reborn into its new body, this body, my body.

I was thinking about the concept of how, in each of our past lives, our soul learns lessons in order for us to become stronger and wiser until we reach enlightenment.

The more I thought about what we had discussed the more negative my thoughts become. Had I been exceptionally bad in my last life? Is this why I had to have all this pain in this life? I allowed myself to think really clearly for the first time about just how difficult some aspects of my life had been for me.

As I ate my food and thought about my life, the tears came again, slowly running down my cheeks like two little rivers. A lovely lady next to me broke her silence. Softly whispering she asked me, "Are you okay?"

"Yes" I assured her, as silently as possible. "Thank you."

After lunch I explained to her why I was crying. Empathetically, the lady shared her own emotional story with me. I was finding that the more everyone was opening up on all levels (through the different aspects of yoga), the more emotions were being released and the more I realised just how much some of my fellow ashramers were also going through.

I was by no means the only person there experiencing a growing pain or a healing crisis. Living in the ashram was stimulating a lot of discussions about life, God and our own personal experiences. I found it an extremely supportive atmosphere to be in, which was just what I needed as my body, mind and spirit rid itself of its toxic waste.

~ * ~

I got an email from my mum. Eagerly I opened it up to see what she had to say to me. After her usual salutation and "Hope you're okay," I read that my brother Philip had fallen against the radiator in his room at the hospital.

"He wasn't able to get up or cry out," she wrote. "He was stuck against the radiator and he's badly burnt on his bottom and his armpit. I've been to see him and he looks really shaken up. He's not walking at all."

I spoke to Cassandra about it.

"His illness prevented him from being able to get up or cry out," I told her. "Can you imagine how it would feel to be stuck against a hot radiator, just waiting for someone to come and find you?" I asked. "I feel so sorry for him, Cass, it's making me feel really sad. My spirits have come crashing back down to the floor. It's making me feel vulnerable and insecure again... Oh God, I'm carrying around so many issues with me. I just want to sort them all out, so I can just be myself!"

"Deb, you've been through a lot in your life," she said kindly. "It's gonna take time to work through it. Anyone would feel really sad at that news, don't be hard on yourself. Here, take this tissue and wipe your eyes."

I took the tissue from her hand.

"Your poor brother," she said.

"I know anyone would be upset, Cassandra," I answered her. "But why can't I just feel the sadness of my brother's pain without then feeling like a lost and immature child who is in pain myself? That's what I don't get. I don't want to feel like that anymore." I looked up at her. "There's got to be an adult lurking in there somewhere, surely."

My comment broke the melancholy mood and we both laughed.

"India will help you, Deborah, don't worry," Cass said knowingly as she took my hand in hers.

I realised that it had been a very, very long time since I'd had no issues and I found myself wondering just how many people might feel the same. There is usually something that holds us back from realising our full potential, stresses us out, makes us act or think in unhelpful ways, gives us insecurities and prevents us from just being ourselves.

I was definitely cleansing myself and was learning new lessons every day. It wasn't as severe a reaction (or healing crisis) as I had in Costa Rica, but it felt similar. I remembered how tough it was back then and how I became a lot stronger for it. I realised at the ashram that I still had a way to go.

One of the things that we learned in the ashram was not to compare ourselves with others. Our ability and our growth is a personal thing that has nothing whatsoever to do with anyone else's performance. This is how it is with yoga and this is how it should be with life. Let's face it, there will always be someone whose ability is greater or less than our own and we shouldn't feel good or bad about that. We shouldn't be competitive and we should not compare ourselves – especially when it leads to pain. It's a valuable lesson.

That evening, Cass and I talked about people whose lives had been quite competitive and whose parents pushed them hard at school and in sport, and had compared their marks, ability and results with others. Could this sometimes leave them feeling as though they were never good enough, whatever they achieved, and result in low self-esteem?

As I lay in bed, I thought about our conversation. Despite my failings at school, I'm pleased to say that I was never put down or made to feel inadequate. I never felt worthless and I always knew that I was good at heart: a kind, loving and caring person that people liked just because I was me. Thinking about it then, I wondered if this was why I was able to love myself and not feel the way so many others seem to, with a lack of self-love.

As I was undergoing my spiritual growth in India, I was starting to see through the cloak of negativity I had shrouded myself in and appreciate the positive things about myself and my life. I realised that, although I'd had

Hummingbird

lots of doubts and fears throughout my life and experienced many varied and quite raw emotions, I had always really liked myself. I fell asleep with a smile on my face and a warm fuzzy feeling throughout my whole body.

~ * ~

Half way through my stay at the ashram, David arrived.

David's brother committed suicide, although in very different circumstances to my own brother, Nigel. David's brother wasn't physically or terminally ill, but he didn't leave a note so nobody knew why he decided to end his life. I guess he was racked with mental and emotional pain and couldn't see a way out of it.

David and I talked a lot about the feelings we both went through at the time of our brother's deaths. It was liberating to be able to put a voice to some of the feelings that I'd kept hidden from my friends and to finally talk about it with someone who knew exactly where I was coming from.

Sometimes we think that we're the only ones who ever feel the way we do about certain things. We can feel isolated, especially if we think that what we're feeling is not appropriate. It's not until we find the courage to voice our feelings (whatever they are) that we discover that indeed we aren't the only ones who ever felt this way and we can start to embrace our thoughts and make friends with them, which enables us to release the emotions and to move forward.

Talking to David was easy. I felt as though our deeply honest conversation had taken place in a wonderful space of pure acceptance and love and that a little more healing had occurred for us both.

As the days went by, I began to feel the synergistic effects of my three bodies coming into alignment.

Physically, I became very supple as the asana practice transformed my body into a pliable instrument, effortlessly persuaded into the postures. Being able to hold the positions more easily allowed me to enjoy the classes even more.

This had the beneficial effect of making sitting meditation easier, which was the original purpose of asana yoga.

As my mind loosened up, I became more comfortable about being with myself and my spirits lifted. As my bodies learned to function in harmony, I felt happier and healthier and – most importantly – more at peace.

It was strange to consider that just 10 days earlier I hadn't known any of the people who were now my amazing new friends. However, I knew that they were just brushing past me, on their own wonderful journeys of self-discovery and with this in mind, my concentration turned back onto myself.

As I shaped my body into each posture, effortlessly moving from one pose to the next, I noticed that I was finally able to focus fully on my movements and my breath. With my eyes closed, my concentration stayed within me for a full two hours, without flitting like a naughty little child from one thought to another.

After that class, I felt as though I was floating in grace: fully at peace with myself and more relaxed and calmer than I could ever remember being. For those two hours, I knew myself.

I was complete. Meeting my new friends had grounded me and balanced me, but my own body wisdom was finally showing up and making friends with me, and it felt AMAZING!

Finally, I thought, I'm getting somewhere.

Hummingbird

The art of surrender in meditation

A poem by Kip Mazuy

Meditation is not about
building yourself up
or trying to be a certain way.

It is not about
becoming a peaceful person
or a wise person
or even an enlightened person.

In meditation
you simply become aware
of what is here.

You turn your focus
back upon yourself
and notice what presents itself.

If you do this,
the ego structure
begins to be peeled away.

Behind all the desires,
distractions, opinions,
beliefs, worries
and emotions.

Behind everything
that the mind has built
upon itself
in order to feel important
and in control
is something
overwhelmingly tender
and vulnerable.

Even painful.

A sense of being
very small and alone
and all of the fear

and helplessness
that goes with it.

And by survival instinct,
you don't want to feel it,
you don't want to see it.

The very drive of the ego
is to get as far away
from this vulnerability as possible.

You want to fit in
or at least stand out.

Nobody wants to be a nobody.

But if you can allow yourself
to feel it.

If you can surrender and
allow yourself to be that small
helpless nobody.

If you allow it all to be as it is
at the very core,
then you fall into the essence
which is behind it.

You become immersed
in what is behind it.

And that is love,
that is peace.

You do not have love and peace
as though it was an object to attain,
you dissolve into it.

It bubbles up
from your essence
and spills into
every level of your being
because you have let go
of the very idea of
trying to be a someone.

Kip Mazuy is the Creator of Bliss Music-Meditation CDs.

Chapter 39

Attachment

Grasping at things can only yield one of two results: Either the thing you are grasping at disappears, or you yourself disappear. It is only a matter of which occurs first – S. N. Goenka

One day at the ashram, my new friends and I had a very interesting and enlightening conversation about attachment. Someone started the discussion by asking us what we thought about the theory of attachment.

"What do you mean exactly?" I asked.

"Well, when we become attached to something, or someone," they said, "it causes us pain because we're afraid that we may lose that person or object. If we lose our jobs, our friends, our loved ones, our house, our car or our designer handbag we feel pain because we have attached ourselves to these people or objects."

"Yes, I know exactly what you mean," someone else joined in. "Our mind grasps at something and puts a label on it. We crave what we don't have, and if we have it and lose it, we feel depressed. Our mind gets tighter and tighter and this is what causes the suffering."

"Mmm… interesting theory," I muttered.

I thought about it. Applying it to myself, I realised that it was indeed true. I had been clinging on to the hope that Cass would travel with me when we left the ashram. I was worrying in case she decided not to and it was causing me pain. When I made a conscious decision to let go of the attachment I felt much better.

Later, back in my room, I decided to visualise myself with a rod of steel running right through the centre of me, from head to toe. I imagined I had wires coming out of my body with the people and things that I care about attached to the end of each one. When I thought about the people or things moving away from me, they pulled at the wires and tugged me right off balance.

Then, I imagined that the wires were ribbons instead. The ribbons were still very close to me, but not physically fixed to my body. I still had the people and objects at the ends of the ribbons, but when I imagined them leaving me, I didn't lose my balance at all. They floated off with the ribbons and I was still strong, centred and grounded. I was still able to love, enjoy and give, but I didn't feel the pain of attachment or loss. It was a remarkable and powerful visualisation.

However, I soon learned that I wasn't fully aware of the people and things I was attached to when Gary left the ashram. As he left, the pull of the wire caused me pain, because I wanted him to stay. So when he had gone, I imagined that the wire had turned into a ribbon and floated off with him. I felt solid and once again grounded and happy. I had discovered a very useful tool.

During the talk that evening, the swami told us to have self-confidence. He said that if we are discouraged, we must come back to our own path. If the path shows contradiction, we must know our own mind and that the truth will come to us.

The swami told us a fable.

A man was walking with his son and his donkey. The son was riding on the donkey and the man was walking. He was very tired. They came across some people. The people said to the man, "You are so tired, why don't you swap with your son and ride on the donkey yourself?" The man listened to what they said and so he swapped places with his son and rode on the donkey as the son walked beside him.

Soon they came across some people. The people said to the man, "How can you ride on the donkey and let your son walk?" So they both got on the donkey and went on their way.

Soon they came across some people. The people said, "Oh, my goodness, that poor donkey, having to bear the weight of two people." So, the man and his son both got off the donkey and walked beside it on their way.

Soon they came across some people. The people said, "Are you mad? What is the point of having a donkey and walking beside it?"

The moral of the story was, of course, that people may criticise us, whatever we choose to do. We can't stop people telling us what they think but we should not let their words stop us from doing what we feel is right. We mustn't worry about what others think of us.

Others will always have an opinion about who we are and what we do. We have to realise that this opinion is based on their lives, not ours.

Hummingbird

Years later, in 2010, I was lucky enough to attend a talk by Wayne Dyer, an internationally renowned author and speaker in the field of self-development. The talk was full of fantastic material that resonated with me wholeheartedly, but there was one particular thing that he said which really stuck with me. That thing was this:

"What you think of me is none of my business."

I like that. If ever I'm feeling concerned about what others think of me, I just repeat that line to myself. I give it no more consideration and I just get on with the business of being me.

~ * ~

Fridays and Sundays were days off at the ashram. We spent the time as we wished, but were encouraged to stay on site.

Although I stayed at the ashram I felt that I needed some time away from my intense spiritual practice (I'm a Libran, I need a balance). I did some washing, wrote some postcards, spent some time at the café with Debbie and Cass and we had a really good laugh. It was very refreshing.

Although I was there to find my own internal stability, I needed to balance it with a bit of what was more normal for me. I met some new people, including an interesting Indian guy. We talked for ages; swapping our knowledge on reflexology and ayurvedic medicine. I allowed myself some fun and for a few days I almost forgot why I was there. And then interestingly I was assigned a new karma yoga.

"Oh, no," I told Cass. "My new job is to mop the floor in the big hall after tea. I won't be able to come to the café with you."

"It's all meant to be," she reminded me. "Just go with it, Deborah."

I sighed. I knew she was right. Mopping the floor was really hard work as it was such a large hall and it took a long time.

"I have a cleaner at home to do my housework," I told a fellow floor-mopper, half laughing but secretly not amused. "I really want to be at the café with my friends."

"That's why you've been given this job," the friendly young man informed me. "The Universe is pulling you back on track."

I chuckled to myself because I knew that he was right. I smiled inside as I let go of what I thought I wanted and dedicated my love and devotion to the job. It made the task a whole lot easier and much more pleasurable.

~ * ~

My time at the ashram was coming to an end. The evening before I left, I joined the others on a long, silent walk to a lake by the Neyyar dam.

"Are you coming Cassandra?" I asked her.

"No," she replied, "I'm going to stay here with Matthew. We only have a few days left together. I'm coming with you tomorrow, Matthew's coming to the main town with us and then he's going off on his own."

"I can't tell you how pleased I am," I told her honestly. I'm sorry you're breaking up, but I'm so glad you're coming with me." I hugged her tightly. "I'll see you later then," I told her and I went off to join the group of walkers.

Finding our way with the light of our torches and the glow of the moon, we walked in a silent group of around 50 people, together in meditation yet alone with our thoughts. It was a beautiful experience. Conserving my energy as I walked in silence, paying attention to each breath and step I took, I was conscious of the powerful energy being created by our collective heightened awareness.

When we reached the lake we all laid down and looked up at the stars. Our voices became united in song, the mantras adding to the magic of the evening. Chanting and listening to the beautiful music our voices were creating, I noticed a harmony that was pure and perfect; the voice of a man lying next to me. As I felt myself melting into his melody, I became totally lost in a state that was beyond my body, and although I was just a small person, against the vast lake and the sky, I felt as big as the Universe itself.

We stayed for a while, basking in the magic of the evening and then walked slowly and silently back to our base, holding on to the incredible energy that had been created.

My thoughts turned to silence and how much my attitude towards it had changed within the past two weeks. When I arrived at the ashram, the silence was my enemy. I craved words and voices as a means of communication and connection. Now I yearned for the peace and power of this silence to last forever.

I felt really weird that night, but I couldn't quite put my finger on it. The walk had been a deeply moving and spiritual experience, which had a profound effect on me. I was aware of my body letting go with a long, low sigh as I drifted off to sleep through my final night in the bare brick room that was now a familiar and friendly home to me.

The next day I woke up feeling quite low and very tired. It was Valentine's Day. I reached into my bag and took out the card that Richard had slipped in there before I left England. His loving words brought me comfort.

It was interesting to hear others say that their mood had also dropped.

"It's because of the phase of the moon," Debbie informed us knowingly. "There's a new moon coming and we're getting ready for a high."

I looked at the moon that evening and the crescent was incredibly small. I couldn't ever remember seeing it so slim.

Being at the ashram was like being on an emotional rollercoaster for me and I was now 100 per cent ready to get off.

We packed our bags and we said our goodbyes.

Chapter 40

Ups and downs in Kerala

Loaded up with my rucksack on my back, my backpack on my front and my yoga mat somewhere in between, I headed for the bus stop with Cass and Matthew and we boarded a bus to the main town. My ticket cost me the equivalent of 20 pence – a bit different from the £14 I'd paid the taxi when I arrived here from the same town two weeks ago.

We tracked down the relevant bus and boarded it. Moving along the aisle to the centre of the vehicle we found some empty seats and settled down: Matthew and Cass on the left side of the bus and me on the right. The seats were very hot, warmed by the sun streaming through the window as it waited for its passengers. As the bus made its way along the dusty road, I relaxed and started to wonder what adventures the next few weeks were going to bring. Warm, sleepy and lost in my thoughts, I was miles away when suddenly there was a loud bang and I was quickly brought back into the moment. My side of the bus had collided with another bus as it was trying to pass in the opposite direction.

"Bloody hell!" I exclaimed. "I thought that the taxi journey had been dangerous enough, but at least we didn't hit anything!"

Thankfully, no one was hurt but it gave us all quite a fright. I said a silent prayer and hoped for the best as we continued on our way.

We arrived at our destination and stepped off the bus into an extremely busy, noisy and dirty place. Looking around I noticed that the sides of the streets were strewn with rubbish and, after the stillness of the ashram, being in the town was a shock to my senses.

To be honest, it was probably what I was expecting, but what I wasn't expecting was to snap right back into the feeling of being like a duck out of water. I just wanted to get rid of that feeling and relax and open up to this wonderful country and all it had in store for me. I was annoyed with myself for feeling like this, again.

"If I'd have been alone," I told my friends, "I'd have got a taxi and gone to a nice commercial hotel on the beach for a week. I would have been more at home there."

"That's crazy," said Matthew, finding it hard to believe that anyone would want to do that. "You may as well be anywhere in the world in a big commercial hotel. You want to experience the real India, Deborah."

I knew he was right but I was fed up of dealing with my insecurities. I actually did want to experience the real India, it was an important point of my trip after all. My maternal grandfather was a quarter Indian. He was born and raised in India, so I have it in my blood. I believe I have cousins in India, but I have no idea who or where they are.

We found ourselves a small hotel and we checked in.

My room was very basic, but it looked clean. It put me in mind of a prison cell. A small, cheap, tatty room with a single bed and an old mattress, a squat loo, shower and a small table and chair. It was bare and despite the hot temperature, it felt cold.

A nicer hotel would've been wonderful, there was no doubt about that in my mind, but I knew that roughing it in cheaper accommodation would allow me to stay in India for longer and it was definitely what I wanted to do, if I could find a way to cope with it. I wanted to prove to myself that I could do it. To stretch and feel the pain, to then become more comfortable with it so that I could expand my boundaries and stretch a little more. Like yoga.

"I knew what to expect," I said to Cassandra. "So, why does it feel so awful again?" I didn't understand.

"It's just not what you're used to," my wise friend told me. "You're accustomed to expensive package holidays, being ferried on an air-conditioned coaches from place to place, having an experienced guide to sort everything out for you, and staying in comfortable luxurious hotels. It takes time to adjust. You came straight off the plane from England to the ashram. I don't know anyone else who has done that. People usually get accustomed to India a little bit first before plunging themselves into such a deep spiritual experience. You've only been here two weeks remember."

"Is that all it is? It seems like months!" I answered. "I think you've hit the nail on the head there. I was a bit naïve I think. I didn't realise what it would be like."

I made a mental note to myself: *don't be so hard on me!*

I reminded myself that I was there to build my character, but I was so glad that I wasn't on my own. A new mantra played over in my mind: "I'm here to build my character, I'm here to build my character..."

"C'mon, let's go out and find somewhere to eat," Matthew said.

"Good idea," I agreed.

The café was basic but the food was excellent. We had four main dishes, three portions of rice, three nan breads, three lassis and two bottles of water for the equivalent of three quid for the three of us. Being in the café lifted my spirits and I felt okay about going back to my room. It's amazing how comforting some good food can be. Back in the room, I showered and got into bed as a wonderful sleepiness came over me. I was happy to drift off and say goodbye to the very eventful day.

I woke up the next morning feeling much better. Despite the hardness of the bed, I had quite a good night's sleep, doubtless due to mental exhaustion.

With every intention of carrying on my yoga practice, I performed some postures and breathing exercises in my room. Cass and Matthew went off to the bank to sort out their money and I went out and had my first ever internet café experience.

A lot of emotional stuff had come up for me in the ashram and I wanted to explain it all to Richard. I'd questioned everything about my life, my past, my present and my future and some of my questioning was about my relationship with him. I'd been having some doubts before I came away and I wasn't sure where I was with it all now and so I wanted to put it down in words for him to read. I was unsure how he would feel about some of it but I had to tell him what I was feeling. I composed my message and, with my heart in my throat, I hit send.

"Can we go to a proper hotel for breakfast today?" I asked Cass and Matthew when we met up again. "I'm getting fed up of Indian food. I just want a normal breakfast for once."

Cass and I overruled Matthew's objections and found a large hotel. It was nothing like the café-style eatery we had been to the day before, but a proper restaurant, the type I was used to.

We sat down on the comfortable chairs at a large dining table laid with serviettes and cutlery.

"Oh, yes, this feels good," I said as I flicked out my napkin and placed it on my lap. I enjoyed the feeling of the air-conditioned room as I looked at the menu of familiar breakfast items. Cass had to admit that it felt really good too, but Matthew was definitely there under protest.

"It's totally lacking in any Indian character or charm," he pointed out as I unashamedly tucked into a breakfast of cornflakes, eggs, toast, fruit juice and coffee. I didn't give two stuffs about its authenticity, I was just glad of its familiarity.

"I totally agree with you, Matthew," I nodded as I bit into a slice of toast. "Great, isn't it?"

Matthew rolled his eyes.

"No, seriously I know exactly what you mean, and actually I agree with you." I said. "But there's nothing wrong with a little bit of what's familiar if that's what you need now and again. And this is definitely what I need right now. Pass the marmalade, please."

Matthew reached across the table and placed the marmalade in front of me.

"Later on," he said raising his eyebrows, "I'm going to take you to a real authentic Indian café."

Having had our western fix Cassandra and I later agreed to go with Matthew to the café where the locals ate. Matthew led us to a compact room filled with simple tables and chairs. We were the only tourists in there and I'm pretty sure that not many white people had eaten at those tables.

The menu was simple – vegetarian meal.

"Three, please," Matthew said to the man who came over to serve us. He held up three fingers.

We were given a banana leaf each to eat our food from and we ate like the locals, fingering the food into our mouths with our right hands. After my much-needed Western breakfast, I was happy to be eating at the Indian café and I really enjoyed the whole experience. The vegetarian meal was delicious and I was touched at the way the staff re-filled our banana leaves as we ate, charging us no more than the fixed price of 40p each. It was quite something to experience and the Indian generosity was overwhelming.

"I guess I could say this is my first eat-as-much-as-you-like encounter in India!" I laughed as I fed myself with the delicious food.

We went back to our digs and I headed for my room. I had a shower to cool myself off and laid on the bed to rest a while. I laid down smiling, glad to be there. Gary was around and was meeting us that evening and I was looking forward to seeing him again. I took out my notepad and worked out what money I had left and I realised that I had a whole £10 a day for living expenses and £70 left to spend on shopping if I wanted to. That was a big budget for India, compared to what my traveller friends had to spend. I figured I could manage on as little as £2 a day if I really, really wanted to. I felt positively rich.

"Hey, Cass, let's go shopping," I suggested when she came to my room later on. "Come on, I'll treat you."

With my newly-found sense of wealth, we went from store to store. In each different shop, we encountered a mass of Indian costumes. We had hours of fun trying on different colours and styles and eventually chose a Punjabi suit each.

"You look great in that one, Cass," I told her as she eyed herself up in the mirror. I went and stood beside her.

"We both look great," she said as she viewed the reflection of the long dresses flowing over the matching trouser bottoms. "It's so nice to get out of our yoga pants at last!"

"I finally feel feminine again," I laughed. "Let's keep them on."

"Oh, yes, definitely," she agreed.

I paid for the outfits and we made our way back through the hot dusty streets.

"I've really enjoyed my afternoon of retail therapy," Cass told me, smiling. "Thanks, Deborah."

"You're more than welcome," I said. "It's what we both needed, I reckon."

I slipped my arm through hers as we made our way back to our digs.

Later that evening, the three of us met up with Gary in a restaurant and it was an agreeable end to a most enjoyable day.

Chapter 41

A little bit of luxury

The next morning, Cass came to my room.

"Where's Matthew?" I asked her.

"He's gone," she said.

She sat on my bed and cried. We talked for a while. I was sorry that Matthew had left without saying goodbye to me.

"Let's move to a better hotel for a few days, Cass," I suggested. "I'll pay the difference."

She didn't need any persuading.

"Yeah, okay Deb. That'd be good, thank you."

The hotel was twice the price at 430 rupees, about £6 for the double room, but I figured that we needed and deserved it. The room had a TV. We liked the fact that it had a TV.

Although they had decided that it was the right thing to do, Cass was understandably feeling sad about breaking up with Matthew and was definitely in need of a bit of TLC.

We jumped onto the large double bed and found the remote.

"Get yourself comfortable, Cass," I said. "We could be here for some time."

Laughing, I flicked through the channels and found a good film. Settling in, we immersed ourselves completely in the movie.

As the credits rolled, I looked at her and suggested, "Another one?"

"Oh, yes," she nodded. "Most definitely!"

It was a totally self-indulgent morning and it felt fabulous.

When the second film was over, I got into the shower.

"This feels amazing," I called out, as I lathered myself. "It's so warm and luxurious."

"And we've got a toilet we can sit on and actually flush!" Cassandra called back. "It's been a long time since I flushed a toilet!"

There was no getting away from it, being at the hotel was great.

We did finally venture out to get some lunch and after we'd eaten we went to the internet café to use the email.

"It's shut," Cass said, pushing the locked door.

"Oh, how strange," I answered. "Let's go to the bank then, I need to change up some money."

The bank was shut as well.

"Excuse me," I asked a passer-by. "Why is everything closed?"

"There's a government strike on today," the local man told us, with the familiar shake of his head.

I looked at Cassandra and smiled, "I think the Universe is giving us permission to go back to the hotel and enjoy the room some more whilst we have it."

"Well, let's listen to it then!" she said. "There's nothing else to do."

Heaven.

We watched another film and then looked at our guide books to work out where our next destination was going to be.

"I'd like to go to Varkala beach," I told her. "Do you fancy that? Gary has recommended a really good place to stay."

"Sounds like a good idea," she said. "Let's have a look at the book."

Using the guide book, we figured out where to go and how to get there.

The next morning, feeling like a couple of naughty children, we had breakfast brought up to our room. After polishing off a Continental breakfast, we checked out of the wonderful room and caught the train to Varkala beach.

"I can't believe that this ticket only cost me 50p," I said, staring at the piece of paper in my hand. "It's amazing, everything's just so cheap out here."

Relaxing back into my seat for the 45-minute journey, I watched the wonderful scenery of local houses and canals as it flashed past the window. It was fabulous.

"I'm beginning to feel as though I'm really on holiday at last," I told Cassandra. "This is lovely. I'm really looking forward to this next chapter of

Hummingbird

my Indian adventure like you wouldn't believe. I wouldn't want to be doing this on my own though. I'm so pleased I met you."

"I wouldn't either. It was all meant to be," she said. "It's gonna be amazing."

We arrived at Varkala and checked into our accommodation. It was cheap and basic, but adequate and clean. It felt good. The building was situated on a piece of land at the back of a small restaurant and we needed our torches to light our way back to the room at night.

We stayed at the beach for one week. I spent some time with Cassandra, and some time on my own. The mornings were hot and the days hotter still. I got up early to walk along the beach before the sun became too much to bear. In the full heat of the day, I went to my room and read or slept and on some days, I did both.

The rest of the time I did yoga and meditation, sunbathed on the beach, enjoyed the great food, visited the internet café and had beauty treatments and massages – paper knickers on this time.

When there was a nice breeze, we sat in the café and just watched the world go by. The line of restaurants sat along the cliff top looking out over the wonderful skyline of Varkala beach and from there we sat in comfort and watched the breathtaking sunsets each evening. Cass and I never missed a sunset in India. In the daytime we looked out over the sandy beach that stretched out between the high rocky cliffs and the Arabian Sea, creating a striking picture that was a joy to behold.

Fish eagles and kites soared above our heads and birds hovered over the fishermen's nets as they pulled them from the water each morning. It seemed to me to be such a huge effort for the 20 or so men to place the large nets out into the water and haul them in again for a catch of such tiny fish.

Taking in the scenery from the cliff top one day, I was thrilled to see my first-ever wild dolphins.

I jumped up out of my seat.

"Oh, wow, Cass!" I enthused. "Look, look – out there."

I pointed out to sea, where the dolphins were playing in the distance and jumping out of the water, showing off their elegant speed and agility.

"I've always wanted to see dolphins in the wild. Oh, God, that's amazing. That's really made my day. Just look at them!"

167

Seeing wild dolphins was definitely on my To Do list for India.

Sometimes beggars would appear on the beach. Some were disabled and some were not. Some were adults and some were children.

"Don't give them any money," we were told. "It encourages them to make begging their way of life."

With that in mind, we gave the children water and shared our pineapple with them.

"I wish I had a book to read," I mentioned to a couple of people I was talking to one day.

"There's a bookshop along the cliff," they told me. "You can exchange your book for another secondhand one. That's what everyone does."

"I don't have a book," I told them. "Can I buy one there?"

"Oh, yes, of course, and when you finish it, you can exchange it for another one."

"That's a good idea. Can you recommend anything?" I asked them.

"Have you read The Journey by Brandon Bays?" the woman suggested. "It's fantastic. She had a tumour in her belly the size of a basketball and she cured herself in just six weeks with natural therapies and emotional release work."

"Wow, really? That sounds interesting."

"Yeah, I know, great, isn't it? Her book tells the story of her life and how she healed herself and then created her own therapy from her personal experience. I think you'll enjoy it."

"I'll definitely have a look for that at the bookshop," I said. "Thanks."

But the shop didn't have The Journey in stock, so I bought a well-thumbed copy of Memoirs of a Geisha instead.

"What a fantastic way to share books and perfect for people who are travelling," I said to Cassandra later on as I showed her my purchase. "I had to pay 200 rupees deposit for it, but the man said that if I finish it before I leave, I can take it back to the shop and get 150 rupees back."

"Well, you can't argue with that," she replied, smiling. "I might get one myself."

~ * ~

A few days after arriving at the beach, I came down with a sore throat and a chest infection. By the next day, my voice had completely gone and I wasn't feeling any better.

"I think I'll go and find the doctor," I whispered almost silently to Cassandra. "I need to get rid of this infection."

"Good idea," she said. "Do you know where he is?"

"I'll ask the guys at the restaurant."

I was sent off in the right direction and I found the local ayurvedic medicine man.

Ayurveda is the system of healing in India, which literally means life (ayur) and knowledge or science (veda). Translated as the art of living wisely or the science of medicine, this ancient method of natural healing is also practiced in other countries around the world as an alternative medicine.

The doctor didn't speak any English, so I pointed to my throat and chest and I demonstrated to him that I'd lost my voice. Thankfully, he understood what my problem was.

He looked at my throat and neck, as I imagined he would do, then proceeded to examine my feet, hands and spine before handing me some herbal pills, liquid and spicy powder to chew, which I think was ginger. Giving me some pain balm to rub into my throat, he indicated that the examination was over and that I should pay him. I held out my money for him to take from me what he required. The doctor took the equivalent of three pounds – not much money for an examination and a handful of natural medicines, but quite a lot of money to the locals.

The medicine he gave me was like a wonderdrug. The next day my voice came back and I began to feel heaps better. My chest infection cleared up within a couple of days and I was feeling good again. I was astonished and very grateful to the doctor.

~ * ~

One evening, whilst at Varkala beach, Cass and I went to see a Kathakali performance. Kathakali means story play and is a classical mixture of dance, acting, music and facepainting. Dating back to the 17th century, these dramatic performances are based on myths and legends and (unlike us) the locals who flocked to watch the show were familiar with the stories being acted out.

If we had arrived a few hours earlier, we could have watched the application of the stunning facial makeup, applied by the artists themselves.

"Putting on the makeup is as much a part of the performance as the show itself and a skill that takes years of practice," we were told.

I found out later that the dancers paint their faces with handground colours mixed with coconut oil. They lay down on bamboo mats to have layers of putty, paper, cork and polystyrene applied to their faces.

The putty (made from cockleshell, lime and rice powder) was delicately applied around the contours of their faces and finally, when the makeup was complete and the elaborate colourful costumes were on, the wooden headgear was put into place.

The show was remarkable and I was mesmerised as the dancers mimed their story with dramatic intensity, accompanied by a rhythmic background of singing and drumming.

We had read in our guide book that the Kathakali performers have many years of training consisting of body massage to keep them supple, dance lessons, muscle control and eye exercises. The eye movements are an important part of the dance and they practise moving their eyeballs in all directions. It was certainly interesting to watch the strange eye and facial movements they performed throughout the show.

It was definitely an experience I would not have wanted to miss, although it was hot in the theatre and the show was far too long for my liking. It was absolutely stunning, but I was pleased when it finally came to an end and we could go back to our room to rest.

~ * ~

I always looked forward to mealtimes at Varkala. Eating there was a joy. I chose to continue my vegetarian diet for several reasons. First, after being in the ashram, eating meat just seemed wrong. Vegetarianism is an integral part of the yogic lifestyle and I had definitely felt the benefits of the fresh, healthy vegetarian food. The yoga way says that the food cycle of nature begins with the plants, which are nourished by the sun, the source of energy for all life. The plants are eaten by the vegetarian animals and the vegetarian animals are eaten by the carnivores. The plants, being at the top of the food chain, have the greatest life-promoting properties and animal flesh is regarded as second best. Natural foods, such as seeds, vegetables, fruits and nuts are regarded as more nutritious and are more easily used by the body.

The true yogic diet is also concerned with the subtle effect that food has on both the mind and the body. The diet avoids foods which are regarded as stimulating, such as onions, garlic, coffee, tea (except herbal), fish, eggs, alcohol and drugs. The yogis enjoy foods that are thought to calm the mind and sharpen the intellect.

Another reason why I chose to stay on the vegetarian diet was because of the discussions my friends and I had had about the theory of past lives. We had contemplated the idea that human beings have had past animal lives and that animals have had past human lives. Looking at it this way, it was hardly surprising that it put me off eating meat.

And a third reason I abstained was because I couldn't be sure that the meat was kept fresh in India and I believed that a vegetarian diet would keep me from getting food poisoning, which in fact it did. I didn't have any tummy problems at all.

Whatever my reasons were, I have to say that I didn't once crave meat as the vegetarian food at Varkala was thoroughly delicious. For breakfast, I enjoyed tasty porridge with banana and honey or a fruit salad. One day, I treated myself to a more expensive breakfast of coffee and croissants. For my evening meal, I ate tandoori vegetables, various vegetable curries, cashew paneer or delicious vegetarian Chinese food. Everything was fresh and tasty. Oh boy, I was in food heaven!

~ * ~

With so much time on my hands, I checked my emails twice a day. I was pleased to see I had a message from my mum and excitedly opened it up.

"Dear Deb," she'd written. "I hope all is well and that you are having a good time in India.

"I've been to see Philip at the hospital and he isn't too good after his fall against the radiator. The burns to his bottom and legs are deep and he is having difficulty standing up for very long. They've said that his liver is failing, but that they have it under control. Unfortunately, he's not able to keep any food down at the moment.

"I thought I'd let you know.

"Mum."

"He sounds in a pretty bad way," I thought. I felt so sorry for him.

Discussing it later with Cassandra, I told her: "I feel guilty about being here at this beautiful place, having the luxury of time and space to sort my head out and to relax and de-stress, whilst my brother's suffering so much back at home."

"There's nothing you can do, Deborah," she reassured me.

"Yeah, I know. It has just upset me, that's all. He never talks about how he feels, he must be feeling so bad right now. I can't bear the thought of it. I'm going to visit him as soon as I can when I get home."

I knew I had a choice. I could choose to be sad or to be happy and enjoy my vacation. I chose to send prayers and loving thoughts to my family back in England, then to let it go and be happy in India.

We always have a choice, we can choose how we feel if we bring our mind and attention to it.

Chapter 42

Respect all living things

One day, as Cass and I were busy doing nothing much, I saw a familiar face in the distance.

"Hey, Peter!" I called out.

Hearing my voice, the man looked over.

"Oh, hi there," he said, coming over to join us. "You're the girls from the ashram. How you doing?"

"Good, thanks," I replied as he pulled up a chair. "I sat next to you at the lake when we went on the silent walk. I was listening to your voice, it was so beautiful."

"Oh, thanks," he said, somewhat surprised. "How long have you girls been here?"

"Nearly a week," Cass told him. "We're leaving in a few days."

"Chilling out after the ashram, eh?" he asked.

"Absolutely," I agreed. "It was great, but a bit strange for me, being as I'd only just got off the plane from London. I went straight there from England."

"Really?" he laughed. "Are you crazy?"

I smiled and raised my eyebrows.

"I guess so. No one could believe how white I was when I arrived."

We talked to Peter for a while about some of the things that we'd learned from the lectures at the ashram.

"I'm a strict vegetarian," he told us. "I really don't believe that it's right to eat meat or fish. We must never kill any living creatures, big or small. We are all connected in the Universe as one," he said. "We are them and they are us. Harming a living creature is wrong."

We could see how passionate he was about his beliefs and we had total respect for them. We chatted more before he went on his way.

"He's such a nice bloke," Cass said.

"Yeah, he's lovely. Everyone at the ashram was lovely weren't they?"

It was more of a statement than a question really but she answered it anyway.

"Yes," she said. "They were."

After a lovely relaxing day and a wonderful meal (vegetarian of course) we made our way by torchlight back to our accommodation.

As I opened the door Cass gasped.

"Oh, my God, look at that!"

My eyes followed her pointed finger and we both stood unbelievably still as we were faced with the sight of a massive spider on the wall in our room. I'm talking huge here. Don't get me wrong, I've seen bigger and better in the tropics, but this spider was big enough and it was on our bedroom wall. And not only that, it was bedtime.

We got up onto the bed, thinking that it couldn't get us there (get us? What did we think it was going to do to us for goodness sake?) and thought about our next move.

"We're going to have to chase it out," I told Cassandra. "I won't be able to get to sleep with it in the room."

Obviously, after our discussion with Peter, killing it wasn't an option.

Carefully and hesitantly, flip-flop in hand, I crept up on the spider. I was quietly poised to nudge him on his way, and then... as soon as I made my move, the spider made his. Down the wall, across the floor and right behind the bed.

We both let out a bit of a squeal and I shuddered from head to toe. Spiders do that to me. We tried again to shoo it out of the room. Well, Cassandra tried and I watched from a distance. The spider moved so quickly and before we knew it, it had disappeared out of our sight altogether. We gave up and went to bed. Knowing that it would be difficult to get to sleep that night, I shuddered as I thought about where it could be or worse still, where it could go.

The next day, with the spider still at large, we bumped into Peter again and told him about our eight-legged lodger.

"We're scared of spiders, Peter," we told him.

"It's not going to hurt you," he assured us. "Would you like me to come and catch it for you?"

Hummingbird

"Yes, please," we answered together.

Peter escorted us back to the room and, after an unsuccessful spider search, the couple in the room next door came out with an empty glass jar. They'd heard what we were trying to do.

"There's a big spider in our room, too," they told Peter. "Would you catch it for us, please?"

"Yeah, of course, no problem," answered Peter. "Maybe it's even the same spider."

Peter took the jar from the couple and managed to catch the spider in it. As that horrible squeamish feeling came back all over me, the spider suddenly escaped from the jar and we all jumped back a little. Peter quickly tried to re-capture it, but to our horror, the guy next door suddenly took off his shoe and splattered the poor spider right into the wall.

It was a tense moment. Our jaws dropped to the floor. No one spoke for what seemed like ages, and then Cass broke the silence.

"I think that's what you call bad karma," she said, looking at the man with part of the dead spider on the sole of his shoe.

Peter looked horrified.

"I suppose you don't need me anymore then," he said and off he went.

Cass and I looked at each other in disbelief. We felt awful.

Back in our room we broke the tension with our laughter, as there, as clear as day and as bold as brass on the wall, was our spider.

"I don't think we should ask Peter to come back and catch it, do you?" I laughed.

Later on that evening we were sitting on our beds talking. It was Cass who saw it first.

"Oh no, look at that!" she exclaimed, jumping back on the bed and pointing at an even bigger spider on the wall.

I looked up in horror and I froze when I saw the extremely large spider.

"I don't believe it," I whispered, thinking that the spider might hear me. "Go next door and get that bloke."

Chapter 43

Preacher Man

It was whilst we were at Varkala that we met the Preacher Man, a tall blonde Danish man who spoke in such a way that completely drew us into his world and made us want to sit and listen to him. He had a spiritual name, which I couldn't pronounce or remember so I just referred to him as the Preacher Man, or the Preacher. He was an amazing person.

"It seems as though he can see inside our minds and read our thoughts," I said to Cassandra. "We don't even have to ask him anything, he just seems to have a way of answering all our questions just by talking to us. All we have to do is sit and listen."

"Yeah," agreed Cass. "It's interesting how he always talks about the things we've been discussing. He makes so much sense."

"I find him fascinating," I said.

"Whoever you worship or follow," the Preacher Man told us, "go straight to the master, whoever that is for you. Don't get attached to any religious organisations."

I'm no expert on religion and I've never been a part of any religious group and I have to say that I am wholeheartedly on board with the Preacher on this one. If you're interested in my personal opinion, here it is. Religion, in my opinion, is faith with man-made rules. I don't apologise to anyone for saying this, it's only my opinion. It seems to me that religion has caused far too much trouble in the world and I find that it's controlling and dictating.

On the other hand, I'm fully aware that being a member of a religious group can bring people comfort and a sense of belonging. It can give them a feeling of being part of a family, somewhere to worship and friends to worship with.

We shouldn't be made to feel guilty if we don't abide by the rules of a religion. Guilt is an extremely destructive emotion. In my opinion, we should make up our own minds about how we feel about God and our faith. It shouldn't depend on what country we're born in or what particular faith our parents or guardians were taught to follow. Having faith is a wonderful thing. What or whom we have faith in should be entirely each individual's decision – with no pressure applied.

I believe that some religions are based on fear and ego, which can get in the way of complete and perfect love and devotion, which comes from our core being – the God within us. Spirituality shouldn't be confused with religion.

Funnily enough, it was at Varkala that I first spoke to God, but I'll tell you about that later.

The Preacher followed his master Krishna.

"If we have desires we should fulfil them," he told us. "This is how we work off our karma. Trying to suppress our desires only works for a while, but if we work through our desires, we will reach a point when we are finished with our deeds and ready to move on to the next life."

India was teaching me a lot about different ways of looking at life and how our beliefs, cultures and spiritual leaders influence our behaviours.

Before I met the Preacher, I had been learning a lot about Buddha and how he sat and meditated on his desires and problems, but it seemed that Krishna had other ideas. I could definitely see the attraction of both philosophies.

The Preacher also suggested that we should listen to our intuition.

"If something or someone doesn't feel right," he said, "you should move on and not let your thinking mind wonder why."

I noted down some of the other things he said so as not to forget them and I'm relaying them here just for your interest. Sometimes, he seemed to make perfect sense to me and some of his lessons were just for me to think about, discuss and then dismiss. However I felt about what he had to say, it definitely gave Cass and I some great topics for discussion, through which we usually discovered something else about ourselves. Maybe some of his teachings will prompt some interesting discussions amongst you and your friends.

The Preacher said that "every person is our brother or sister."

The theory that we're all connected and are one with everything and everyone was one of the topics we had already been discussing.

He pointed out to us that we had to experience the dark before we could see the light and that the more darkness we have, the quicker we will elevate to the light.

He suggested that we should travel more and should leave home alone, as a person from home will be an attachment to that place, people and things. This would inhibit us from getting the most out of the experience as our minds would be constantly referring to home and our familiar things and preventing us from expanding and growing. Because of my own experience in India, I understood exactly what he meant. If I had been with someone from home, it would have been easier for me and I don't think that I would have learned as much about myself as I had done by being there alone.

He also said the following things:

> We mustn't analyse but accept what is. 'What is', is always the right path.

> To be attached to anything causes pain. We should free ourselves of material possessions as they hold us back and tie us down.

> We have nothing to fear. We were always with our best friend – ourself, and to know ourselves, we have to be alone.

> The material body is just a vehicle in which we travel, we never die.

> We should get up early, before sunrise, and cleanse ourselves, washing away our dreams.

Keeping a completely open mind, I enjoyed sitting and listening to the Preacher immensely.

~ * ~

We spent seven days at Varkala Beach before we decided to move on. I had a great time there and the days had been long and interesting. We went to the local carnival in a rickshaw, rode on an elephant, had a few beauty treatments and, with my newly hennaed and beautifully conditioned hair, we reluctantly left the beach resort and headed to our next destination – Alappuzha.

Chapter 44

Total heaven

Love is what we are born with. Fear is what we have learned here. The spiritual journey is the unlearning of fear and the acceptance of love back into our hearts –
Marianne Williamson

Alappuzha is a town in Kerala with beaches, picturesque canals, wonderful lagoons and breathtaking backwaters. Life in Allepuzha moves around the water and because of this it's known as the Venice of the East. I heard that the children there learn to swim before they walk and that they sail boats before they ride bicycles.

It was the backwaters that had drawn us there and we spared no time in organising ourselves a house boat for a couple of days.

Our quaint little rice boat was the smallest vessel available and it didn't take us long to get acquainted with it. We looked around and saw a compact but charming bedroom, a kitchen, bathroom and a dining area. There was a small deck at the front of the boat, which was almost entirely covered with a double mattress.

The hired boat came with three members of staff – two punters and a chef. We sat ourselves down on the mattress and we set off. The punters used bamboo poles to gently propel us through the water. The scenery was stunning.

Costing the equivalent of £21 a head, renting the boat was the most expensive thing I did in India, but it was worth every rupee. As we drifted through the quiet canals lined with coconut palms I felt the most perfect sense of calm.

"I feel as though I'm truly in paradise," I said to Cass, soaking up the whole tranquil experience.

As we glided through the wonderful scenic backwaters, Cass and I studied our spiritual books and talked about the Hindu Gods Shiva, Brahma and Vishnu. Shiva is associated with destruction: destroying the old and bringing in the new. Brahma is the creator and Vishnu the preserver. It opened up an interesting and lengthy discussion between us.

As the heat of the day began to subside, we dropped anchor and went for a swim. The water was cooling and refreshing after the long hot day.

When the sun went down we drank a little bit of rum and then meditated on the mattress until dinner. The chef prepared us a delicious meal of authentic Keralan food and we savoured every mouthful of the flavoursome curry, rice, vegetables and chapattis.

"That was delicious," Cassandra said, licking her lips. "Let's go and sit at the front of the boat and watch the sun set."

We never missed a sunset in India.

The sunset was gorgeous against the backdrop of the palm trees and being on the boat enhanced its beauty even more.

"This is the most beautiful sunset I had ever experienced in my entire life," I told her.

To this day, I have never seen a sunset to rival it.

"I feel quite emotional to be honest – I could quite easily cry right now. I feel so free here in India Cassandra," I told her "and I still have half of my holiday ahead of me. I feel as though I have all the time in the world to do exactly as I want, with no time restraints and deadlines to meet. It's as though my mind can totally relax in the luxury of space and time. It's a fantastic feeling."

"Yes," she said. "I know exactly what you mean. It's not often you get the opportunity to feel that way, is it?" She looked at the horizon. "What an amazing sunset."

When the sun had finally disappeared behind the palm trees, we laid down on the mattress at the front of the boat and looked up at the stars. We started to sing, one song after another until we drifted off to sleep with the cool breeze on our skin and the sound of the water gently stroking our ears.

I felt completely at peace and at one with myself on that boat and for a while I didn't mind about anything at all, I was so blissfully happy. The day had been completely perfect and as I fell asleep, I whispered to my friend, "I hope I will remember this day forever."

Although I had only known Cassandra for just three weeks, I absolutely loved her with all my heart. From the moment I met her, I felt the connection, as though I had known her all my life. If it's true that we have lived past lives, I have no doubt that we were connected in those former existences. Whatever our connection was or had been, there was no denying that she had a fundamental role to play in my life at that time.

Although we were just friends — and nothing at all more than that — that night on the boat was the most romantic evening I've ever had. The combination of the stunning landscape, the tranquil water, the most exquisite sunset, meditating and singing, laying under the magnificent night sky together, gazing up at the stars and the feeling of closeness that we had built up over the past three weeks, left me totally enchanted. It's no wonder they call Kerala God's Own Country.

I was totally in love. In love with myself, in love with India, in love with God, in love with Cassandra and in love with my life. By now I was beginning to fully appreciate that it was the simple joys of life that make us truly happy, not the material things that we get so hooked on back at home. The real joy of life is about what we feel not what we have.

It was idyllic to wake up on such a beautiful lake and watch the sun rising between the palm trees. What a scene to wake up to.

"Fancy a dip?" asked Cassandra. It was early and there was a nip in the air, so I declined. Whilst Cassandra swam, I put on my cardigan and picked up my book, *Memoirs of a Geisha*.

"My mother, my father and my sister were gone," I read. 'And I could do nothing to change it."

That sounds familiar, I thought to myself. I continued to read...

"But I suppose that... I've been dead in a way too. (They) were gone, but I wasn't gone... I felt as though I'd turned around to look in a different direction, so that I no longer faced backward towards the past, but forward towards the future. And now the question confronting me was this. What would that future be?"

A shiver ran down my spine. It was exactly how I felt about my own life. I was letting go of the sadness and uncertainty that had always been such a huge part of my life. Loved ones had gone, but I was not gone. I had changed my direction of thought and was now taking a different path. It was a path where I could be content and happy, whatever I endured in the future. I knew it would be a long and steep climb, but I had no doubt that I was now on the road to inner peace.

~ * ~

I felt so content on the boat that I didn't want to leave it and move on to our next destination.

"I'm grasping again," I said to Cassandra. "And it's making me feel unhappy."

"If you let go of the grasping and allow the feeling to leave you, you will give way to peace again," Cassandra reminded me.

She was absolutely right. I let go of the grasping of wanting to hold on to the experience and the unhappy feeling was replaced with peace.

"In any case," said Cassandra. "Surely it's better to move on whilst you're feeling so good."

The wonderful feeling I had on the boat was so strong that I knew I would keep the memory of it for a long, long time. If I allowed myself the time to get used to it, the feeling may become diluted and my memory of it could be less intense.

We left the boat and made our way back to the train station.

Chapter 45

Nothing is a coincidence

"What time's the train due?" I asked Cassandra when we arrived at the station.

Looking at the information board, she read out that we had two hours to wait.

"Let's get a drink and a bite to eat," I suggested seeing the station café.

We were used to having time to spare, to sit and chat and think. Chilling out no longer felt like a luxury, but completely the norm. Hearing the train approaching, we got up from the table and gathered our belongings together.

"Wow, that's a long train," I observed as we watched one carriage after another pass by us by before the train finally came to a halt. "There must be about 40 carriages."

"Come on," said Cassandra as she walked along the platform towards the back of the train. "Let's go further down."

"It doesn't matter where we get on," I told her, looking through the windows into the carriages. "It's quite an empty train."

"I know, but I feel as though I want to go down a bit," she said, walking ahead of me.

I shrugged my shoulders and followed her down the platform. There was no reason I could see why she didn't want to get on the train where we were, but I followed her anyway because it didn't really matter. I boarded the train behind her.

"Let's sit here," I suggested, getting ready to offload my backpack onto a seat in the empty carriage.

Cassandra carried on walking.

"Let's just go a bit further down," she suggested.

My jaw dropped when I saw him. Sitting on the seat in the otherwise empty compartment was the Preacher, cross legged in his meditation pose. I couldn't believe my eyes; Cass must have had a sixth sense about it.

It may be what some call a coincidence, but I believe that there was a higher force at work. The Preacher had no idea where we were heading after the beach. Even we didn't know what our exact plans were when we left. Of all the days, of all the trains, of all the carriages, of all the times, how did it come to be that this spiritual man was sitting right there in front of us? It was as though he was just waiting for us.

Which brings me nicely to another subject I'd discussed with my friends at the ashram. Are we really in control?

Some people think that we all have a higher consciousness, much greater than our human awareness. We talked about how our higher consciousness is leading us to the places we need to be and the people we need to connect with.

Seeing the Preacher that day sent the questions whirling around in my mind again. Are we fully in control of the choices we make? Are these choices really made by our earthly mind and body or is it our higher consciousness that is guiding us to where we need to be?

Is the body merely the vehicle that enables our spirit, or higher self, to physically move around in this incarnation?

Was this meeting with the Preacher merely a coincidence or was the reason for it to confirm that we truly aren't in control and that everything is in the hands of a higher power?

"Hi," he said when he saw us, not looking one bit surprised.

"Hello," we replied as we took off our bags and sat down with him.

I was extremely surprised – struck dumb in fact – and it was Cassandra who spoke.

"Fancy seeing you here. How you doing?"

Once again we were blessed by the presence of the Preacher Man. He spoke directly to Cass during the journey and I listened with interest, still trying to get my head around seeing him there on the train.

"Everything before now is a memory and everything in the future is a dream," he told us. "The present moment must be experienced calmly, with no thoughts of the past or of what is to come. The more we meditate and learn to be in the present, the easier it is to be sattvic (pure and spiritual).

"The way we are feeling is reflected back at us in the material world. Our fears confront us. Doubts are our enemy and can lead us to insanity. If we feel in our heart that we know the right path, we must not listen to the doubts of the mind. If we are very fearful, we must get to a calm place and still ourselves."

When Cassandra got up and went to the toilet, he turned his head and spoke to me.

"You have come a long way on your spiritual journey," he said. "You are much closer to the light than Cassandra is. It's her I need to speak to, she has a lot of doubt and confusion around her, a lot of questions to be answered."

I understood completely. She'd just broken up with Matthew and was unsure of what direction her life was heading. She had been talking to Matthew by email and they were remaining friends. She didn't know what she would do when I went home to England or what she would do when she finally left India. She was re-discovering herself and she had a lot to think about.

I looked deep into the Preacher's eyes.

"I'd like to take his photo," I thought. "So that I can remember him forever."

Somehow I knew that his work was done and that I'd never see him again. But just as quickly as the thought entered my head I realised that it didn't matter if I never remembered his face. It was the experience of his soul that I would never forget.

"Do not question why coincidences happen," he told me, as if he'd read my mind. "Just accept them."

We disembarked at Ernakulam. Standing motionless on the platform I looked at my friend.

"I feel as though I've had a dream and I can't quite digest it," I told her.

Unable to move, I allowed the feeling, this new proof (as I thought of it) that nothing was a coincidence, to work its way into my body. It was a wonderful spiritual experience that totally blew me away.

"I wasn't surprised to see the Preacher on the train," Cass said casually. "Things like that happen all the time here in India. You get used to it, Deborah."

Chapter 46

It is what it is

To get to our next destination, Fort Cochin, we wanted to catch the ferry. As there was a government strike on again that day and there were no ferries running, we were forced to spend our money on an expensive taxi. It was a popular place to visit and we were lucky to find a nice room (with of course enough space to practice yoga in) for £2.25 a night.

I immediately liked Fort Cochin. It had a comfortable feel about it with its mix of more familiar Portuguese, Dutch and British houses.

The Portuguese Fort (Fort Emmanuel) is no longer there after being destroyed by the Dutch and the name Cochin is derived from the pre-colonial Kingdom of Kochi. With a rich and varied religious and cultural history, Kochi became one of the most important harbours on the west coast of India, focusing its attention on trading spices with China and the Middle East.

Fort Cochin itself is famous for its large Chinese fishing nets, which is the main reason I had it on my list of places to visit in India. The nets are thought to have been introduced by Chinese traders in the early 14th century.

After a good sleep, we woke up to a bright and sunny day.

"Let's walk down the road and find the nets on the waterfront," I suggested at breakfast.

I hadn't seen any pictures of the shore-operated structures beforehand and they were nothing like I had expected. I was surprised at the scale of the huge wooden frames and was mesmerised as I watched the team of fishermen hauling the nets up and down in a slow and rhythmic manner that was quite hypnotic. Using ropes counterbalanced with large rocks, the nets were lowered and raised from the water. Each net was at least 10 meters high, reaching out over the sea, poised and ready for the next catch.

"Would you like to have a go?" a fisherman asked me.

"Oh, yes please, I'd love to," I replied. "Cassandra, get my camera!"

Having a go at operating the nets was fun, but I preferred to sit and watch the men as they worked, leaving the nets in the water for just a few minutes before raising them to view their modest catch.

Soaking up the laid back atmosphere of the place, we strolled around the busy fish market before entering the church. Kneeling down I said a prayer.

"Thank you for this body and mind that houses my soul. Thank you for bringing me to India and for bringing Cassandra into my life. I pray for peace. Peace for myself, peace for all who know me and peace to the world and the Universe. Shanti, Shanti, Shanti. I pray for everyone, anywhere in the world who is suffering. Please bless them all with your divine love and presence."

It felt good, praying in the church.

Outside some lads were playing cricket. We sat in the cool shade of a tree and talked as we watched the match.

"I've been thinking about my brother Philip," I confided in Cassandra. "I wonder how much time he has left in his body."

"I guess it's difficult to tell," she said.

"I think that he must have had quite a miserable life," I told her. "I wonder if he's ever been really happy. He was always causing problems before he became sick, creating some trouble or disturbance, manipulating and controlling those around him. He's never seemed to be able to understand how to live in harmony with people, Cass."

"Well, how do you think he felt about it?" she asked me.

"It's impossible to know how he felt, I can only guess I suppose. I wonder if he felt very isolated. He never talked about his feelings or emotions. I've never had any idea what he was thinking or feeling. It makes me so sad when I think about him.

I had so much time to think in India.

I know it doesn't do me any good," I told her. "It won't change anything, that's just how it is. As Larry in Costa Rica used to say, 'it is what it is', but I just feel a bit low when I think about him."

"Why are you thinking about him right now?" Cassy asked.

"I don't know. I think it's because I prayed in the church. I thanked the Universe for my life and it made me think about my brother."

"Were there any good times in his life?" she asked me.

"I guess so," I said. "He was actually a very popular guy. He always had good friends around him, loyal and true friends. They enjoyed his pranks and he made them laugh. He was always messing around. I guess he enjoyed his life at times, like I did when I was with my friends. But I saw a different side to him Cass, the side he showed when he was at home. An angry, aggressive side, controlling and manipulating. I never felt safe around him when we were at home."

~ * ~

We stayed at Fort Cochin for two and a half days. I did some yoga, walked, meditated, talked with Cassandra, wrote in my diary and read my book. We went to see the palace – which cost us just three pence each to get in! – and we went to the synagogue, which was closed. We got a bus to the busy town of Ernakulam so that Cass could do some shopping, before getting a rickshaw to the bus station to find out the times of the buses to Munnar. Munnar, we'd decided, was to be our next destination.

We got on a bus back to Fort Cochin. It was packed solid and I was forced to stand right up the front next to the driver as the bus sped its way through the chaos of the day's traffic. It was a hair-raising journey. Pressed tightly against my fellow travellers, I had a first-rate view out of the forward-facing window and the oncoming traffic.

"Bloody hell, Cassandra," I gasped as I finally fell off the bus exhausted. "That was a top position to witness every swerve and near miss that bus made! It was scary. You know, I was actually wondering – quite calmly as it happens – if it was my fate to die today, on that bus!"

Safely back in our room we packed our bags to leave for Munnar. It had been nearly four weeks since I had left England and I had just over two weeks of my journey in India still ahead of me. The time was passing slowly.

"I think it will be good for me to spend the final week alone, Cass," I told her. "I need to see how I feel being here on my own."

Cassandra agreed.

"Yes," she said. "It'll be good for you, Deborah."

We started to think about what we would do when we parted company.

"I'd like to travel north to Bombay," she told me, looking it up in the book. "Blimey, it looks as though it's 30-40 hours on the train. I don't much fancy that on my own. I think I'll email Matthew again, he's going north tomorrow. Maybe we can travel together. There are things I want to talk to him about anyway."

"That's a good idea," I agreed.

Hummingbird

In truth, I desperately wanted her to come to Munnar with me. I sat quietly and asked myself why. The answer that came was that I was nervous about travelling on my own in case I couldn't find my way. I'm absolutely hopeless when it comes to finding my way about on my own. I have no sense of direction and I wasn't confident about asking for help.

I knew that Cass had to follow her own path and so I let go of my own grasping to allow fate – and Cassandra – to decide. If she was to go north the next day with Matthew or come up into the mountains to Munnar with me, so be it. I wasn't in control of it and I didn't try to persuade her either way.

After dinner, we sat by the river overlooking the naval base and watched the sunset.

"This isn't the most picturesque setting to watch the sun go down," I said.

"No, not at all," replied Cass. "But we never miss a sunset, do we?"

"No," I agreed. "We never miss a sunset."

After sundown Cassandra checked her emails. "Matthew hasn't replied yet," she told me. "Looks like I'm coming to Munnar with you tomorrow."

"I was secretly hoping you would," I confessed. "Although I'm sorry you're not meeting up with Matthew of course. To be honest, I'm relieved that I don't have to travel on my own."

Chapter 47

An unexpected detour

When you have completed 95 per cent of your journey, you are only halfway there (Japanese proverb)

The next morning, we got up early and caught the 6:30 bus. The four-hour journey up into the mountains was beautiful. I thoroughly enjoyed it and was thankful that it wasn't too hot on the bus that day.

Munnar is situated at a place where three rivers meet. The land used to be covered by a thick jungle before a British lawyer and tea planter arrived there in the 1870s and cleared the forest for the tea plantations.

When we arrived, we quickly found a reasonable place to stay, unloaded our bags and wasted no time in getting back outside again. The town itself had a really nice feel to it and we walked around a bit before sitting by the river to watch the locals wash their clothes.

The cool mountain air was welcoming after the stifling heat of the past month. Periodically, the clouds would clear and the sun would peak out for a while, making the day quite pleasant indeed. It was understandable how the area was a favourite summer destination of the British rulers in the colonial days.

After some time, we left the river and walked up to the temple where we sat for a while, just being. My mind was clear and I felt at peace with my world.

The next morning, after meditating, we went for a wonderful walk up and around the tea plantations. On returning to the town we discovered that everything was shut due to yet another strike. There were no buses, taxis or rickshaws. We had to go to the big Western hotel for breakfast and were disappointed with the stale cornflakes and below-average, very sweet, coffee.

My mood started to drop. I'd felt so good the day before and I was disappointed that I wasn't feeling so positive. We couldn't sit and relax in the hills, as I'd imagined doing, because the tea trees were in the way and there were dogs and cows wandering around freely which made me feel nervous about going off on my own.

Hummingbird

I went back to the room and ironed my washing. I managed to borrow an iron from the hotel – what a luxury it was to iron clothes! It didn't take long, I had very few clothes with me. As there was nothing to do and nowhere to go because of the strike, we went up on the roof of our hotel to sunbath. Cass liked it on the roof because of the views, but I hated it because there was a lot of junk up there. It was interesting to see how the two of us had such different perspectives of the same place. I wished that I could see beyond the mess, like Cassandra could, and just admire the more distant views.

During the day, my spirits fell further. I didn't want to be in Munnar anymore and I felt homesick. I went back to the room and slept for a while before going out for a walk. Cass came and found me at the church.

"I think I'm suffering from my expectations," I told her. "I was expecting something different than this. How on earth people travel in India for months and months I really don't know."

"You have to let go of the expectations and take it for what it is," she told me. "Some people just like each different experience, no matter what it is. It's all a learning curve, don't worry, Deborah. Some are better than others at adapting, that's all. C'mon, let's go back and get something to eat."

On the way back into town, we came across a white-skinned man at the side of the road. The man had a motorbike with him, minus a tyre.

"Hi," we said as we walked up to him.

"Hello," he answered back in an English accent.

"Have you broken down?"

"I've got a puncture. I'm waiting for my mate to bring my wheel back. He's taken it to get it repaired. My name's Simon," he said, extending his hand.

"Hi, I'm Deborah," I told him, shaking hands with him.

"And I'm Cass, nice to meet you. What are you doing in India?" she asked.

"I'm travelling with three other guys and Fiona," he told us. "We're planning a route for a motorbike rally."

"Wow, that's sounds interesting. Have you done this before?" I asked him.

"No, it's our first one. We're planning on bringing loads of people out here next year to do the rally. We're just sussing out the route, hotels and stuff. What are you girls up to here?"

"We're just hanging out really. We met at an ashram and now we're just doing a bit of sightseeing."

After talking to him for a while, Simon invited us to join them that evening at their hotel. "Fiona could probably do with the numbers being evened out and a good girlie chat!" he said.

He seemed like a nice enough guy.

"Okay, thanks. See you later then," we told him as we walked away. "Hope your mate comes back soon!"

As there was nothing else open that day, we ate at the roadside café. For the equivalent of 30p each for a meal, the food was exceptionally good.

"Fancy coming to meet Simon?" I asked Cassandra after dinner.

"No," she said, "I think I'll stay here. I don't really fancy any company tonight."

I was definitely feeling in need of a bit of stimulation so I walked down the road alone to Simon's hotel. There was a power cut which had left the way quite dark and a little scary but I arrived at the hotel safely. It was much bigger and posher than the place that Cass and I were staying in.

Simon and his friends were sitting at a dining table.

"Ah, glad you made it," he said as I entered the room.

He introduced me to the others. They all seemed really nice and friendly. "This is Fiona," he said pointing to the only lady amongst them.

"Hi, Fiona, I'll sit next to you if that's okay?"

"Yes, of course it is," she said, pulling out a chair for me.

I talked to Fiona for most of the evening. "It's great to have the numbers balanced a bit more," she told me. "The boys are great, but I have really been missing some female company."

"What exactly is it you're doing here?" I asked her. "Are you on a motorbike too?"

"No," she told me. "I'm in a jeep with a driver. A local guy. The boys are on the bikes checking out the route and I'm mapping it from the jeep and clocking the miles from one place to another."

"Where are you off to tomorrow?" I asked her.

"Periyar Wildlife Sanctuary. Why don't you come with us if you're fed up here," she offered. "There's room in the jeep."

"I'd love to," I told her excitedly. "I'll ask Cassandra. I really hope she wants to come, it'll be great!"

"I'll give you a lift back to your place and you can ask her," she said.

Back at my basic hotel, Fiona waited in the jeep whilst I woke Cassandra up and told her about Fiona's offer.

"Yeah, okay," she said. "I don't mind, it sounds good."

"See you tomorrow then, Fiona," I said as I waved her goodbye.

My mood had lifted no end and I was excited about the next leg of my journey with Fiona and the boys.

~ * ~

It was the 2nd March 2002. I was sitting in the back of the jeep on my way to Periyar National Park. Cass was in the front with Fiona, looking ahead to where we were going. I was looking back down the road from where we had come, trying to visualise one hundred and fifty motorbikes riding along the route behind me.

"Oh, no," I thought suddenly, feeling really queasy. "I'm going to be sick!"

"Stop the jeep!" I cried out.

Crouching at the roadside moments later, I was vomiting up my breakfast.

"How embarrassing," I said to Fiona when I'd stopped being sick. "I've only known you five minutes!"

"Don't worry about it," she said. "I think you'd better swap with Cassandra and sit up front with me."

Thankfully, once I was facing forwards, I was fine after that and Fiona and I got to have a good chat.

The scenery on our four-hour journey was beautiful and when we arrived at our destination we checked into a lovely hotel with a swimming pool. Fiona had negotiated a really good price with them on the promise that they'd be back next year with lots of people.

"This is bliss," I said to Fiona as we swam in the pool. "You have no idea. This water feels amazing. After the accommodation I've been staying in, this hotel is like pure heaven to me!"

It was great to be travelling with Fiona and the guys and I felt really pleased to be there, in India, on such a fantastic trip.

Speaking to Simon, I discovered that he had given up his City career to pursue his dream.

"I'd have gone crazy if I'd have stayed in the City," he told me. "I wanted to do something I could be proud of."

Simon wanted to make a difference in his life.

In the morning, I had my first hot bath since leaving England and boy it felt good.

"If we always have everything we want," I said to Cassandra, "we wouldn't appreciate anything as much. It's good to deprive ourselves of certain things sometimes because the pleasure of experiencing them again is so enhanced." I laid back in the tub. "I never thought I'd enjoy a bath as much as this. It's the best bath I've ever had in all my life. Ever!"

We stayed with Fiona and the boys for another day. Cass rode on the back of one of the bikes and I stayed in the Jeep with Fiona. We stuck to the smaller back roads, passing rivers, forests and a couple of amazing dams and I took some beautiful photographs. Fiona was interesting to talk to and I enjoyed her company immensely.

"What's the most adventurous thing you've ever done?" I asked her.

"I once spent a month in the jungle in Borneo," she told me.

"Why did you do that?" I asked.

"It was for a TV documentary called Jungle Jane," she said. "It was an extraordinary experience."

"I bet it was! Have you travelled a lot, Fi?"

"Yes, quite a bit."

"Ever been to India before?" I asked her.

"Actually, I have," she said. "I've ridden a motorbike here a few times."

I thought Fiona was fantastic – so adventurous and talented. I must admit, I was a bit envious of her life.

We spent that day travelling to a place called Angamaly and after some negotiation on Fiona's part, we spent the night in a wonderful suite of a really posh hotel.

"Oh, okay, if I really have to!" I laughed as I stepped down from the jeep and looked at the entrance to the magnificent hotel.

The next day, we said our goodbyes. Fiona had really enjoyed having us around for a couple of days and was sorry we couldn't go on with her. After travelling with the boys for some time, she had been feeling in need of some female company and, just as if by magic, we appeared from nowhere. Or did we?

I felt pretty sad to say goodbye to them all, I'd had a fabulous few days of much-needed fun and luxury with some wonderful and inspirational people.

~ * ~

Simon and Fiona finished organising the tour and went back to India the following year with a large group of people. It was the first-ever tour they had organised.

Fiona eventually left the group, but Simon continued to build up his company, Global Enduro, which celebrated its 10th anniversary in 2012.

The company expanded its portfolio to include motorbike adventures in Africa, the Himalayas and Cambodia, as well as running arctic dog sled and snowmobile endurance adventures in Finnmark, 400km north of the Arctic Circle.

Simon's organisation specialised in charity challenges and donated an impressive £3.4million to charity.

In 2008, Simon and his company took Princes William and Harry to South Africa on a motorbike challenge to raise money for their chosen charities. I mean, come on, how cool is that! Simon is also the founder of the charity Adventure Ashram, a non-profit organisation helping children of India to a better standard of health and education.

He's quite a guy is Simon Smith! I feel privileged to have crossed paths with him, Fiona and the boys on my travels, at the very beginnings of their own special and unique adventure.

~ * ~

I was feeling a bit low the day I met Simon and the others and my spirits were really lifted by those few days on the road. It was exactly what I needed – to come off of the spiritual path for a while, let my hair down and have some fun.

After the guys left the hotel, Cass and I went to visit Attirapally waterfalls. Despite being told that they were the second highest falls in

India, we couldn't find them in our guidebook. Two bus journeys and an hour and a half later, we arrived at our destination.

The road leading up to the falls was scattered with palm trees which invited us to an area of great natural beauty. It was absolutely gorgeous there. The falls were spectacular and the river was stunning. As we sat by the river cooling our bodies for a while, we were aware of some Indian guys looking at us, but we didn't mind so much, we had become quite accustomed to it by then.

We sat on the rocks, our feet dangling in the cool river water, the sun shining down on our bodies and I was in heaven again.

"It's so peaceful here," I said to Cassandra. "I'm surprised that there aren't any tourists about."

"Well, it's not in the guidebook," she reminded me. "So I guess no one knows about it. There aren't even many locals here," she observed.

"I wish we could stay here for a few days," I sighed

"Yeah, so do I but we have to get back to Fort Cochin this evening because of the strike," she reminded me.

Chapter 48

Back to Fort Cochin

After a couple of tranquil hours by the river, we made our way back to Fort Cochin. We took two buses back to the posh hotel and collected our backpacks, which we'd left there earlier. The hotel manager tried to arrange for a car to take us back, but unfortunately it wasn't possible. It seemed that he couldn't do enough for us because we had arrived with Fiona and the boys. He didn't know that we had only just met them and we certainly weren't going to put him straight on that account. We tried to get a bus, which would have cost us 30p, but it was full and we couldn't get on it. So, we had to get a rickshaw at the added expense of £3 and then a bus on the final leg of the journey back to Fort Cochin.

We did like to get the bus wherever possible as, apart from being exceptionally cheap, it was just so much fun. The bus drivers and conductors seemed to have quite a stressful job, racing against the clock and hardly stopping to let people on and off. It was quite amusing to see them haul the old ladies onto the bus, the driver's foot barely hesitating to come off of the gas pedal!

Trying to find the right bus was always an interesting challenge. We soon learned not to say, "is this the bus to...?" because the locals always answered yes, whether it was or not. I don't think they ever liked to say no when asked a question by a foreigner. We had to choose our words carefully. "Which bus goes to....?" was a much better question, although we were still sometimes given the wrong answer.

When we were on the bus, we soon learned to check with two more locals to confirm that we were actually on the correct bus. It was great fun as long as we weren't too hot and tired. When we were hot and tired and just wanted to get to where we were going, it was no fun at all.

"Everyone's staring at us as though we are as naked as a jaybird," I said to Cass when we were finally on the right bus back to Fort Cochin.

"That's because we're the only white people on here," she said. "I guess they don't see many white faces around here."

On the bus or off, Indians always seemed either too embarrassed to talk to us (women and kids just looked and giggled) or wanted to ask us lots of questions.

The young men liked to practice their English on us. They would often approach us, interrupt our conversation and start to ask a string of questions that usually went something like: "What is your good name? Where is your place? Where are you from? What are you doing? What is your job? Are you married? How old are you? Have you been to India before? How do you like Kerala? How long are you staying here? What hotel are you at?

Write down your home address, please."

~ * ~

We finally arrived at the hotel in Fort Cochin and thankfully they had a room for us. We were too late for cooked food, so I just ate a bag of crisps. After eating so healthily since I arrived in India, the crisps were a welcome treat. Apart from the Garibaldi biscuits I'd brought with me from England, the only other snack I'd had since arriving in India was the peanut brittle that most people at the ashram were addicted to.

We spent a few more very hot days in Cochin, mooching about, eating the most delicious vegetarian food, meditating and wandering into the shops to get our daily dose of flattery. We could always guarantee that we would hear how beautiful we were and how we would break Indian hearts if we left Cochin. Oh, how those boys loved us, but I knew that as soon as we left, their undying love for us would easily be transferred to the next Western lady to enter their shop. It was nice to be complimented nonetheless.

I adored Fort Cochin, with its wonderful big fishing nets, its wild dolphins, the green parakeets that settled in the trees above us, the goats that wandered around, the fish stalls displaying the catch of the day and the local men performing their daily keep-fit classes along the water's edge each morning.

It was an extremely interesting place. There was so much going on and yet it had the most wonderful relaxed feeling about it. Apart from the intense heat, it felt perfect to me. It felt like the ideal place to hang out.

I started to spend more time on my own. Not because Cassandra was annoying me, quite the opposite actually, I loved her more and more with every passing day. But I kept my mind focused on what I had to do. And that was to find the true me and to seek out the God within me. And finding ourselves and God can only be done when we're alone.

After much soul searching, I decided to go back to Varkala to spend my last week in India alone.

Cass's train to Delhi was not for a few days so it would have been easy and quite pleasant for me to stay there with her for three more days, but I wanted to experience some time completely on my own in the hope that that I would be more focused on my yoga and meditation practice. I was finding it difficult to discipline myself, although that was partly due to the heat, which was making me feel lethargic.

My plan for my last week at Varkala was to get to bed early and get up at 5:30am to meditate and then go to the beach to do yoga whilst it was still cool enough. Then, I would maybe walk for an hour, swim, sunbath then sleep when the heat became unbearable.

On our last day together at Cochin, Cass and I met a guy with a wonderful big smiley face. Big smiley face man, as I called him, couldn't stand up as his legs were crippled and paralysed and he bumped himself along the pavement on his bottom, using the backs of his hands because his arms were all twisted.

He coloured in pictures and sold them to make his living. It was admirable to see that he didn't beg, but was doing something constructive to earn his living.

"Would you like to have coffee with us?" we asked him after purchasing a picture and chatting to him for a while.

"Yes, please, that would be nice."

He shuffled his way to the table and Cassandra lifted him up and onto the chair.

"It's nice to be on the same level as other people, instead of having to look up at people all the time," he told us.

I tried to imagine what it would be like to be him, but my mind wouldn't allow me to go to that place, it was too frightening.

"What else do you like to do apart from colour and chat, drink coffee and smile?" I asked him.

"I listen to music at my house, big smiley face man told us. I particularly like Bob Marley," he said. "Do you know Bob Marley?"

"Well, not personally," we laughed. "But we certainly know who you mean!"

"He has so much sunshine in his spirit," I said to Cassandra as we were making our way back to our room. "It shines out through his wonderful infectious smile. You know what I've decided?"

"What's that?"

"If ever I'm feeling low, I'm gonna think of our smiley friend. If that guy can keep his spirits up, I'm sure that it's possible to keep mine up as well."

Yes, I felt good about that. It's so easy to forget just how lucky we are.

"India is full of things that remind me to be thankful and happy," I said. "Having an attitude of gratitude is an essential and important aspect of our personal growth."

Cassandra wholeheartedly agreed.

~ * ~

It was our last evening together.

"Tell you what," I said to Cassandra, "let's celebrate with a bottle of wine. I know it's extravagant, but I'll pay for it. It'll be a lovely treat for us."

I hadn't had a glass of wine since I left the UK and the thought of it now was very appealing.

Dressed in our finest Indian attire we walked into an expensive hotel and ordered a bottle of wine. Sitting down at the table, I carefully poured the first glass of cold crisp white wine and felt my taste buds coming alive at the thought of drinking it. I lifted the glass to my mouth, slowly. I wanted to savour the moment.

Boy that wine tasted good! After five weeks of abstinence it was like nectar on my lips.

The wine cost the equivalent of five nights' accommodation, but it was so very worth it. Oh, yes! It was cold and delicious and I savoured every mouthful. Feeling rather more than tipsy, we went back to our digs and spent our last night together in Fort Cochin.

Chapter 49

Being by myself

The next day Cass got the bus with me to the train station. I anticipated that I would find it difficult to leave her, but was surprised that I actually felt okay about it. I knew that it was the right thing for both of us. We were relying on each other; taking comfort from knowing that the other person was around. We had to find out how it was to be on our own.

I knew that I would definitely see her again and that this was not the end of our friendship. I had learned about the pain of attachment and I let her go with surprising ease. She was the most perfect person I could have met and travelled with and I acknowledged that. Not once did she irritate me or do anything to upset me. Not once did I feel uncomfortable in her presence, feel bored by her conversation or feel intimidated by the silences between us. As my train pulled out of the station, I looked at the woman standing alone on the platform and I thanked God for sending her to me as I calmly and happily waved goodbye.

I settled down for my four-and-a-half hour train journey back to Varkala. It was long and hot, but I was feeling in total balance. I watched the beautiful scenery, listened to some music and talked to some locals to pass the time. When I finally got off the train, I took a rickshaw to the beach and felt confident in dealing with the driver, who tried to overcharge me by 15 rupees. I negotiated the price down with the expertise of a well-seasoned traveller.

I went back to the place we had stayed before and was delighted to receive a warm welcome from the owners of the rooms and restaurant. Thankfully, they had one room left and they even gave it to me at a reduced price.

It felt strange to be there on my own. I watched the sunset that evening and for a moment I wanted to be back in Fort Cochin with Cassandra. However, I knew that that was the old pattern of behaviour and the easy option and that it was right for me to be on my own for a while before I went home.

I thought again about what Matthew had said at the ashram. I was out of my comfort zone and was stretching myself.

Like yoga, you stretch a little and it feels tight. You hold that pose and it becomes more comfortable, and then you can stretch a little bit more.

"Feel the stretch," I said to myself. "Let it hurt a little, it won't kill you. Relax. You can't grow without stretching yourself."

I was grateful to the owners of the rooms and restaurant for being so kind and friendly to me. Each day, when I returned to my room via the restaurant, they made me feel at home and welcome and they treated me like their good friend. They were my balance wheels.

The next day, I got up at 5:30 as I had planned. I showered and then meditated. An hour later, I went to the beach and did my yoga practice. It was such a beautiful setting to practice in. As I performed the asanas, I looked at the many fishermen on the beach and out in their boats. I saw a couple of Indian guys practicing tai chi. After I finished my yoga routine, I sunbathed a bit and I swam in the warm sea.

Although now on my own in India, my mind was still easily tempted by distractions. I was invited to the Italian restaurant one evening to listen to some live music. I was tempted to go for the company but I managed to decline the invitation, as I wanted to be alone to still my mind. After all, spiritual practice, like any discipline, takes dedication. I knew that over time, with daily practice, meditation could become the foundation of a more fulfilling spiritual life for me.

We can easily forget the importance of a healthy soul. We realise the benefits of healthy habits for our bodies and minds, but quite often tend to neglect the soul. Unless we specifically seek it out, we don't get taught how to connect with the source of all life and live from our higher selves.

To get to know myself, I knew that I had to be by myself. I had to still my mind and listen to the whisper of my soul. I wanted to know what it was telling me. I was still confused as to who I was and what I now wanted.

If I started to socialise, I'd meet more people and they would be a distraction. I heard my inner voice speaking to me: "If you can't be with yourself here, where can you be with yourself?"

So, I spent the week alone. I stuck to my routine. I got up at 5:30 every morning and meditated before going to the beach to practice yoga. I found it much easier to be disciplined when I was on my own. It allowed me the space and time to face my truth as I started to contemplate my future. I knew that I was changing and growing, clearing my way out of the fog and through the barriers that my unconscious mind had kindly put up to protect and shield me. I knew deep down that I would escape the disease that had devastated my family and now I had to think about my future. A future I hadn't even known existed until recently.

As I allowed the truth to surface, I felt sad and I felt scared. I knew in my heart that something was wrong and that for some reason I wasn't happy in my relationship any more. I decided to email Richard to try to explain that I felt confused and that, although I loved him dearly (which I did and still do to this day), I wasn't sure if being with him was still what I wanted. I had changed a lot since my breakdown in Costa Rica and it had made me feel differently about every aspect of my life.

I hoped with all my heart that he would understand, and that he would reply.

Do you remember I told you that it was at Varkala that I first spoke to God? It was Monday 11 March 2002. I was sitting on the sandy beach, looking out over the vast sea in front of me and allowing myself to open up into my meditation. I was aware of a huge presence of love and my voice was whispering: "I put my trust in you. I have faith in you and I give myself to you so that I may realise my truth."

I knew there was a powerful and loving presence within me, which I had first experienced in Costa Rica, but what I felt at that moment was different.

It was totally and absolutely an external expression and definitely not addressed to myself, as was usually the case. I was addressing the force of nature and of life – the Universe or God – the entity that is all and everything. I felt it resonate through my entire body and above and beyond my being as far as I could imagine it to be and further still. The surrender was peaceful and full of love. And it was totally unintentional. I was at another turning point in my life.

Nowadays I mostly refer to this immense energy as the Universe or Grace, because I feel that if I use the word God, it can be so easily misinterpreted by each individual in their own way, whereas the Universe fits my idea of God so much better.

~ * ~

I had an email reply back from Richard. As I looked at his message in my in box, I felt tense with the anticipation of what he might say. I steeled myself to open it and was relieved to find a comforting message and I got the feeling that he understood what I was trying to say to him. I took some deep breaths and as I breathed out, I felt tension leaving my body.

"Thank you," I whispered.

Six weeks after leaving for India, a different Deborah went home to England. A more confident and peaceful Deborah, a woman who was totally at ease with herself, with no need or desire to connect with anyone on the long journey back.

I knew that I had grown up a lot in India and was sure that it was the best therapy I could have ever spent my money and time on.

I had a small bottle of wine with my meal on the plane. I felt a wonderful warmth within me, not simply from the now unfamiliar buzz of the alcohol, but for me, for Deborah Goodman, for the huge steps I had taken over the last six weeks.

"Oh boy, what an enlightening trip that was."

My life would never feel the same again.

Chapter 50

A new life

I returned from India into the loving arms of my boyfriend. I was pleased to see Richard and he was pleased to see me. I had no job and a little bit of savings left, but I had a new respect for the material things I possessed and the knowledge that I didn't need many of them anyway.

I planned to start working for myself as a masseuse and reflexologist, but as yet I had no clients. Because I grew up in Essex and I worked in London, I didn't know any local people apart from my next door neighbours. I had to start totally from scratch.

I spent the first six weeks of my time back in the UK marketing myself. I posted adverts in local shop windows for clients wanting home visits and I contacted health clubs in search of a therapy room to work from. I advertised cut-price offers and I started work on the creation of my website. I designed some leaflets and business cards and I searched online for free websites I could advertise myself on.

I drew up a business plan, detailing how many treatments I would have to carry out in order to make enough money and I was naïve enough to think that it would all fall into my lap from the beginning.

But it didn't, and business was slow – very slow. When the work trickled in, I soon realised that I was going to need a Plan B. Letting my cleaning lady go, I started to boost my income with a cleaning job myself. Boy, what a turn-around!

I cut right back on my outgoings, taking packed lunches if I went out and a flask so that I wouldn't have to spend any money on a drink. Needless to say, I wasn't buying any clothes, shoes or handbags.

Richard took me out for dinner and treated me sometimes, but I was determined to pay my half of the bills at home.

"If I can't do that, Richard, then I'm not making it work am I?" I told him.

"No," he replied. "I guess not".

It was important to me that I was self-sufficient but I was extremely lucky to have his support in every way possible.

One day, as I was looking through the local newspaper, I happened to notice an article about the opening of a health club at the nearby hospital. It was a gym for the National Health Service staff. I gave them a call to find out if they had a treatment room there.

"Yes," the manager answered. "We do actually. Would you be interested in coming to have a look at it?"

"Yes, please," I enthused and made the arrangements to view it.

The gym was small, but it had everything needed for an all-round workout. It had an adequate-sized aerobics studio and a small reception area, behind which was the treatment room.

From inside the treatment room, I could hear conversations being held in the reception area, which wasn't very conducive to a relaxing treatment. However, the manager offered me the room on the basis that I paid the club 10 per cent of whatever I earned there. This arrangement was a godsend, as most other establishments wanted anything between 40-60 per cent of my takings or a daily fixed rate, which I could hardly afford without existing clients.

I took the room. My work was still slow but at last I was managing to give some treatments. I was allowed to use the gym for free and continued to practice yoga in the aerobics studio. I mingled with the gym members to get myself known and I advertised discounts to encourage people to try my treatments.

I was frustrated, but I was determined to make my new career work. I was still cleaning my neighbour's house and was desperate to get a bit more money coming in. I went for a few interviews for part-time office jobs, but it wasn't really what I wanted to do with my time. I was sure that something more suitable would come along.

My faith paid off.

I was walking around Covent Garden in London with my friends one day, talking to them about my situation and my need to earn more money. My friend Daxa suddenly stopped outside a shop.

"Look, Deborah," she said, pointing to a sign in the window. "They want Sunday staff in here."

What a stroke of luck. The shop just happened to be Culpeper, a herbalist shop selling not only herbs but aromatherapy oils and products. I enquired within and was elated to be offered the job.

Culpeper was a tiny little shop situated opposite St Paul's church in the

Hummingbird

heart of Covent Garden. It was one of a small group of shops, the first of which appeared on Baker Street in 1927. The business was founded by Hilda Leyel, a practicing herbalist and a truly inspirational lady.

I absolutely loved working at Culpeper each Sunday. The money wasn't brilliant, but it gave me a regular income and I worked with two amazing people, Dan and Vicky. I learned so much about natural healing from them as they were actively using nature's remedies in their day-to-day lives. I had a lot of fun working there and we had many interesting customers. I started to learn more about aromatherapy by selling the oils in the shop and I began to study aromatherapy at college one evening a week.

I loved the job so much, I'm sure that I would have happily worked there for nothing.

Chapter 51

The Journey, Brandon Bays

I was gathering and reading quite a lot of books at this time – books on natural health, therapies and inspirational stories.

I remembered about the book *The Journey*, which a lady had recommended to me when I was in India.

"The woman who wrote it (Brandon Bays) cured herself of a massive tumour in six and a half weeks," the lady had told me. "It's an amazing story."

I bought the book and read it.

My fellow traveller was absolutely right, I did find the story of Brandon's life and work truly inspiring. Having the football-sized tumour growing inside of her led Brandon to begin a remarkable journey of self-healing.

Just six and a half weeks after her diagnosis, she went back to the hospital to be told that, not only had her tumour disappeared, but that there wasn't even a trace of the tumour to be seen. She was textbook perfect. Amazing herself and her doctors, Brandon had intuitively listened to her body wisdom and completely healed, without any drugs or surgery and with no pain at all.

Brandon used her experiences to develop a remarkable process that can be used by anyone and everyone to facilitate emotional and physical self-healing.

After I read Brandon's story, I was eager to attend her workshop to be guided through the process myself. I knew that I still had some healing to do and I was eager to release any emotional trauma that was left in my body. However, at the time I had no spare money and so I put it off for a while. It was a few years later, in April 2004, when I attended the Journey Intensive Workshop in London.

The only money I've ever borrowed in my whole life was for my first second-hand car and my mortgage. That's just how I am, I never borrow money and I only spend it if I have it. But I have to tell you, if I'd have known then what I know now, I would have borrowed that money and attended Brandon's workshop a lot sooner than I did.

The workshop was hosted by Brandon herself. I remember clearly the first time I saw her that weekend, she was absolutely radiant. Her energy was shining bright and filling the room with pure love and grace. It felt wonderful to be in her presence.

I'm not very good with estimating numbers, but I guess that there was possibly a couple of hundred people there that weekend, all searching for a way to improve and enhance their lives and their health. After registration, we all gathered together in the large room to begin our healing journey with Brandon.

Brandon is an excellent speaker and was easy to listen to. Her story was captivating as she took us through her personal journey of her life and her work. She explained the Journey process to us and demonstrated it live with one of her delegates, who bravely volunteered to get up onto the stage and bare her soul for the sake of everyone's own healing process. That couldn't have been an easy thing to do and I'm grateful to that person for doing that, enabling us to be able to witness first-hand how the Journey would work for us.

~ * ~

You have to leave the city of your comfort and go into the wilderness of your intuition. What you'll discover will be wonderful. What you'll discover is yourself
– Alan Alda

Inevitably the time came for me to experience the process for myself.

Taking my script, I paired up with another lady and we found a space to put our chairs, side by side and facing one another. We were close together, so that we could speak softly to each other.

It was my turn to be guided on my journey. I felt a bit anxious, but was eager to free myself of any emotions that were holding me back from an abundance of health and happiness. I closed my eyes.

"Think about the issue that is bothering you," my partner told me.

"Yes," I said. "I'm doing that."

"What are you feeling?"

Brandon had explained that it was important for us to name the emotion we were experiencing.

"I'm feeling sad," I told her.

"Where in the body do you feel this sadness?" my partner softly asked me.

"All over."

I felt the tears coming and I allowed them to flow freely from my eyes and down my cheeks.

Bringing all of my awareness to each emotion as it arose allowed it to be fully experienced and I was surprised at how quickly each emotion melted away, being replaced by a different feeling.

By holding them down, we are keeping our emotions — and ourselves — stuck. We try to move on, but we can't because the emotions and issues that we haven't dealt with keep coming up to remind us that they are still around.

Unless we open the door to them, they will just keep on knocking and if we stop listening, they will find another way to show themselves, usually in depression or emotional breakdown or in a physical manifestation of ill health and disease. The Journey technique gives us the tools to access the emotions that we are so used to pushing back down inside of us and allows us to fully experience and finally release them.

My process continued for a couple of hours. I was getting stuck a lot, not knowing what I was feeling, experiencing nothingness and sometimes just being stuck in a pleasant emotion; my conscious mind coming into play and liking where it was, not wanting to move on. I was becoming more and more exhausted and part of me wanted to give up and stop the process altogether. Until... hold on... what was this? I found myself having an unfamiliar feeling. A very unfamiliar feeling indeed.

"What are you feeling now, Deborah?" my partner asked me, noticing the change on my face.

"I'm angry," I said. "I'm really, really angry."

I knew instantly why I was so angry. Without the Journey, I had never seen it before. I just thought I was someone who didn't get angry. I hadn't really thought about it, but suddenly it was all so crystal clear.

"I'm angry at my dad."

There, I'd said it.

I was guided to fully experience the emotion and it came up with a vengeance. And then, quite quickly, the anger dispersed and was replaced

Hummingbird

by love.

The method guided me though more emotions after that, and re-visited some I'd already been to — sometimes many times over. Eventually, I broke through a blackness to experience an overwhelming joy and peace. I had finally broken through to source.

Source is the ultimate destination — a place where we experience boundaryless freedom and joy. It's a place of unlimited peace, pure love, pure being. It's a universal vastness of beauty and grace.

I sometimes explain source like this. Imagine the first moments of infancy when we are pure and untouched human beings. This life has not had a chance to put its stuff on us yet. We haven't been influenced by our parents, relatives, teachers, siblings or peers. We don't know any jealousy, grief, cruelty, or pain. Put-downs, pressure and competition are stresses of the future. We haven't had an opportunity to experience any unwanted negative emotions or energy and, if we are fed, cuddled and loved, we are most probably hanging out in that magical place… that is source.

Being there felt utterly amazing.

As I experienced myself as this joyous peace and love, I allowed the feeling to wash right through each individual emotion as I was guided back up through the levels of my emotional journey. Knowing myself in this state of grace, I spoke to each emotion from this new place of joy and the words came straight from my core being.

"Don't be afraid," I told my fear. "There really is nothing to be afraid of."

And to the feeling of emptiness I whispered, "there's no need to feel empty ever again. There is too much love within you for you to ever feel empty again. Allow the love in."

As I spoke to the emotion of despair, my voice softly said, "embrace it, experience it and then let it go."

Up through the levels I continued, until I reached the sadness that was at the very beginning of my journey.

"There is no sadness any more, only joy and love."

And knowing myself fully as that joy and love completely blew me away.

When my emotional Journey process was coming to an end, I was guided to imagine a campfire of unconditional love and acceptance. I imagined a much younger me sitting around the campfire and in my mind I brought my father to sit by the fire alongside me.

I listened for the gentle voice of my partner as she continued to guide me through my process.

"What does the younger you want to say to your father?" she asked.

In my vision, the little Deborah turned and looked at my father.

"I'm angry," I said. "I'm so angry that you weren't there for me when I was growing up. I'm so angry that you were sick and that I didn't have my dad with me. I'm angry that you had that horrible illness and that I had to visit you in that mental hospital. It scared me to see you like that dad and I'm angry that I was so scared. Scared of going to see you there. Scared of the other patients at the hospital. Scared of getting the illness myself, so scared and so angry! I can't even tell you how angry I am right now."

Now that I was allowing myself to feel it at last, the anger was having a field day. I could almost hear it cheering: "Ah, finally, she's letting me out! Halle-bloody-luyah! I was suffocating in there!"

My partner was taking it all in her stride. Calmly she asked me, "and what does your father have to say to you, Deborah?"

"He says that he's pleased that I've finally allowed the anger to come up. He says that he's so very sorry for the way it was and it's perfectly okay that I'm angry. He understands. He says that he's sorry that he wasn't there for me."

That familiar feeling came to me. First, the lump in my throat, then the stinging in my eyes and finally the tears came.

"He wanted to be there for us all," I sobbed. "And he was angry about the illness, too."

"How does the younger you reply to that?" I was asked.

Addressing my father again I whimpered, "I know you're sorry, I'm sorry, too. I know it's not your fault, that's why I couldn't allow myself to be angry with you, Dad." My anger was now replaced with tears of relief. "I love you, Dad."

"And what does your father have to say?" my new friend asked me.

"He says it's all okay now. It's all going to be okay now. He's proud of me and he loves me."

When the conversation was over and we were completely exhausted of words, forgiveness was given and I sent him my blessings.

Hummingbird

Finally, I understood what anger was. I knew where my anger had been hiding and I knew why.

When my Journey was complete I was asked to imagine how I would be feeling in the future – in a day's time, a month's time and in six months' time. How could I see myself in a year from now, in five and 10 years' time? Was I feeling free? How was I handling things?

I could picture a whole new me. Free from the sadness and pain and experiencing perfect health and wellbeing. I was at peace and full of joy and grace.

I was asked to write a letter to myself, from that place in the future. A letter from the all-new future me, to the me of today. This is the letter I wrote to myself that day.

Dear Deborah

Don't be afraid. There is nothing to be afraid of. Love is around you and within you. Source is boundless and wonderful.

It's no-one's fault. There is only freedom to be found. You are growing stronger each day.

I love you and am here – waiting for you. I know you will come to me. I trust completely, now you must trust too!

Since I did the Journey process, I am able to experience anger when it's appropriate. I don't feel angry all the time and the emotion only arises when it's justified. This is because I allow myself to fully experience it when it does show up.

I practice this method with each and every emotion on a daily basis. This is the gift that The Journey has given me. It's a whole new way of looking at my internal world. I believe wholeheartedly that, what seems like a simple thing – the discovery and release of a hidden emotion – could well be a key to avoiding future illness.

~ * ~

When the emotional journey was fully complete, I was guided on another journey. This time it was a physical journey. As I used my imagination, powered by my own body wisdom, I took a look inside myself in order to discover any areas of disease and to heal my physical body.

I could actually see the areas of distress within myself and I watched as they healed, before I was guided back to my outside world.

Brandon Bay's Journey process is powerful. It's being used in hospitals, in prisons, in schools and in addict centres. It's being used with victims of violent crime. Mainly it's being used by people from all walks of life who know that in some way they feel held back or blocked.

If you haven't experienced this type of healing work before, it may seem a little difficult to understand. In her book, The Journey, Brandon explains the process to us and details the script for us to work with ourselves. I would thoroughly recommend The Journey to anyone and I would suggest that you begin by reading Brandon's book before you either attend the Journey Intensive weekend or find yourself a qualified practitioner in your area to guide you through the process.

I'm by no means a qualified practitioner, but I've used the script that Brandon developed to take a handful of my clients on their own emotional journeys. Each time I have done this, I've seen significant results. One man finally forgave his abuser and a lady who had been attending the Priory clinic for the past two years with only a slight change in her progress, went to the police the next day and reported her abuse in full detail – the first time in 25 years that she had told anyone the whole story.

Another lady did the Journey process with me and saw a marked improvement in her self-esteem, learned to say no and now has more time and energy for herself, resulting in an even higher self-esteem and a better quality of life. She's no longer petrified of getting cancer every time she feels an ache or pain and is now doing things for herself and not just for everybody else.

It is remarkable.

Chapter 52

Determined to succeed

You never fail until you stop trying – Albert Einstein

My work at the health club slowly picked up. I was determined to make a success of my new career and I kept telling myself that I wasn't going to give up or fail. I searched the internet for any information I could find to help me succeed and I contacted all the local schools to find out about any fundraising pamper days they were having. I had no idea that it would be so difficult to build up my client base, but I never gave up and slowly, little by little, I got busier.

It was at a pamper day that I met Jane. I instantly liked the tall, slim beauty therapist with her attractive face and her long blond hair. She seemed very genuine, warm and open.

"Would you be interested in working with me to give pamper evenings in people's homes?" I asked her. "I've done a few with my friend in Essex, but I'm looking for someone more local to work with."

"That sounds interesting," she said. "Yes, why not. Shall we get together and work something out?"

Jane and I swapped numbers and we went from there. It was the start of a great friendship. Jane started working at the health club with me and at last I had a colleague of sorts. Going it alone is rewarding, but can be quite isolating at times and thankfully Jane turned out to be a loyal friend and confidante.

Chapter 53

Infant massage

Being touched and caressed, being massaged, is food for the infant. Food as necessary as minerals, vitamins and proteins – Dr Frederick Leboyer

"It would be lovely to teach mums how to massage their babies," I thought unexpectedly one day. I literally just woke up one morning with the idea on my mind.

I don't know where the thought came from, maybe I'd seen baby massage classes advertised somewhere or perhaps someone had said something that had planted a seed in me. I really don't know, but the thought stuck in my mind and I looked on the internet to see if there were any courses I could attend.

I was thrilled when I found a course in London, studying with the International Association of Infant Massage (IAIM). It was exactly the training I was after and I signed up for it immediately.

The first day of my instruction with the IAIM soon came and I took the train into London. Arriving at the hotel, I found the relevant conference room and entered enthusiastically, I couldn't wait to get started. Looking around the large comfortable room I took in the surroundings and the faces of the other delegates – all women.

I chatted to a few people and discovered that my fellow classmates were made up primarily of mums, health visitors, yoga teachers and therapists; much as I had expected.

Our Swedish tutor, Mia Elmsäter, was a warm and wonderful teacher. (She has a remarkable story of her own to tell; please see Appendix C.) I spent four interesting and thoroughly enjoyable days on the course with her and my fellow students.

After introductions and a presentation on the history of massage and infant massage, Mia settled us down to teach us the baby massage routine.

"Okay everyone, let's get started on learning the strokes," she told us. "If you can all sit on the floor, in a semicircle, with your babies in front of you, we can begin."

Hummingbird

Pretending to take some oil in our hands, we looked into the glass eyes of our dolls and lovingly asked them if they would like a nice massage. We watched for the cues – signals that indicated that the babies were happy to be massaged or were not quite in the mood at the moment: maybe they were hungry, or needed changing or just needed a cuddle right now. Not surprisingly, our baby dolls were very well behaved. Yes, it was clear that none of them were complaining!

"It's not quite this straightforward with real babies," Mia was quick to point out as she guided us through each movement.

We practiced a mixture of Indian and Swedish massage techniques on the dolls and when we came to massaging the feet I already had an advantage because I knew all of the reflexology points.

When we finished the routine we thanked our babies for the wonderful massage experience we'd had with them and we gave them a cuddle. They were happy dolls indeed. Well, we had good imaginations.

Mia talked to us about the positive effects of baby massage and I wasn't at all surprised to learn just how much a loving massage will benefit not only the child, but also the parents and how important the massage can be for the process of bonding. I was reminded how I'd experienced this for myself when I started to massage my brother Nigel at the hospital. Sadly our bond had been breaking down, but when I started to massage him, it strengthened the relationship between us again. It was quite remarkable.

It was one thing learning the baby massage routine for ourselves, but now we needed to learn how to actually teach others to massage their children and this was another matter altogether. Thankfully, because of my experience of running workshops, teaching a group wasn't a totally new concept to me.

Mia guided us through the principles of how to instruct others in the art of baby massage and I learned some important points about the teaching techniques. We talked about valuing and supporting the parents, which I found extremely beneficial and I learned some communication and group facilitation skills, which I was soon to discover were necessary tools to have when you have a class of real life babies in front of you.

There were many different components to the instructors course, one of which was to learn how to adapt the massage for babies born prematurely. Vimala McClure, founder of the IAIM, states the following in her book Infant Massage: A Handbook for Loving Parents:

"In one study, 20 premature babies were massaged three times a day for

15 minutes each. They averaged 47 per cent greater weight gain per day, were more active and alert, and showed more mature neurological development than infants who did not receive massage. In addition, their hospital stay averaged six days less."

How remarkable is that? With this information available to us, it's surprising to me that every Special Care Baby Unit in the country doesn't have a qualified infant massage instructor on its staff.

I began to realise that there was so much more to infant massage than I had first imagined. After a very productive four days on the course I came away with a lot of new knowledge and plenty to think about. I also came away with plenty of homework – an essential requirement for completion of the training.

I had four to six months to complete and submit my coursework. I read two books, one on the first year of child development and one all about the importance of touch.

Touching: The Human Significance of the Skin by Ashley Montagu is an amazing read. It's a whole book dedicated to the wonderful power of touch, backed up by scientific studies.

I absolutely love this book and I would encourage anyone who cares about humanity to read it or at least to have a look through it. The author, a British-American anthropologist and humanist, was passionate about the study of human behaviour and in 1995 the American Humanist Association named him the Humanist of the Year.

Ashley Montagu's book leaves us in no doubt of the importance of tactile stimulation on our mental health, our physical health, our sex lives, our immune system and our ability to thrive. It's no wonder that so many of us love to receive a massage and a cuddle.

There are numerous passages from Ashley Montagu's book that I would love to share with you. Compelling evidence about the power of touch is filling its pages from cover to cover, but for now I'll just leave it here with a reminder that everyone, at every age, needs a loving word and a loving touch.

The coursework I had been given required me to complete 10 short answer questions, 35 multiple-choice questions, seven essay questions and a practical teaching self-evaluation.

The 10 short answer questions related specifically to the massage itself and I found them quick and easy to complete. The 35 multiple-choice questions were also fairly easy for me and I received a mark of excellent for both sections.

The seven essay questions were a lot more time-consuming, but I thoroughly enjoyed working on them. For a girl who didn't like school, I was absolutely loving the study of complementary medicine and infant massage.

I worked hard on the essay questions and at the same time I was required to organise and run my own five-week course of baby massage classes. With REAL LIVE BABIES! The thought of running the classes was daunting. Where and how should I start?

"Okay, Deborah," I said to myself as I sat down with pen and paper. "Let's make a list." I always seem to start a new project with a list. "Now, what's the first thing I have to do?"

Find a venue, I wrote.

"And then?" I asked myself.

Find parents and babies, came the next item to appear on the sheet of paper in front of me, quickly followed by dates and times of the course, list of things they need to bring with them, structure of the course week-by-week, get oils and flip chart.

There, I'd made a start.

I took the advice of the handbook and decided to hold five weekly sessions and structure the course as suggested. It seemed like the best approach. I rang a friend to find out the times that the older children were at school and decided to hold the classes on Monday mornings. I looked around for a venue, but I couldn't afford the hire charges so I decided to hold the classes at my home and to keep my fingers crossed that there would be enough room.

So, with the dates, times and venue decided on, all I had to do was to find mothers with babies of a suitable age.

"Ah, how do I do that?" I wondered, not knowing any local people with children. In a moment of inspiration, I decided to make a flyer advertising free baby massage classes and find the relevant people to give it to.

The next day was a cold and wet Monday morning, but I didn't let that dampen my enthusiasm. I went to the local supermarket car park and, trying not to get my leaflets too soggy, I handed them out to all the women I saw with little babies.

I left a couple of leaflets at the local hospital and I contacted the

National Childbirth Trust. Within two days, I had four ladies booked onto the course. A couple of the ladies knew other mothers who wanted to come on the course so I soon had more than enough people.

I put together a course plan, structuring the sessions week-by-week and two days before I was due to hold the first class, I staged a dress rehearsal. I emptied my dining room, laid down throws and arranged cushions on the floor. I had three dolls to practice with, so I gave one to Richard, had one for myself and placed the other one on the floor by a cushion.

I ran through the whole of the first session, with Richard playing the part of all five mums. It went well and Richard acted the parts wonderfully. We had fun with the rehearsal, but I wondered what it would be like when the babies were there, controlling the flow of the class. I was excited and was looking forward to it, whilst at the same time I felt a bit anxious.

The day of the first session soon came. I started the day with some yoga and meditation and I felt calm and relaxed. I got the room ready, lit candles and put on some relaxing music. I had total faith that everything would be okay, whatever happened.

I was all set up and feeling extremely positive when, half an hour before the first class was due to start, two mothers cancelled due to chicken pox. I crossed my fingers that the other three would come and thankfully they did.

I was surprised at how well the class went. I felt quite calm and I really enjoyed teaching it. The mums were all lovely and the babies were absolutely gorgeous.

Interestingly, working so closely with the mothers and babies started to bring up feelings in me that I hadn't felt before. Feelings about how I wasn't a mum and never would be. Maternal questions about the choices I'd had and the decisions I had made because of the illness that affected my family. All of a sudden I was being forced to face the issue and to deal with it. It was time for me to find out about myself as a childless woman.

Throughout the five weeks of the course I explored my feelings deeper. Was I jealous of these ladies? Did I have a gap in my life that needed or wanted to be filled by a child? Would I have enjoyed being a parent? How is it going to be when I'm older and have no children to visit me or grandchildren to love and enrich my life?

I thought about it a lot. I imagined myself with a baby and also with an older child. As I meditated, I asked my inner self to bring forth the truth.

By the end of the course, all of the initial feelings and questions had completely gone. I was left with a sense of peace and the realisation that I had made the right choices. I was reminded that everything was in divine order, exactly as it was supposed to be.

The infant massage teacher training fitted into the journey of my life perfectly. It was in no way a replacement for not having a family and I knew that I absolutely wouldn't change anything at all. I loved working with the babies and the mums, but for me it was and is about educating and empowering people, so that their children can grow up to be well-adjusted individuals. It's about helping people to better cope with parenthood and about the whole concept of holistic therapy and loving touch.

As I diarised the weekly course sessions for my exam submission, I noted down my feelings. When I received my exam folder of work back from Mia, I was delighted to see that she supported my sentiments. I looked down at the page and read her words:

"Remember that being a good instructor does not depend on whether you have children or not. It's the passion you have when teaching and the respect for babies and parents that makes the difference."

And there I was, a qualified infant massage instructor and thankfully I knew myself a little better for it.

Chapter 54

Crying - a happy release

We have learned that crying is anti-social and a sign of weakness. This was probably one of our earliest lessons – Vimala McClure

My study of baby massage covered the very important and interesting topic of crying, a subject that I'm obviously extremely interested in and very experienced at.

As Vimala McClure explains in her book, Infant Massage: A Handbook for Loving Parents, we have become obsessed with the idea that we need to get our babies to stop crying. Whether it is our way to leave them to cry themselves to sleep or to rush to their smallest noise, it is our sometimes misguided feeling that, if they stop crying, they are feeling better. We don't only apply this to our babies either, but sometimes to ourselves and our friends, too.

Think about it and imagine this scenario. You're at work having a particularly bad day and someone or something upsets you. You get the prickling at the back of the eyes, indicating that the natural response of your body is to cry, but you stop yourself because you're at work. You shove the feeling down inside you and you carry on with a half-smile because you don't want anyone to know that you're upset. Would you feel better for that? No, I very much doubt it. You'd probably feel unbalanced for the rest of the day.

And let's just say that you hold it all in until you go home. And then on the way home your train is delayed and you can't get a seat and your handbag breaks and you lose your phone. You're still holding it all in because you're in public and you don't want to be seen crying.

Oh what a bad, bad day you've had. You go home and you talk to your best friend or partner and you let it all come flowing out. Your friend or partner listens to you with loving attention and maybe gives you a hug and a tissue. You have a good cry, you talk about what's upsetting you and you release all the tension. Would you feel better then? Of course you would, because you've allowed the emotion to come up and out and after a day like that it's just what you needed. The stress is released and the body, mind and spirit can reset itself back to normal.

Hummingbird

Now, imagine a different scenario. You go home, eager to talk to your loved one and that person isn't in the mood to hear what you have to say. Maybe they've had a bad day themselves and they're using up all of their energy to push and hold down their own unwanted emotions.

You know immediately by the way they use their avoidance tactics, that they are unable to listen to your problems. They change the subject or they say that often-used phrase, "Come on, don't cry." Maybe they give you a cup of tea and a biscuit so that your mouth is distracted or they suggest that you both go out to see a movie to take your mind off of things.

How would you feel then? Do you think that you'd feel loved and listened to? Would you feel able to freely express your emotions and feelings, letting go of the stress of the day? Would you feel as though that person was one 100 per cent ready to listen to your story? Or would you push the feeling down inside again, and carry on with your evening as best you could. Or maybe you'd go to your room and let it all out by yourself, alone with no one to listen to you. Or would you ring another friend, one who you know would be able to listen to you?

What do you think happens to those emotions that get pushed back down into the body? Do they eventually disappear or do they get stuck within us? Could there possibly be a potential for them to manifest themselves in a physical illness? Many holistic therapists, including myself, believe that this is exactly what could happen to them.

~ * ~

Years ago, I had a client who came to me for a relaxing massage. As I took her case history and talked to her before her treatment she told me about her negative experience of childbirth. Although many years had passed since she had given birth, the incident was still clearly in the forefront of her conscious mind. It had left her with an extremely bad memory and a negative view of the lack of care and compassion she had felt from the people involved. Despite this, as she conveyed her story I detected no visible signs of emotion at all, which really surprised me.

The woman got undressed and laid facedown on my couch ready for her massage. The room was warm and the soft lighting and relaxing background music created a peaceful and soothing atmosphere for the treatment.

Taking three deep breaths together, I laid my hands gently on her back as I proceeded to guide her softly though a progressive relaxation to encourage the release of physical and mental tension. I massaged her back, neck and shoulders before moving to the backs of each leg. Holding up the towel to give her cover, I asked her to turn over and, as she did so, I looked down at her face. The corners of her mouth were slightly turned up and she looked happy and totally at peace.

I proceeded to massage the front of her legs and her feet. She was almost purring with pleasure by the time I took her arms in my hands and guided each stroke towards her shoulders. Carefully placing a towel across her chest to cover her breasts, I lowered my hands gently onto her abdomen. Slowly and rhythmically I massaged her tummy in a clockwise, circular motion and suddenly she burst into tears. It completely took me by surprise.

Thankfully, because I had experienced the Journey therapy, I knew exactly what to do. I kept my hand placed softly on her tummy and calmly and gently I asked her, "What is it you're feeling?"

"I'm so sorry," my client said, still crying. "I don't know where that came from!"

"It's okay," I told her. "Just allow it to come up... What are you feeling?"

I stopped and waited for her to experience the feeling.

"What's the emotion?" I asked.

The woman continued to cry. I waited.

"I'm just feeling so angry," she said. "Angry at the midwives and the doctors and at everyone involved with the birth."

I allowed her to express her feelings, without giving any opinions or advice, but by just listening and reassuring her that it was okay to cry and to talk. I kept on asking her to tell me what she was feeling until all of the emotion that had been stuck inside her womb had been allowed to surface and she became calm again.

"Wow!" she exclaimed, after getting up and dressed. "I haven't cried like that since my baby was born. I've cried, of course, but not like that."

"Well, it obviously needed to come out," I told her, pleased that I had helped, and we booked her into the diary for another treatment.

The next time the lady came to see me she told me that, since her massage with me, she had been feeling so much better than she had been before.

"I hadn't quite realised just how much it was affecting my mood," she told me.

Hummingbird

I was so pleased that I knew exactly what to do to help her fully unblock and release the emotion. We will never know what might have happened to it, had it not been released and was allowed to remain stuck in her body, but I'm pretty sure in my mind that it could have found a way to manifest itself, in either emotional or physical disease.

~ * ~

From observing hundreds of babies in massage classes and in other cultures, Vimala believes that babies' feelings are as deep as ours and that their fears, their sorrows and their frustrations are no less and I agree with her. Crying is their only release and what better way to allow our babies to release their tension than by holding them close and giving them permission to cry?

So next time your baby cries (and it's not a hungry cry), try this. Calm yourself and hold them close in a loving and relaxed embrace and say to them: "Tell me all about it, I'm listening to you."

As your little one's emotional need to release some tension arises, say to him or her: "I may not understand the problem, but I do understand that you need to tell me about it. It's okay, I'm here. Let it all come out."

Vimala writes in her book that: "research has consistently shown that babies who are responded to promptly – not by hushing but by listening and acting – cry less frequently and for shorter periods as they grow older. It is not only an expression of pain or discomfort but seems to be an inborn stress-management and healing mechanism. If allowed and responded to with relaxed, loving listening, crying can help babies regulate their own stress levels and grow to be more relaxed and stress-free children and adults."

We can apply the same strategy to anyone, whatever their age, and – whether crying or not – allow ourselves to actively listen to our loved ones (and our clients) with compassion and empathy, showing genuine love and respect for the person's experience.

It makes perfect sense.

Chapter 55

A difficult decision

I was finding my new line of work really interesting and – at last – I was doing a job that truly fulfilled me. I was compelled to study and I was happy and passionate about my work.

But however certain I was about my new career path, I was equally as unsure about my personal life.

Since my breakthrough in Costa Rica I had found that I was changing – continually growing and discovering myself – and I knew that something had to change in my private life. In one way, things were becoming clearer to me, but in another I was still so confused. Not allowing myself to listen to my inner voice of truth, I tried to ignore it, for I knew that if I acted upon my feelings, I would experience a great deal of pain.

Richard had been a great friend to me – a true gift from the Universe – and I will always appreciate the support and love that he gave to me. But a part of me wasn't happy and, no matter how hard I tried, or how much it pained me, I could no longer pretend and ignore it.

Something was missing and I didn't know what to do about it. My mind and my heart struggled to find an answer as we carried on regardless, the love and friendship that we had for each other as strong as before, but the partnership breaking down under the tension that I was placing upon it. I wasn't being fair to my boyfriend and it wouldn't have been right or honest of me to stay with him.

Richard was kinder than I could ever have hoped for. He knew that I was like a bird that had to fly, and he would never have tried to clip my wings.

"I can't keep a bird in a cage," he told me, unselfishly.

The break-up was amicable. By this time, Richard had left his job at BT and was studying for a career change. He had one year left at college and so, for convenience, we continued to live together, but separately, as friends, for a year after we broke up. It was a difficult time for both of us, but I was pleased that he was still in my life.

Telling my family about the break-up was difficult. My family all adored

Hummingbird

Richard and I knew that they would be upset. They were happy that I was with him because they knew what a good and kindhearted person he was and that they would never have to worry about me whilst I had him by my side.

My brother, Stephen, lived in Gloucestershire and worked in London. Richard and I both loved to go and spend a weekend with him. Usually, we would start the short break by visiting the farmers market in Stroud on a Saturday morning. It's a fabulous multi award-winning market that is well worth a morning of anyone's time, especially on a sunny summer's day. Richard and I used to look forward to finding the organic burger stall, with its wonderful burgers and sausages, sold by the farmers who reared the animals themselves. We knew that the animals had had a good life and the meat, along with the homemade chutney, was delicious. Our mouths used to water as we got nearer to Stroud – a burger was a real treat for me and this was just about the only time I would eat one – I'm very fussy about where my meat comes from.

Stephen was just about the most enthusiastic person I'd ever seen at the market. He'd go from stall to stall, tasting the produce and chatting to the stallholders. He always came home with shopping bags full up to the brim with his purchases. He absolutely loved that market and going around it with him was a real joy.

Sometimes, if we were eating out in the evening, we would go to The Mad Hatters for dinner – a wonderful organic restaurant in the town of Nailsworth (now with new owners and re-named Wild Garlic) and we sometimes enjoyed our breakfast at Hobbs House Bakery, another fabulous award-winning eaterie, where we'd relax in the upstairs room with our delicious eggs on toast, croissants, coffee and the daily papers.

When we weren't eating or shopping, we went walking in the countryside to burn off some of the many calories we'd consumed. Yes, we liked to visit my brother in Gloucestershire, we liked it a lot.

Because of the distance between us, I tended to only see Stephen when we were both with our partners, it was never just the two of us.

After Richard and I split up but were still living together, Stephen asked me when we were next going to visit him in Gloucestershire. I kept on putting it off – making excuses as I hadn't told my family about the break up yet. I didn't want to tell my brother over the phone, I wanted to speak to him properly about it. I was constantly wondering how I was going to be able to see him on my own.

One evening, I went to London to meet up with a friend who was there on business. My friend was staying in a posh hotel in Green Park, so I had a few drinks and stayed over at the hotel with her for the night. I woke up the next morning to be greeted by glorious sunshine. It was the first warm and sunny day of the year and, as I didn't have any clients until 3pm, I decided to go and sit in the park for a while. I'd never been to Green Park before and it was wonderful to sit on the grass with my coffee and pastry, soak up the sun and just people watch.

A lady was doing her exercises. I watched her for a while and was reminded of a time when I did yoga every day. I hadn't done much now for about a year because of a painful lower back problem and I decided that I would try to do some yoga whilst I was there in Green Park.

It was wonderful to feel the stretches again. Slowly and carefully I eased myself into each position as I felt the warmth of the sun on my body and a gentle breeze on my face. I decided to try for the headstand, a position I hadn't managed to get into for a long time. I knelt on the grass, sat back on my heels and brought my elbows to the floor. Interlacing my fingers, I placed my head in the cup of my hands and prepared for the manoeuvre. I imagined going through the different stages of the asana, bringing my hips up, my knees to my chest and straightening my legs, feet pointing up towards the sky.

With my mental preparation done, I performed the move. After such a long time, the position felt amazing and I held my body upside down for as long as I could manage.

As I was holding the headstand position, I was thinking about my brother. How was I going to tell him that I'd broken up with Richard? When would I get an opportunity to see him alone? How would I create that opportunity and when and where could it possibly be?

When I brought my knees back into my chest and my shins and the tops of my feet were firmly on the ground, I rested back on my heels. With my head in my hands once again, I felt a spiritual shift and I stilled myself to allow the feeling to wash through me. I felt more connected and at one with the energy of the universe than I had felt for quite a while. It was a powerful feeling.

I started to pack up my things to go home. A man came over to speak to me and delayed me for a while. When I eventually left the park, I went to Green Park tube station and I boarded a train. The trains were frequent, but it's a busy station and there were no empty seats. I stood by the doors and looked over at the people sitting down. As I looked around, I saw a familiar face and I couldn't believe my eyes. It was my brother, Stephen, sitting on the seat right by me!

"Wow," I said as I tapped him on the shoulder. "Hello! What are you doing here?"

"Oh, hello," he said, lowering his newspaper. "I'm just on my way back to work, I've just been out to buy something."

"That's so weird," I said. "I've been thinking about you this morning – wanting to meet up with you – and here you are, on the train."

Steve laughed. He didn't believe that our chance meeting was anything but a sheer coincidence.

I wasn't so sure.

"I want to talk to you about something, Steve," I told him. "You wouldn't by any chance have time for a coffee, would you?"

"Yes, I'm sure I could have a coffee with you," he told me.

We got off the train and found somewhere to have a hot drink and a chat. I told him about my break-up and about how I'd been feeling lately and I felt much better for our meeting. Somehow I felt a little closer to my brother afterwards.

I left London with a renewed sense of wellbeing. Was it really possible that the yoga had opened up some kind of channel in answer to my prayer and that a power greater than any other had brought my brother and I together that day? I felt wonderful for the rest of the day and for days afterwards. My energy levels were really high and I was filled with a joy and a peace – a knowing.

It was the same kind of knowing that I had in India, when I came across the Preacher on the train.

~ * ~

Richard and I both began dating other people and when Richard left college, he moved in with his new girlfriend.

For as long as I live, I swear to God that I will always have the greatest love for him in my heart. After 14 years together – and six years apart – I still miss him and think of him often, but I am so pleased to tell you that he is now married and settled into a new and happy life.

Chapter 56

The law of attraction

I managed to get myself another mortgage and stay in the home that I loved.

My friend, Jane, introduced me to modern jive and to her friend, Jo. Once a week, the three of us went dancing together and through dancing I met more people and made new friends. It was on a dance weekend away that I met Stuart.

Stuart and I hit it off immediately and spent hours talking to each other that weekend. We swapped details and it was the start of a great friendship.

Stuart introduced me to *The Secret*. He lent me a DVD and told me to watch it. I would imagine that many people reading this will have at least heard of *The Secret*, if not read the book or watched the DVD. It's a very popular self-help book (it's sold more than 21 million copies) and it's based on the law of attraction.

The law of attraction is a natural law. It works by attracting to us the things that match the frequency of our thoughts.

I watched the DVD with great interest and attention. I nodded as I watched, finding the content consistent with what I already believed and found to be true – that the energy we put out into life reflects back at us in our wealth, health and our happiness.

As I've mentioned before, we are all vibrational energy. Our thoughts and feelings are vibrating on a frequency that goes out into the universe. If we are negative and pessimistic, we exist from a low level of vibration and will therefore attract low-level vibrational situations, which translate as negative experiences. But if we are positive and optimistic, we will attract higher-level vibrational experiences, such as health, wealth and happiness.

The Secret encourages us to imagine ourselves already in the situation that we want to be in – driving the car, having the successful business and seeing the money in the bank; with the perfect partner by our side, in our dream house, at our perfect location; with the good health that we desire, and the life that we dream of.

As I was sitting watching the DVD of *The Secret*, I was silently agreeing with its every word. I was aware that I was already practicing the law of attraction to some extent as I was imagining myself with plenty of clients and enough money in the bank to be comfortable. I was already changing my lifestyle and working towards a happier and healthier me. The important message was to picture myself already in the situation I wanted to be in and that the visualisation of my future life would manifest itself to be true.

Then something happened. As I was watching the DVD, my phone rang.

I answered the phone.

"Hello."

"It's Jane," said my friend. "Are you busy?"

"I'm just watching a DVD that Stuart lent me," I told her. "It's brilliant. I can speak to you though, Jane. What's up, hun?"

"Nothing," said Jane. "I just wondered if you had a few moments. I wanted to talk to you about a book my client has just been telling me about."

"OK, hold on," I said. "I'll just pause it."

A moment later, I was back on the phone to my friend.

"Okay, I'm with you. What's the book called?"

"It's called *The Secret.*"

"Oh my God!"

That's the honest truth, I swear. Just as I was watching the DVD, Jane was talking about the exact same thing with her client.

The next day, the phone rang twice with new clients wanting to book treatments with me. In the following weeks, I booked in more new clients and from that very day my work took a turn for the better. I got busier and busier and I never looked back.

I gave up cleaning my neighbour's house and with a little reluctance left my Sunday job at Culpeper.

I'm not at all surprised that the book has sold so many copies and been translated into 44 languages. Since being introduced to *The Secret*, I have met and heard about so many more people whose lives have changed for the better because of it.

Another wonderful thing that Stuart put me onto is Mikes Dooley's

Notes from the Universe. Mike is one of the teachers in *The Secret* and is also a creator of the TUT Adventures Club (TUT = Totally Unique Thoughts). TUT's motto is a mantra I use often these days: **Thoughts become things, choose the good ones.**

I put this in bold because it's probably the most important message I could ever pass on to you. Thoughts truly do become things. It's imperative to our health, wealth and happiness that we choose the good ones – wisely, positively and continuously.

In TUT's own words…

> "TUT believes that everyone's special, that every life is meaningful, and that we're all here to learn that dreams do come true. We also believe that "thoughts become things," and that imagination is the gift that can bring love, health, abundance, and happiness into our lives."

Each weekday, I receive an email message from the Universe that is inspirational, motivational and fun. It's a daily reminder of how to live and how to think. I'm far from alone in my love for Mike's daily notes as they are sent to more than 450,000 subscribers in 185 countries.

I have the *Notes from the Universe* perpetual calendar in my treatment room, so that I can now read two notes each day, one on my email and one on my calendar. Many of my clients love them too and have also signed up for the email messages. Each day, Mike Dooley and the Universe make me smile and are instrumental in helping to keep me happy and healthy.

I just LOVE them.

Chapter 57

Another life lost

After various disasters in local small care homes (usually due to his behaviour), my brother Philip was moved to a unit in St Andrew's Hospital, Northampton, where there is a specialist unit specifically for people with Huntington's disease. As I have mentioned before, Philip was lovingly cared for there and, unlike Nigel, he was quite happy to be looked after. My two brothers were very different in this respect. Nigel was such an independent man and Philip never wanted to leave the nest and go it alone.

For the first time since being in care, Philip settled down in his comfortable surroundings. The nurses and carers treated him (and the other patients) like a member of their own family. They took him to the café and to the swimming pool, which are both situated in the hospital grounds. They played him the music he liked and they talked to him, laughed and joked with him and he seemed content. Sometimes they took him on outings – to the London Eye and to other locations. Mum visited him regularly and I went to see him about four times a year, mostly with my mum, but sometimes on my own.

Philip was chair-bound by now and could no longer speak and I wasn't afraid of him anymore. The nurses and staff on his unit always made me welcome and thanked me for visiting. Some of the people in the unit never had any visitors, even though they had a family.

In 2008, Philip suffered a series of chest infections and became a lot weaker than he already was. He lost the ability to swallow food and could only drink sips of water. We went to St Andrew's to be with him and were up and down to Northampton and back as he became weaker and weaker.

Mum was there most of the time and stayed overnight with him. When the weekend came, I went up with her to see him and we slept on the sofa and chairs in the hallway. After that, Mum was given a spare bed in a nearby ward, as she wanted to stay close to her son. We realised that he was slipping away.

As we sat with him, holding his hand and gently talking to him, I started to softly sing the blue ridge mountains of Virginia to him.

It was a song that Philip used to sing with his friend. Mum joined in, our voices were soft as we joined together in saying goodbye to a brother and a son, our eyes moist with tears as we remembered how comical it was when Philip and his friend did their Laurel and Hardy impressions. They did a fantastic take off of the comedy duo.

We looked at each other and smiled.

"He loved Laurel and Hardy," I said, looking at my mum's sad face. Philip had all of their films on video tape.

"Yes," she said. "He did."

The doctor informed us that Philip would need to be taken to the regular hospital if he was to be put on a drip. At the hospital, Philip would have been mostly left on his own and, as he could not speak, he would not have been able to communicate with the staff.

Philip could no longer do anything for himself. He had no control over his body. Huntington's disease was in its latter stages and most of the family didn't believe that keeping him alive by false feeding him would be a kind thing to do. It's a very controversial subject I know, but I believe that we made the right choice. Some people will not agree I'm sure, but there are no benefits to prolonging the suffering that my eyes or my heart can see or feel.

We didn't want Philip's last few days to be spent at the general hospital, with strangers who didn't know him and who had little time to be with him. At St Andrew's, he was loved and well cared for and in his final few days he was with the people he knew and trusted. He had someone he knew with him at all times, was carefully monitored and fed sips of iced water.

He passed away peacefully.

Mum fetched Philip back to Essex to be cremated and his funeral was well attended by many of his friends. I was surprised but pleased that so many people turned up to pay their respects to him. Many of them had not seen their friend for quite a few years. A short while after the service, St Andrew's held a special memorial service for my brother in the chapel that is situated in the grounds of the hospital.

My second brother was finally at peace.

Chapter 58

The treatment triangle

With the many wonderful and compassionate friends in my life I was surrounded and supported by love.

My client base was growing and my clients were wonderful. I was blessed to have such an amazing job and to be working with such fabulous people – I couldn't have had nicer clients if I'd have handpicked them myself. They came back month after month for their regular chill-out time and treatment with me.

I greeted each day with an attitude of gratitude and a positive mind set and the Universe answered my prayers.

One day a lady called Jan came to see me. She found my website whilst searching for a massage therapist and she instinctively knew that I would be the right person to massage her. Jan is a hypnotherapist who thinks along the same lines as I do and we soon became friends. Jan kindly sent her friend Kim to me for a massage and that was the start of what is now known as the Treatment Triangle. Kim is a five element acupuncturist, who specialises in fertility. She has an extremely busy practice in Orpington, as well as a clinic at Harrods in London.

Kim, Jan and I recommend each other to our clients and we quite often work with the same individuals to help improve their health and wellbeing. In fact, it was a client of ours who first came up with the nickname of the Treatment Triangle. I now have many clients that the Treatment Triangle has sent to me and I thank my dear friends Jan and Kim for that. They are the best advert I could ever wish for and I love the nickname they gave me, Magic Hands. Now they just call me Magic for short and I must say – I like it!

As well as working with private clients, I started to offer massage to people in care homes. I work on their bodies with my aromatherapy oils and creams and I talk to them with kindness and love. Most of the people I work with have multiple sclerosis, dementia or locked-in syndrome and are unable to speak to me, so I watch their faces for signs of pleasure or discomfort. Two of the people I see who have locked-in syndrome can move their eyes to indicate yes or no, so I am able to get permission from them for the massage and communicate with them throughout the treatment.

Working at the care homes provides me with a constant reminder of how blessed I am to have good health and brings forth the joy in my heart to know that I can do something nice for those less fortunate than myself.

Chapter 59

Lavender man

After breaking up with Richard, I had a few relationships that didn't work out. I was happy on my own, but I visualised my life with a partner to share my world with. Someone whose life I would enhance and vice versa.

One day I was talking to my friend Angie about relationships – or rather, the lack of.

"I wonder when I'm going to meet my perfect man," I said to her, somewhat despondently.

For some strange reason I thought that she might know the answer. Of course, she didn't know the answer, but she was very helpful nonetheless.

"Don't worry," she assured me. "You will meet someone I'm sure. And he'll be just like you, Deborah."

Throwing her hands up and twirling around in a childlike way she laughed.

"He'll be into therapy and energy and love the things you love." She looked at me and continued. "And I see him wearing a lavender T-shirt," she laughed.

"Oh, I hope so, Angie," I answered, trying to conjure up a picture in my mind of the man in the lavender T-shirt.

A few weeks later, I was at a 40th birthday party. I'd gone on my own and was really enjoying myself. I was dancing along with everyone else on the dance floor to some fabulous tunes (did I mention that I love to dance?) when suddenly I found myself dancing with a stranger.

A nice stranger.

A stranger with a sparkle in his eye and an energy that was vibrant, yet warm and loving. A stranger with a kind heart and a beautiful aura – I just knew it and, even though I couldn't see it, I felt it. All too soon the dance was over and he was gone.

"Who was that?" I asked the hostess.

"That's Mark," she told me. "He's a therapist, Deborah, like you."

"Really?" I replied, interestingly. "Who's he here with?"

Her reply was the reply that I wanted to hear. "He's here on his own."

I looked up to the ceiling. "Thank you, Universe," I said, silently.

I sought Mark out at the bar.

"Can I get you a drink?" I asked him.

"No, no, let me get you one," he insisted.

"Angela tells me you're a therapist," I said, accepting a glass of wine from him.

"Yes, I'm a cranial sacral therapist," he told me.

"Oh, how interesting. I'm a therapist myself," I informed him, feeling slightly tipsy all of a sudden.

Mark was absolutely lovely. We talked for ages at the bar and we swapped email addresses. Well, actually I gave him my email address, my website address and my phone number, just to make sure that he could get in touch with me. He was as passionate about his work as I was about mine. He understood exactly everything I said about our energy, our thoughts and our healing paths. He seemed to be perfectly in tune with me.

I left the party feeling great. I was over the moon that I'd met him. The next day, I rang my friend Angie and told her about Mark.

"I think I've met my lavender man," I said excitedly.

Mark and I talked a bit on email and I plucked up the courage to ask him if he was single.

"No," he told me. "I live with my girlfriend."

At first I was really disappointed, but I knew that it wouldn't stop me from being his friend, he was such a wonderful person.

We kept in touch and we meet up occasionally to talk about our shared interests and passions. He's a wonderful gift in my life and I love him dearly. He is known to me and my circle of friends as Lavender Man, a title he accepts with humour and pride. Lavender Man is a shiny gem who continues to bring sparkles and beautiful love into my world.

I'm always fascinated and eager to talk with Mark, he's such an interesting person. I love to hear about his experiences of his trips to America, where he interacts with dolphins in the water to assist with the healing of human beings.

Hummingbird

I love the fact that he spends his spare time playing flutes. He's flute-mad and at the last count he was the proud owner of 22 Native American flutes. Lavender Man never goes anywhere without a flute or two in the boot of his car. When he plays them, the music is enchanting and so beautiful to listen to and I sit back, close my eyes and go to another place in my mind. Mark has created a CD of his music and now I can listen to him whenever I want to. Sometimes I play it when I'm giving a treatment and my clients find it very relaxing and healing.

I don't see Lavender Man as often as I'd like to, but when I do, I feel as though I've come home. He's totally on my wavelength and he seems to get me one hundred per cent. I feel so in tune with him. I thank the Universe and celebrate the fact that he came into my life and is my dear, dear friend.

Chapter 60

Fundraising

Feel the fear and do it anyway – Susan Jeffers

As my ex-boyfriend was busy planning his wedding, I met a guy out dancing and we dated for a year. Although we got on well and had lots of fun, it didn't work out for us and so, as Richard was walking down the aisle with his new bride, I broke up with my new boyfriend. Richard's wedding day reminded me that I needed to feel special too, and I didn't.

I was feeling flat and I needed something to focus my mind on, a project or a new hobby. I was wondering about what to do when the Huntington's Disease Association (HDA) Newsletter landed on my doormat. Flicking through it I came across an interesting article inviting me to Trek the Great Wall of China and raise money for the HDA.

That's what I'll do, I decided as I read through the article. I'll raise money for the HDA and I'll have an amazing experience at the same time. I'll do something I can really be proud of. It's a win-win situation. I'll raise the money for my charity. I'll have a project to focus my mind on. I'll do the training and I'll get fit in the process. It'll really give me something to get my teeth into.

Some of us have silent saboteurs. These are the voices that give us doubts and hold us back from achieving our goals. They are the nagging insecurities that are lingering deep inside our subconscious, waiting to pounce. They are old patterns of behaviour that belong to our past, limiting beliefs that are loitering, just waiting to sabotage our hopes and dreams.

I was apprehensive about signing up for the trek, as I soon discovered that my silent saboteurs were not so silent after all. I ignored the little blighters and in August 2008 I signed up for the trek or to put it another way, I closed my eyes and jumped!

And then the doubts got the better of me and I panicked.

Would I be able to raise the money? Would I be able to get fit enough for the trek? Would I be okay on my own? The saboteurs were chattering away in my head…. on and on…. and as much as I tried to silence my negative thoughts, the doubts kept on popping up.

Hummingbird

I went to bed that evening and stilled my mind.

"It will be okay," I told myself. "Just think positively and it will all be okay."

I focused on my breath and I felt the calmness come back to me.

"Other people do it," I told my saboteurs. "What's different about them? If they can do it, I can do it! Anyway, I've sent off the registration form and a £300 non-refundable registration fee so now I *have* to do it!"

After a good night's sleep, I woke up and I felt completely different. I was absolutely sure that I could achieve my new goals. The answer to the questions of the day before was loud and clear. YES, I WOULD and YES, I WILL!

Sometimes you just have to jump.

~ * ~

All journeys have secret destinations of which the traveller is unaware – Matt Buber

At that time, I didn't really appreciate just how amazing the whole experience was going to be. All I knew was that I had to raise a minimum amount of just under £3,000 and I had nine months in which to do it.

I lost no time in setting myself up with a blog and creating a JustGiving page and I put it out to the Universe that I would raise the money and get myself fit enough to do the trek.

"Please, Universe," I pleaded. "Get on board with me on this one. I'm gonna need you."

I felt a calmness flow through my body and a voice inside me told me that it would all be okay. I knew that I would raise the money, get fit and complete the trek.

I had no idea how quickly things would escalate. I sent out an email to all of my friends, clients and contacts, telling them what I was doing and exactly why I was raising money for the HDA. I was very honest and open about my family history, as I knew that this would evoke empathy and compassion and entice people to put their hands in their pockets.

I printed off leaflets and gave them to everyone I didn't have an email address for. My friends rallied around with phenomenal support and passed on my emails to their friends and within two weeks I had raised over a thousand pounds in sponsorship alone. Every day, I thanked the Universe for the sponsorship and the momentum kept going.

JustGiving was a godsend, making it simple for anyone to make a contribution, wherever they were in the world. I had donations from friends in America, Australia and Japan. Friends of friends donated very generous amounts and I made sure that I emailed and thanked every single person who gave their hard-earned cash to support me and my cause. I was astounded and humbled at the level of response I received.

I decided to hold a party to raise some of the money for my charity trek so I hired a hall, printed off some tickets and once again asked the universe to help me. Taking the advice of *The Secret* I visualised myself hosting a very successful event.

My friend kindly offered to DJ for me free of charge and one of my clients offered her services in another way.

"If you can get a blackjack table," she told me, "I'll croupier for you."

"Oh, wow, thanks, Helen," I said surprised. "That's so kind of you. I didn't even know that you did that. I have no idea where I'll get a table from, but I'll ask the Universe and I'm sure I'll get one."

We laughed and hoped for the best. The next day, I happened to mention to another client that I needed a blackjack table. I figured that the sooner I put it out there, the sooner it would manifest. And manifest it did.

"My friend's son has a table," she told me, to my astonishment. "I'll ask her if you can borrow it."

Later that day, I had a phone call confirming that I could indeed borrow the blackjack table, so within two days of asking, I was on my way to collect it.

Identifying the correct house, I walked up to the door and rang the bell. A friendly-looking lady answered.

"Hi, I'm Deborah," I said, offering my hand.

"Come on in," the lady beckoned me, smiling warmly.

"It's so kind of you to lend me the table," I said as I took the carry case from her hand.

"It's no problem," she answered kindly. "I don't mind helping someone who is raising money for charity. What charity are you doing it for?"

I took the opportunity to tell her my story and before I knew it she was writing me out a cheque.

"Here," she said handing it to me. "It's a donation for your cause."

I looked at the figure on the piece of paper in my hand. It was a donation of £200.

"Wow, thanks," I said, overwhelmed for the umpteenth time since I started the project. "Would you like to come to the party?"

"That sounds fun, how much is it?" she enquired.

"It's £10 a ticket. We're having an auction there, as well."

"I'll have 10 tickets, please," she said as she wrote me out another cheque.

If I hadn't been carrying a heavy blackjack table, I think I would have been tempted to skip back to my car. I couldn't believe my luck, I was grinning from ear to ear.

"Thank you, thank you, thank you," I said to the world.

The tickets for the party just flew out of my hands. Within three weeks, I'd sold them all. I had no idea just how fabulous the party was going to be. Stuart set up one of his chocolate fountains and he held an auction for me on the night. After tugging on some heartstrings and a little bit of begging, I had been given some fantastic items for him to auction, including:

Two golf days
A website designed and hosted for a year
A holiday apartment for a week at the beach
A guitar lesson
A signed and framed Millwall football shirt
A tour of Wandsworth Prison
A spa day for two people
Photography vouchers
A box at Old Trafford football ground for eight people, with lunch included
Five sessions of acupuncture
Coral betting shop vouchers
A quad bike session
Three tickets for an Arsenal v West Ham football match.

Stuart really did me proud that evening. The auction would never have raised as much money as it did without his outgoing personality and superb powers of persuasion pushing up the bids, along with the guys from the local Round Table tactically bidding to raise the stakes. It was such a fun evening.

Helen was a marvellous and beautiful croupier and she raised £300 for me on the blackjack table.

With the money from the ticket sales, auction, blackjack, chocolate fountain and raffle, the evening raised a grand total of £4,756.

With all this money banked, my target had been reached and surpassed. I upped the target on JustGiving and was now on a mission to see just how much I could possibly manage to raise for the HDA within the nine months leading up to my trek.

I had some raffle tickets printed and I raffled off some of my treatments, adding another £200 to the pot.

My ex-boyfriend Richard had been kind enough to forward my email to his friends and a guy from his car club, who I'd met only twice, donated a thousand pounds. When I saw what he'd done, I rang him in Holland immediately.

I was so excited that, when I heard him answer the phone, I forgot my introduction and just blurted out my words.

"Oh, my God I can't believe what you've done! That's amazing, it's so kind of you!"

"Hold on," he interrupted, in his Dutch accent. "Who is this? I can't understand you. Speak slower, please."

"Oh, sorry, it's Deborah from England," I said, slowing down a little, but not much. "Richards's ex-girlfriend. Thank you so much for your donation, it's AMAZING! I just can't believe you've done that. Thank you *so, so* much. I had to call you to thank you. An email wouldn't have been sufficient. I'm so grateful, you have no idea. You are so kind."

"Oh, hello Deborah," he laughed when he realised who I was. "It's okay, it's no problem. It's a great cause and I'm happy to do it for you. I hope you raise lots more money."

I spoke to him for a while and then put down the phone, still trying to get my head around the fact that someone I hardly knew would make such a large donation towards my charity trek.

Hummingbird

My vibrational level was obviously good, I was putting it out there and it was coming back in abundance. Grace was indeed smiling upon me.

People gave me items for a boot sale, which I held one sunny Sunday morning in September with my friend Carole by my side.

I wrote a press release and emailed it off to a few local papers and before I knew it, I was on the front page of the *Bromley Borough News*. The article generated more donations from local residents and neighbours.

I was a very busy lady. The fundraising was taking up a lot of my spare time and by now I was also well into my training schedule. I had a workout plan and I was sticking to it. My first training walk was a two-hour round trip in the pouring rain, but I didn't let the wet weather put me off. I put on my waterproofs, turned on my iPod and got myself out there and I actually found it quite enjoyable. I never would have gone walking in the rain if it hadn't been for the impending trek. It was quite nice actually.

Two mornings each week I got up early and walked for an hour or two before starting work. And on Sundays I did a longer walk of three to four hours, building up to a long walk on both Saturday and Sunday. Towards the end of my training, I was doing regular walks of five to six hours. I printed off cross-country walks from the internet and discovered more of the local area. Rain or shine I went out walking to ensure that I would be fit enough to complete the trek. True to form my friends were very supportive and came out with me, but I sometimes walked for five or six hours on my own. It was wonderful to get out and about.

I joined the gym and my friend Kelly helped me out with some personal training sessions.

"You'll be doing those walking lunges on the Great Wall of China soon," she joked, as I puffed and panted and complained about her tough training tactics.

"You're gonna be glad of this training," she told me. "You have to do it, Deborah, you know you do."

I didn't like the personal training sessions because they were such hard work, but I knew that she was right and it must have been doing me good – surely! Nothing that hurt that much could *not* be beneficial.

My initial fundraising target of £3,000 had been blown out of the water by the total amount of £10,430, with more than £1,000 in Gift Aid on top of that. I was as pleased as Punch. The money has been raised and the training had been done. I just needed to get my kit together and I'd be ready to go to China.

Chapter 61

Andy

Only those who will risk going too far can possibly find out how far they can go –
T. S. Eliot

It was at this time, as I was fundraising for China, that I met Andy. On Monday 23 March 2009 Andy came to me for a massage, four days before he was due to head off to the Sahara Desert to run an endurance race for charity. Seriously, I thought I was taking on a challenge with the Great Wall of China Trek, but I was astonished at what this guy was planning to attempt – The Marathon des Sables.

Check this out:

The Marathon des Sables (MdS) is a 151- mile endurance race across the Sahara Desert in Morocco. It's equivalent to five and a half regular marathons in just six days

"Have you done anything like this before?" I asked him.

"No." he replied.

I'm certain I noticed a slightly pensive look on his face.

"But I have been training and have now run three official marathons with another six runs of 25 miles around Bewl Water, just on my own."

"Are you crazy?" I couldn't help but to ask the question.

"Possibly, a little…" came his reply.

"Are you all set to go? Ready and prepared for the challenge?" I asked him.

"More or less," he said, unconvincingly. "I just have to sort out my pack. I have to run with everything I need in a bag: food, clothes, medical kit, sleeping bag etc. So I need to work out precisely what I need and bag up all my food for each day."

As he was telling me more about his challenge, I swear that my mouth was gaping open wider and wider as I listened to what he was about to attempt.

Hummingbird

Even before leaving for Morocco, deciding what to take with him seemed a huge challenge in itself.

"When you're running with your pack, you need to keep the total weight down," he told me. "I have to decide how much food to carry." Carrying more food would mean that he wouldn't be as hungry and that he'd have more energy for the race but the downside of that would mean that he'd have more weight to carry on his back as he ran, which would slow him down - at least until he'd eaten his way through it!

He had to work out what clothes to take with him, as he would be wearing the same outfit day and night for the duration of the race.

My mind conjured up a comical picture of a desert camp, in which there were many people, steam and odour evaporating from them in a misty haze, pegs clipped tightly onto their noses.

"Boy, it's gonna stink!" I thought.

My mind was quickly brought back into the room as Andy told me that he had to decide what type of food he would need to take and what snacks and trail mix he'd need.

"What's trail mix?" I asked him curiously.

"It's a mixture of nuts, dried fruit and sweets that you can pop in your mouth along the way to keep you going between meals," he told me.

"How can you carry all your food for a whole week?" I asked.

"Well, you have to take dehydrated food and a little stove. You need to take some fuel and they supply you with water each day for you to boil up to cook with, for your breakfast and evening meals.

"I've been reading the online forums and they say that you have to be disciplined to eat as soon as you finish each day, no matter how tired or trashed you are, because it helps your recovery, which is vital to help you to go again the next day and the next."

I didn't much fancy the thought of living on dehydrated food for six days and I couldn't imagine running in that kind of heat.

"Surely, in the desert it's going to be pretty hot. How are you going to cope with the heat, Andy?"

"Oh, I'll be okay," he said seemingly trying to convince himself. "But they reckon the temperature could get up to a 120 Fahrenheit by midday."

Rather him than me, but as crazy as I thought he was, I was fascinated by his forthcoming challenge.

The hardest day of the race was going to be on the fourth stage, when the competitors would set off across the barren wilderness to complete a whopping 57-mile stage. Few people would complete it before dark, many would rest overnight and finish the next day.

This was to be followed by a mere 26-mile stage – just a humble marathon distance.

"Blimey, this makes my trek sound like a walk in the park." I said, finding it extremely difficult to get my head around what he was telling me.

I'd never known anyone who'd done anything like that before.

"Oh well, it's all about the personal challenge and it's all relative," he said nonchalantly.

I liked his positive attitude.

So, that's how I first met Andy. I massaged him and hoped that it was going to help a little and off he went to do his ultra-marathon race through the Sahara. Meanwhile, I continued training hard for my own challenge and my meeting with Andy spurred me on and made me even more determined to do my very best.

A few weeks later, Andy was back from Morocco and he emailed me to tell me all about it. He'd completed the race without too much of a problem and he thoroughly enjoyed the challenge. I thought he was amazing.

Andy and I emailed each other regularly after that, as he was really interested in my training and extremely supportive and encouraging. We were email buddies for a few months in the time leading up to my departure to China and I looked forward to receiving his messages.

Meanwhile, I'd been in contact with one of my trekking buddies on Facebook. Although we hadn't met, Stacey and I got on really well and we were encouraging each other through our online support. Stacey was raising money for the mental health charity, Mind. I just knew that we were going to hit it off and as soon as I met her at the airport my inkling was confirmed. I had a buddy to trek with.

Chapter 62

The Great Wall of China

The trek itself was extremely hard, but it was fabulous. It was much more treacherous than I'd imagined. The Great Wall of China that you see in all the pictures is the bit that the tourists visit. As a trekking group, we mostly walked on broken bits of the wall, on steep narrow paths and on overgrown paths that ran alongside the wall and up through the forest. Most of the time, the walking seemed relentless – walking, walking, up, up, up – one step at a time… on and on.

Hour after hour.

The second day of the trek was hot. It was 116F and we walked more than 970 metres. It was a long, long day. At times the journey was quite emotional; at times it was just fabulous. I was extremely thankful that I had done so much training.

With over 40 people walking – each for their chosen charity – we were quite a big group and most of the people were absolutely lovely. We had a group of Scottish ladies with us who were always singing and were fun to be around.

A few people in the group had a problem with vertigo on the trek. The height and narrowness of some of the paths made them freeze with fear. Thankfully, I was okay but I could understand why they felt that way. There were times when I was a bit unsure of the path myself, but we just had to stay steady and keep looking at our feet.

There were a few incidents where people lost their footing and slipped completely off the path, but there were so many trees in the hills where we were walking that they couldn't actually fall too far. They were scratched, bruised and a bit shocked, but apart from that – well, let's just say that it was all part of their experience. Needless to say. I was glad it wasn't me who'd fallen.

The training that I'd done paid dividends and ensured that I could manage most days without too much of a problem and I was thankful for that. Silently I apologised to my trainer, Kelly for all the names I had called her under my breath in the past few months.

I had three good buddies on the trek: Stacey, Sophie and Laura and between them they helped me to get through each long and laborious day. We all helped each other. We laughed a lot and we each had our moments of reflection. I suppose it was inevitable that I would think about my brothers as I sometimes walked on my own along the rocky or grassy narrow paths in the scenic hills of China. I remember a particular incident when the girls were talking about their favourite Laurel and Hardy scenes and the song that we sang to my brother as he was dying came back into my mind.

Blue ridge mountains of Virginia.

It brought tears to my eyes and I couldn't shake the song out of my head for hours.

I was surprised to discover that there was a young guy on my trek who was also raising money for Huntington's disease. His mum has the condition and he is at risk of developing the disease himself. One afternoon I walked with him for hours and we shared our stories.

"I've never talked to anyone else with HD in their family before," he told me. "I've only ever talked to professionals about it. You're the first person I've met who is at risk of it like me, Deborah."

He was an absolutely lovely, lovely guy and I'm so glad that he was with us. Meeting him and talking with him was one of the highlights of the trip for me. I was so pleased that I had helped him by listening to him and sharing my own experiences with him.

It was an emotional afternoon and that evening I felt the consequences of the day in my body as my hip locked up and caused me terrible pain and stiffness. Thankfully, Laura is a physiotherapist and she worked her magic on me and I had no problems after that at all.

Alongside the pain in my hip, I was having a particularly bad emotional wobble that evening and was really worried that I wouldn't be able to go on. Thanks to Laura, Stacey and Sophie's kindness and support, I recovered sufficiently to carry on the next day and I continued to trek to the very end.

On the final day of the trek, as we walked back along the restored part of the wall and to the finishing point, our leaders popped open bottles of champagne and we celebrated on the Great Wall of China with plastic glasses of bubbly. The hard work was over.

I enjoyed the trek so much that I didn't want it to end. As we celebrated with hugs and congratulations, I just wanted to go back to the beginning and start it all over again. It was a fabulous experience and I'd thoroughly recommend it to anyone.

Hummingbird

The whole journey, from the beginning of the fundraising to the end of the trek was such an incredible adventure for me and I was overwhelmed by everyone's support from start to finish.

On my return from China, my friends organised a celebration for me in the garden of a local pub. It was a beautiful sunny day and lots of people came to congratulate me for completing the trek and raising the money. I was on such a high after my hugely successful project.

Taking on a challenge – a proper challenge that you have to work hard for – can give a person a really fantastic sense of achievement and worthiness. Completing a difficult challenge makes us feel good about ourselves and that in turn raises our self-esteem and boosts our immune system. I would recommend it to anyone and everyone, but especially to those people who feel that they need a lift in their lives. If your life feels a bit flat or dull or you feel that you don't have much to look forward to in your life – whoever you are and whatever your circumstances – I'm sure that there's always some kind of goal that you can set yourself to work towards. It's hard (but that's the point), it's fun and believe me, it's worth it!

Chapter 63

A test of endurance

When I returned from China, I settled down into my routine again. The experience had left me feeling proud of myself and full of self-love and joy.

I hadn't seen Andy for a few months and so I met up with him to tell him all about my trek. Andy has seen a lot of the world and has travelled and trekked in some fantastic places himself. In that respect, we realised that we had a lot in common as we shared our stories of places we'd been to and things we had done. After a few weeks, at the end of May 2009, we started dating.

Andy had continued his running. He'd joined a local running club and started to run regular marathons. I had never met anyone as focused and determined as Andy, for whom failure is never an option.

He became hooked on his sport and looked for bigger and better ways to challenge himself. The stronger and fitter he became, the more he wanted to do. His body was changing as he ran more and he went to the gym after work most days. I worked most evenings so it suited me, too. I worked, and he went to the gym. We saw each other at the weekend and we took one evening off during the week to spend it together and that worked out well for us.

Andy is a great example of what can be achieved if we focus our minds on a goal. Okay, maybe some may say he's a bit obsessive or maybe he has an addictive personality. Sometimes I think he's slightly crazy for all the things he does, but he's also totally inspiring.

He's a constant reminder to me that when we set our minds properly to do something, whatever that is, we can reach our goals and bring our dreams to successful fruition. We can improve our self-worth by achieving these things; things that we may never have imagined we could achieve.

Not only physical challenges, but practically any challenge or goal that we set out to achieve can be reached if we want it enough. For example, I've never written a book before and I didn't really know how to go about it, but once I decided to do it (and jumped) I took each step at a time. I Googled how to use punctuation, I constantly used a thesaurus, I went on a workshop to find out how to publish and promote my work (thank you

Hummingbird

Joanna Penn), I asked people to read my work and give me honest feedback and I found out how to publish my story on Amazon by Googling some more.

I like to think of these challenges as little mini journeys on the larger journey that is our life. When we embark on our mini journeys, it gives us something to talk about with our friends and the people we meet and it's important to have some conversation that is interesting and engaging. We are building a meaningful life and making positive memories for ourselves.

After coming home from the Marathon de Sables, Andy went through a short phase of feeling down, which apparently is not uncommon after completing a challenge of this type. In his case, this was probably due to the five and a half months of increasingly intensive training and focus that almost consumed his life.

He had seen less of his family and friends during the months preceding the event as his weekends were taken up with the necessary training, which would sometimes include running almost a marathon distance on both Saturday and Sunday.

Completion of the challenge left him with a void. With no specific focus he found it difficult to get back to normality and the gap that was left just preyed on his mind. It was like an interminable itch that needed to be scratched. Maybe it was a mid-life crisis, who knows? He was soon to be turning 50, after all, and he wasn't feeling too happy about that.

Andy soon signed up for his next challenge and in May 2009 he embarked on a via ferrata climbing trip in the Austrian Dachsten Alps. For someone with a fear of heights, that was quite a brave thing to do.

In October, he was off again. This time to take part in the Jungle Marathon, another endurance race of 124 miles, which took him through the Amazon rain forest in Brazil. Again, it was a self-sufficient race, only this time there was no tent or cover provided and so he had to pack and carry an additional item, a hammock.

To be fair, this wouldn't be my idea of fun. During that week in the jungle he was chased by killer bees, stung by an army of ants (oh dear, he really shouldn't have put his hammock where he did that night) and forced to wade through many swamps, some of which were neck deep. He swam across two 400m-wide rivers, leapt and stumbled over thick tree roots and slept in his clothes every evening, which were sometimes wet and swampy. It's got to be said, it wouldn't be my idea of fun.

Before even completing the Jungle Marathon, Andy had entered an

Arctic one, the 6633 Ultra, to be held in Canada in March 2010. The organisers tell us that this race can quite genuinely claim to be the toughest, coldest and windiest extreme ultra marathon on the planet. That was like a moth to a flame where Andy was concerned.

Unfortunately, he didn't complete the arctic ultra because he pulled his back after 50 miles of sledge pulling. But he didn't let that put him off. He rested for two days then did one more day just for the fun of it. ·

The next challenge he signed up for was a Sahara Race in Egypt in October 2010. It was about the same deal as the MdS although with much fewer people.

As you can see, Andy was really hooked by now. The more he did, the more he wanted to do. He was becoming faster and stronger and in between each endurance race he ran a marathon (mostly cross-country) about every other week. Sometimes, he'd run a marathon two weekends in a row.

In July 2011, he went off to Mongolia to take part in the Gobi Challenge, a six-day, self-sufficient endurance race cumulating in an ascent of the highest dune in southeast Asia.

You probably get the idea by now – Andy is hooked on running and loves a difficult challenge. He's completed eight triathlons and the Tough Guy assault course challenge.

Usually people train for a marathon. Andy's marathons are his training for his endurance races. In just under four years from when he started running, Andy completed his 100th official marathon and is now a member of the 100 Marathon Club.

I've suggested that he writes a book himself – I think it would be quite an interesting read.

~ * ~

After my trek in China, the dust had barely settled when people started to ask me what my next challenge was going to be. At first, I wasn't thinking about another challenge. I was just so happy that I'd raised so much money and had such a wonderful adventure.

Andy, as I've said, is a truly amazing person, but his focus and dedication to his continuous challenges were getting more and more intense and I started to question if this was what I really wanted in a partner. I was once again fighting with myself to determine what it was that I needed. I wanted someone that I could share my life with and do things with –

together as a team. It was difficult to really understand what was driving him to push himself as much as he did. We talked about it, but I'm not sure that even he knew the full answer to that question.

To be fair, Andy and I did have a couple of trekking holidays together, which were really hard work, but fabulous experiences. I felt safe with Andy on our treks – over the stunningly beautiful Dachstein Mountains of Austria and across the Atlas Mountains in Morocco. It was exhausting, but fantastic. It was vastly different from the exotic and luxurious holidays that Richard and I used to go on.

But despite Andy's good efforts to continue with his passion and to have a successful relationship with me, the situation wasn't making me happy and I decided to break up with him. It was sad – we were both sad – but I couldn't see any future in it.

When I broke up with Andy, I signed up for a trek on Mount Kilimanjaro. I figured that, if I wanted people to sponsor me again, I would have to have an even bigger and better challenge than before. And what bigger and better challenge than to trek to the summit of the world's highest free-standing mountain – Kilimanjaro!

I'm pleased that Andy and I remained friends and we gave it another go but a month before I left for Africa, we broke up again.

Chapter 64

Kilimanjaro

Oh-my-God – I'm going to be sick!

We'd only been on the mountain for a day and a half and I was the first in the group to be throwing up. Typical.

I'd been hanging back for a while, as I felt that things were not looking so good. Heather, a lovely young lady doctor, was always the last one in the line of walkers heading to the top of Mount Kilimanjaro and she was fast becoming my new best friend.

The rest of the group of 24 trekkers, plus the guides and Rhiannon (the expedition leader) made their way slowly up to the lunch stop, as Heather and I found ourselves alone for a while on the mountain.

"Just rest for a bit," she suggested.

I sat down on a rock and was aware of nothing but my breath, as I tried to stifle the feeling that was welling up inside me.

"Oh no, here it comes." I turned my head to the side and was horrified as my breakfast forced its way out of my stomach and onto the mountain path beside me.

The relief I felt from the sickness was wonderful, but brief. I was shocked and upset that it was only the second day of the trek and already I was being sick. Suddenly, I became aware of a different kind of insistence.

"I need to go the toilet," I informed Heather, with a sense of urgency in my voice. "I'm sorry, I have to go now!"

The path we were on that day was long and tedious, continuously meandering its way through dense bushes of giant heather plants (not to be confused with Heather the doctor). My thoughts went back to what I'd said just an hour ago.

"We're definitely not going to lose anyone today, there's nowhere to go but upwards on this path."

The heather bushes were thick and impenetrable and there was no possibility of just nipping off to find a rock to squat behind.

The doctor waited for me around the bend, and just as I pulled my trekking trousers down I heard a group of porters coming up the path behind me. Oh no!

"STOP! WAIT THERE!" I shouted.

Luckily, they heard me.

"Okay, we'll wait, no problem," they replied.

I felt sure they were pretty used to this kind of situation and knew exactly what was going on.

They waited out of sight. I went to the toilet on the side of the path feeling upset and worried about the trek ahead of me.

As I covered up my business with branches from the heather bush, I felt the nausea coming back... oh no, not again.

After being sick for the second time, Dr Heather decided that I needed some help.

"Here, take this," she said as she delved into her bag and brought out a tablet for me to swallow. "It'll stop the sickness."

With six and a half days still ahead of me, I was starting to wonder if climbing Mount Kilimanjaro was such a good idea after all.

It's the altitude that does it. Some people suffer, some people don't. The problem is that you just can't tell if it's going to affect you until you've started the trek.

John, the chief guide from the African company that was looking after us on the mountain, came back to find us.

"How you doing?" he asked in his deep African voice.

"Not so good," I told him. "I've been sick twice and my tummy isn't feeling too great. I can't believe it, it's only the second day."

"Don't' worry," he told me, placing a reassuring hand on my shoulder. "I've seen people make it to the top after being sick this early on. It doesn't mean that you won't reach the summit, I'm sure you'll be fine." His words were comforting and I wanted desperately to believe him.

For the past eight months, I'd spent all of my spare time training extremely hard to ensure that I would be fit enough for my forthcoming challenge. Once again, I was going to the gym twice a week, swimming and jogging and I was spending practically every Sunday going for long country walks. As before, my friends had been supportive, taking it in turns to accompany me on my walks when they were able to, and I would often go out walking for four or five hours on my own.

I'd put an enormous amount of effort into raising another £5,000 for my charity and the whole project had been all-consuming. I really wanted to do this trek.

"How are you feeling?" asked Heather.

"Pretty bad actually," I told her, truthfully.

Heather and John walked with me slowly up to camp where the rest of the group were eating lunch. I sat down on a rock and sipped a cup of hot soup. Thankfully I started to feel better.

"Please, God," I prayed. "Get me up this mountain!"

I'd arrived in Tanzania so excited about the challenge ahead of me.

Just a month ago, I'd broken up with Andy and was certain that this challenge had come at just the right time. I was looking forward to some space and time away from home to think about myself and my future.

I knew I'd done enough training to cope with the physical demands of the trek, but it was finally beginning to sink in that it was the mental stamina I would need to take me all the way to the top.

After that day I wasn't sick any more. Each morning my fellow trekkers would greet me in the same way.

"Hey, Debs, how you feeling this morning?"

And I'd always reply along the lines of:

"Okay, thanks. My tummy is a bit dodgy, but I don't feel sick."

Then, every day, a few hours into the trek, the nausea came back. I spent most of my time fighting back the urge to be sick, and constantly stopping to sit down until the feeling temporarily passed. The further up the mountain we were, the worse I felt.

I was by no means the only one to feel the effects of the altitude. Others were sick after me, or at best they felt sick and bloated. Most people were suffering with dodgy tummies, but somehow they managed to keep smiling – well, at least whenever I saw them they were!

The main body of the group was made up of a team of people from the Isle of Man. Apart from me, my tent buddy, Heather and Rhiannon, everyone already knew someone else on the trip. Feeling unwell (and thinking a lot about Andy) made me feel vulnerable on the mountain and without a close buddy to confide in, it was a constant battle to keep my

Hummingbird

spirits up.

Each frosty morning I was woken by the familiar tones of my African friend, assigned to look after me and my tent buddy whilst we were at each different camp.

"Washy-washy," he'd call as he placed the bowl of hot water in our doorway. However, as we unzipped our tent to greet him, it was the hot drinks that we were more grateful for.

"Thanks so much, this is just what we need," we said as we wrapped our cold hands around the hot mugs of tea that he'd placed on the floor next to the bowl.

In order to keep warm at night, I slept in my thermal top and leggings, my wooly buff, my hat, gloves, socks and long sleeved top.

"Keep your batteries on you at night to keep them warm," I'd been told. "And keep your clothes for tomorrow in the bottom of your sleeping bag, so that they aren't freezing cold when you put them on in the morning."

It was good advice, but it was very busy in my sleeping bag. With all that was packed into it, there was only just enough room for me to snuggle down inside.

Each day brought with it a new landscape to feast our eyes upon. The lush green forest at the bottom of the mountain turned into the giant heather moorland where I had stopped to be sick. Coming across a few gentle streams, the African guys had a chance to fill up the water bottles for the cooking and washing water.

On the third day, I crawled out of my tent to be greeted by a cold and frosty morning.

Wrapped up in my hat, buff and gloves I set off with the group for the long day's trek. The route turned east and we found ourselves in a semi-desert with fewer trees and more rocks. After a long, slow and pretty tedious five-hour walk through the barren and dry expanse of the desert, we finally reached camp.

"I'm too cold to change this morning," said my tent buddy the next day, deciding to walk in her thermal long johns and pink pyjama bottoms.

It was Sunday. As the sun began to warm the day, we gathered around in a circle for a service on the mountain. The African men were on one side and my group of trekking buddies were on the other, facing them. As the locals began to sing and pray, I listened to their beautiful voices and looked out into the distance at our snow-capped destination.

I had only one prayer on my mind that morning: "Please, Universe, let me get to the top."

We were lucky to have a guy in our group who was a fabulous singer. His classically trained voice was as operatic as it was deep and powerful. There was something very moving about praying on the mountain that morning. I swallowed hard as the magical voices of the men drifting through the air brought a lump to my throat. As I felt the emotion stinging the back of my eyes, I moved out of the circle and wiped away my tears.

"Are you okay, Debs?" someone asked.

"Yes, I'm okay. I'm just moved by the service."

My jumbled up thoughts were being fed directly from the joy and pain in my heart. The positives and negatives were coming into my head, hand in hand like two old friends, reminding me of why I was there.

"I'm so lucky to be here. I can't believe I'm standing here, being a part of this special service, heading for the summit of this famous mountain and treading in the footsteps of others who had a dream or a tragic story to tell. It feels surreal. It's amazing. I'm amazing... I feel so alone up here. I'm missing my friends. I don't know what to do about Andy. It hurts so much... I'm so lucky to be here. It could have been so different. I could be dead now.

"I'm doing this for you, Nigel, you were so brave. And for Dad, Aunty Babs, for Philip and for me. I'm doing it because I can. I'm the lucky one. I'm so happy. Thank you, God, thank you so, so much for giving me my life. This life. Thank you, Universe, I love you ... Oh, God, it's hard. It's too emotional, I don't want to cry."

I wasn't the only one with a tear or two in my eye that morning, that's for sure. The service was extremely moving and I could tell that others were thinking about their lives and loved ones, reflecting on their own personal stories and challenges.

I had tears, but I was feeling happy, almost ecstatically so. The joy and pain were as one. It was the opposite, but the same. This happy/sad feeling wasn't at all new to me, I had got used to it a long time ago.

With the service over, I hoisted my rucksack onto my back, picked up my walking poles and took a few deep breaths.

"Okay, let's go."

And off we went, walking one behind the other, onwards and upwards, singing happy songs.

Hummingbird

We had been told that, next to summit day, this would be our toughest day. At an altitude of around 4,600 meters we finally came across Lava Tower, a 100m tall formation jutting out of the mountain that was created by cooling lava at some point in Kilimanjaro's past. In the shadow of the tower, we were relieved to put down our backpacks, find ourselves a rock to sit on and rest our tired legs, some of us in shorts or trousers and one 23-year-old young lady in pink pyjama bottoms.

After lunch, we descended into the Barranco Valley and the scenery changed yet again. With more vegetation it became a bit more interesting as we entered an amazing area known as the Garden of the Senecias.

"I've never seen anything like this before," I remarked to one of my fellow trekkers as I looked upwards at the tree-like plants.

"These are huge!"

The senecio plants were spectacular, towering above our heads with stout woody stems that split at the top forming two or four more branches with giant rosettes of green cactus-like leaves on the top. I read somewhere that they looked like candelabras the size of telephone poles and I think that's a pretty good description.

Each day now, we were having wonderful views of Kilimanjaro's summit, reaching 19,342 feet (5,895 meters) into the sky. On most days we were lucky enough to have a clear view of the top.

~ * ~

On day five, I woke up feeling really upset. I was dehydrated, I had a big fat lip (sunburn I suspect) and a headache.

Fed up with the nausea, the bloatedness and the diarrhea, I was struggling to keep my morale up. I'd had enough of sleeping in a tiny tent, being frustrated at not being able to find anything in my bag, having to sleep in all my clothes, not being able to wash properly and thinking about my broken relationship with Andy, which felt as rocky as the mountain I was climbing.

I had a block.

Trying desperately not to disturb my tent buddy, I gently slipped out of my sleeping bag and, with a slow and steady hand, unzipped the tent as quietly as I could. Exiting into the glorious morning sunshine, I let out the long, slow breath I'd been holding onto. Finding myself a large flat rock, I sat facing away from the camp and sobbed, releasing the block and allowing the tears to flow freely down my cheeks and onto my warm down jacket.

It was the right thing to do. When it was over, I felt that the pressure had been released and that I was ready to carry on. I felt more positive about the forthcoming summit day, which we were all excited about, but at the same time dreading. We had already been briefed about how tough it was going to be.

For the first time the long breakfast table was set up in camp without the protective tent being erected over it and we ate our porridge, eggs and bacon with the glorious warmth of the sun upon our faces.

After breakfast that day, Rhiannon had some sad news for us all.

"Unfortunately," she said, "due to breathing difficulties because of the altitude, the decision has been taken to send one of the guys back down to the village. It's too dangerous for him to continue the climb."

Everyone felt sorry for our teammate who had to turn back. We all knew what a tremendous effort it had taken each and every one of us to get there in the first place and our hearts went out to him. We didn't have to imagine his disappointment, we knew what he would be feeling. Just two days beforehand, I had wondered myself if I would actually be able to make it to the top.

"I'm so sorry," we all said as we hugged him and said our goodbyes. "Take care, we'll see you at the bottom. Well done for getting this far."

As I gave him a hug I whispered in his ear: "Enjoy the pool at the hotel you lucky sod, I wish I was coming with you." And I almost meant it.

With one team member down, we continued our long, slow journey upwards on Mount Kilimanjaro.

After such a rocky start, that day actually turned out to be the best day of the trek for me. The walking was the toughest we had encountered so far, as we started with an hour and a half climb up the steep and rocky Barranco Wall. I relished it. I had found the walking a bit too easy up until then, the training I'd done had obviously paid dividends. My headache went, the swelling on my lip went down, I had no nausea and I felt on top form. I really enjoyed every minute of the trek that day. We were now at 3,900 meters and I felt great.

The next day was my 48th birthday. All week I'd been looking forward to opening the cards I'd brought with me from home and I woke up early to look at them. Reading the cards gave me comfort and I was so glad that I had decided to carry them to Africa with me. I didn't leave my tent until I'd opened them in peace and had soaked up every bit of love that they contained. They were full of words of encouragement, poems and sketches of me up a mountain! They grounded me and gave me a renewed confidence in my ability to get to the top.

I got changed and sorted out my bag for the day before joining the others in the breakfast tent. I was greeted to a chorus of *Happy Birthday* and was handed a card signed by my fellow trekkers. How wonderful!

Mealtimes on the mountain were always a bit of a balancing act. The tables were pushed together to make one long surface and the chairs were set precariously on the rocky ground. Sometimes we were lucky enough not to be on too much of a slope and sometimes we weren't so lucky.

As I finished my birthday breakfast of porridge and eggs, I heard the familiar sound of Rhiannon's voice saying my name.

"Can you pass that down to Deborah, please?"

I looked over, wondering what it could be and I watched as the envelope went from hand to hand until it reached its destination in front of me.

"I wonder who this is from," I whispered as I opened what I assumed was another birthday card and read the words inside:

> *Hiya Deb. I hope that you have had a great trip so far, made lots of new friends, have not been sick at all and are enjoying every moment on Kili.*
>
> *After all the hard work and effort you have put in over the last six months (and before) with training and fundraising, moments of anxiety that passed and <u>finally</u> the big day is about to begin. Just remember, Deb, pole pole [slowly, slowly in Swahili – the mantra of the mountain] one foot in front of the other and you <u>will</u> get there, to the summit of Kili.*
>
> *What an achievement that will be for you! I'm sorry that I'm not there with you to offer support and encouragement, but I <u>am</u> doing so from here, I'm with you every step of the way, willing you on to the top.*
>
> *Take care babe, I'm so proud of you.*
>
> *Andy.*

After letting go of my emotion on the rock at camp the morning before, I was determined not to cry any more, but Andy's card brought a lump to my throat. Bless him, he had contacted the organisers beforehand and arranged to post a card to them, so that Rhiannon could give it to me on my birthday. He knew that I would be leaving camp at midnight for my final push to the summit.

I was thrilled and extremely moved that he had done that for me. I felt a nice warm glow inside to know that so many people were thinking of me that day, especially him.

We were one day away from the summit. I trekked that morning with a bright pink Birthday Girl banner across my body and balloons tied to my rucksack. I wasn't going to let my birthday be forgotten that day, mountain or no mountain! I was having my own little celebration, in my own special way.

We reached camp that afternoon and were now at 4,600 meters above sea level. My tummy was bloated and upset and it was making me feel bad again. The camp was extremely rocky and screedy and, although there was no rubbish there, it reminded me of a tip, because of its messy appearance and the negativity of my mind. It was difficult to clamber over the rocks and screed to get to the Porta Loos and my spirits had started to plummet again. It seemed as though I was in a constant battle with them on the mountain, continuously trying to raise them up.

I needed to find Rhiannon and have a word with her.

"C'mon, Debs," she encouraged me. "You can do it. You've come this far and I know that you are more than capable of getting up to the summit. You can't stay here at camp on your own. You have to come with us. We'll make sure you're okay. If you feel sick I'll get someone to carry your bag for you. Just think how amazing you'll feel when you get to the top. You can't stay here. Come on, you'll be fine. You can do it, I know you can."

I absolutely knew that she would say that, but I felt better for putting a voice to my feelings and she did manage to reassure me somewhat.

After dinner, we were given our usual briefing about what to expect the following day or in this case, that night:

"Set your alarm clocks so that you are up at 11pm tonight. We'll be having breakfast back here in this tent at 11.30pm and you must all be ready to leave camp at midnight.

"Everyone, make sure that you wear your full thermals under your trekking clothes and wear your hat, gloves, buff and layer your clothes. You'll need thick socks and your down jacket. It's going to be extremely cold out there. You need to pack your sunglasses, sun hat, sun screen and lip balm in your bags. Do not forget them. Take three litres of water and put your bottles upside down in your bag as they freeze from the top. Take plenty of snacks and rehydration sachets. Put a sachet in your water as it slows down the freezing process.

"It's going to be a long day. It will probably be the toughest day that most of you have ever experienced, so you'll need to dig deep within yourselves to find the strength and will to get through it. You are a great group and I have no doubt whatsoever that you will all get to the summit.

"We'll be walking for the first five hours in the pitch dark, so we all need to wear our head torches. Make sure you have spare batteries with you. When the sun comes up, it will lift your spirits and give you the boost that you'll definitely be needing by then.

"Tonight, we'll be ascending 1,295 metres and then, when we have reached the summit, we'll be coming back down to camp for a meal. After that, there'll be another couple of hours walking down to our next camp. We'll be descending 2,145 metres and the day will involve a total of between 12-15 hours of walking.

"It may be the hardest thing you've ever done, but it may also be the best thing you've ever done!"

We were all feeling apprehensive about the journey ahead that night and I have to say, nearly everyone looked really worried.

Alongside the notes I was making in my notebook, I wrote these words, in huge capital letters, sprawled diagonally across a whole page.

POSITIVE MENTAL ATTITUDE!

IT'S ONLY ONE DAY OF MY LIFE

When the briefing was over, I was aware of some quiet excitement outside the tent and I didn't have to wait long to find out what it was all about. As the singing began, the cooks brought in the birthday cake and passed it along the row of people to rest on the table in front of me.

"Can you believe it? They baked me a cake!" I said to the lady sitting next to me. "We're 4,600 metres above sea level, up a mountain and they've baked me a cake."

It even had candles on it and the words 'Happy Birthday Debora' across the top. They'd missed out the 'h', but I totally forgave them for that.

I cut up the cake and passed it around so that we could all have a piece. After we'd finished the delicious cake, we all went to bed to rest for a few hours and to mentally prepare ourselves for our toughest day yet.

Our tent was on a bit of a slope so it was tricky to stay in one place in my sleeping bag. I was having problems with my tummy again and, under normal circumstances, I would have let nature take its course. However, this was by no means normal circumstances and so I took an Imodium tablet and hoped that it would work.

The mood in camp at our 11.30pm breakfast was oddly quiet and apprehensive. The darkness was littered with the lights from our head torches, dotted around camp and coming into line as we took our places for the final summit push.

Now that I was ready to leave camp, I was mentally prepared for the day. Fully resolved to the challenge ahead, I left camp at midnight with the group. We walked in a line, one behind the other, snaking our way *pole pole* up towards the top of the mountain.

We walked slowly in the darkness for five and a half hours. Our guides were fantastic, singing a lot and encouraging us all the way up. Periodically I had to stop and sit down as the nausea got the better of me. Resting for a moment relieved the sickness feeling and allowed me to continue. I went in stages like this all the way up, stopping and starting, constantly focusing on my breathing.

When the sun came up, just as Rhiannon had predicted, it lifted our spirits no end. It was one of the most spectacular sights I've ever seen. I don't believe I can find any words to do it justice.

A famous saying popped into my mind.

"Life is not measured by the number of breaths we take, but by the moments that take our breath away."

This was definitely one of those moments. I stood in awe as I watched the beautiful orange and red glow appear in the distance, lighting up the blanket of cloud below me and taking away the chill of the night. As the sun rose further into the sky, the darkness faded and I could finally see my fellow trekkers and our position on the mountain. With the sea of cloud below us, and blue sky all around us, it felt surreal. It was a scene I had only ever witnessed from an airplane before.

It was the boost we all needed to push on to the top.

Suddenly, I now had a guide to myself that I guessed Rhiannon had organised for me and for the final few hours, as my symptoms got worse, I gave in and allowed him to carry my backpack.

My guide and I kept on walking slowly upwards. It was as though we were in an imaginary bubble, the group were around me, but I was aware only of the two of us as we journeyed on and on in the daylight, stopping to rest when the nausea took hold. I was fully focused on the task, it was the only way I could do it. Step-by-step, breath by breath, *pole pole* – my personal guide and myself. Nothing and no one else came into my mind. He was extremely patient, encouraging me all the way, until eventually we reached Stella Point, our final resting place before the summit.

We were an hour away from the roof of Africa. The whole group was finding it difficult to breath now. Every step to the top from Stella Point was as slow as a snail's pace and now the actual walking and breathing was the most difficult part. Everyone was in the same situation. The air at the top of Kilimanjaro contained only about half the amount of oxygen that it did at sea level, and was so thin that we could hardly walk at all.

As I made my way to the summit, I was unable to think about anything but breathing and walking.

"One foot in front of the other (right foot forward). Just keep going (left foot forward). One foot in front of the other (right foot forward). Just keep going (left foot forward). With this new mantra repeating in my mind, I literally focused on every word and every step until I finally reached the wooden sign, which read:

CONGRATULATIONS!

YOU ARE NOW AT

UHURU PEAK, TANZANIA 5895M. AMSL.

AFRICA'S HIGHEST POINT.

WORLD'S HIGHEST FREE-STANDING MOUNTAIN.

ONE OF WORLD'S LARGEST VOLCANOES.

WELCOME.

"Oh, thank God for that!" I said as I ripped off my jacket and fleece and threw them on the ground. It was unusually hot at the top of the mountain that day.

My personal guide was full of congratulations for me and everyone was excited, hugging and kissing, relieved and elated to have finally reached their destination.

"Wow, we made it to the top!"

"Congratulations!"

"Hey, give us a hug, we did it!"

"Yeah! We made it."

"Well done, everyone!"

Much as I tried to feel good about it, I just didn't feel like celebrating. I was grumpy and irritable and I felt that the quicker I could get back to camp the better it would be. So, I had my photo taken as soon as I could and grabbed my guide to start our descent.

I found Rhiannon.

"We're going back down," I informed her as I left the summit celebrations behind me and I didn't look back.

And then came the moment that no one ever warns you about. Just when I thought that the hardest part was over, I was suddenly 'skiing' down the mountain on loose dusty scree. The scree slope was pretty intense and I guess it could have been fun, were it not for the fact that I was totally exhausted and still feeling sick. I found the steep and dusty slope impossible to walk on and used my poles to steady myself as I went down, in a kind of half-running, half-skiing fashion. I almost fell a few times and it was the last thing I needed.

It felt like it was never ending, but it was actually the best part of two hours. I think I was more relieved to see the back of that scree slope than I was to see the summit! My poor legs hadn't worked so hard all week.

Thankfully, as I descended, I began to feel my body getting back to normal again. The nausea left me and my tummy started feeling better.

At exactly midday, 12 hours after setting off from camp, I was the first of the group to arrive back at the tents. I found my temporary dwelling, got into my sleeping bag and instantly fell into a deep sleep. After the sleep and some delicious lunch, I felt so much better than I had done for days. I felt my spirits rise again.

After lunch, we had another three hours of walking back down to the next camp, and I enjoyed every moment of it. Having a sleep and some lunch, combined with being lower down the mountain, had improved my morale (and my unfortunate altitude symptoms) no end and I felt absolutely fine again – at long last. It was so wonderful to feel normal again.

The next day, we walked for eight hours to get to the bottom of the mountain. In contrast to our climb, the descent was rapid. The scenery was beautiful, as we came down through the wonderful forest, the warm sun finding its way through the vegetation and warming us with its smile.

I was very happy and proud of what I had achieved.

Chapter 65

My life now

A few years ago, my family was surprised to discover that it wasn't in fact the doctors who had wanted to keep my grandfather's illness a secret from his family members. Recent contact with a long-lost cousin of my father's in Canada has uncovered the news that it was in fact my grandmother who had requested that her husband's illness was to be kept a secret from the family.

This was quite a revelation for us. For years we had blamed the health professionals for not telling my father that he was at risk of Huntington's disease. Not knowing about it caused my family a lot of pain and upset when my dad first became ill as no one knew what was wrong with him. Not only that, when he did eventually go into hospital, he was given the wrong medication and treatment – including electric shock treatment – which I'm sure was detrimental to his health.

So, it was my grandmother who had asked the doctors not to tell anyone about Huntington's disease. When my grandmother received news from her brother-in-law to say that his wife (my granddad's sister – are you keeping up?) had been diagnosed with HD and that he was writing to everyone in the family to tell them about the risk, my grandmother's reaction was to believe that they were lying and to cut herself off from the family and she asked them not to contact her again. There was obviously a reason why she took this action and what that reason was, well, I can only speculate.

Maybe she was trying to protect her children from living their lives under a cloud, as I did, scared about their future and worried about their own families. Maybe she truly thought that it was the best way to deal with the awful situation or maybe she was just burying her head in the sand and refusing to believe the truth. Ignorance is of course no protection – once the dice has been rolled, nothing can be changed.

She must have been scared. Maybe she remembered how one of her husband's parents had suffered with a mental affliction and the stigma that had been attached to the mental illness of the parent was too much for her to face up to.

Maybe she felt guilty for giving life to her children – children that were at risk of a devastating and debilitating mental illness.

I guess I'll never know what was going through her mind at the time, but I can only assume that it was the mind of a very frightened woman. A woman so scared of the affliction and the stigma that she attached to it, that she closed the door on it and kept it firmly locked away for as long as she lived.

I wonder what would have happened if she had accepted the truth and told her children about HD? Would my parents have had children of their own? Would they have even been married? Would I have ever been born?

But why ask why or what if? The fact is that I'm here on this amazing journey that is my life.

~ * ~

Spiritual Response Therapy

And my journey just gets better and better. A couple of years ago, I met my lovely friend, Jo Constantinou. Jo is a therapist of a different kind. She uses a combination of Spiritual Response Therapy (SRT), Neuro Linguistic Programming (NLP), Emotional Healing and Spiritual Restructuring to work with her clients to help them to live the life they desire and deserve. Jo and I became great friends and we have often worked on each other to assist with our own healing. Jo's work is amazing. SRT is a type of healing that I had never come across before.

I am totally captivated each time I see Jo for a clearing, which she carries out by using a pendulum, a set of charts and a series of questions that research the subconscious mind and soul. After identifying issues that may be affecting my life and health, she uses the pendulum to clear blocks and negative energies that are hindering me and holding me back from experiencing perfect health and balance.

Having a session with Jo is a truly fascinating and educational experience. I inevitably learn something new about myself each time I go to see her.

One of the benefits of the way Jo works is that a clearing can be completed remotely or via a phone consultation or Skype, as well as in person, so you don't even have to travel anywhere to see her. You don't even have to be in the same country to benefit from her work.

I find that the Universe is constantly offering me opportunities to grow myself in every way and to experience new and wonderful challenges in my life. Jo and I now run workshops and retreat weekends to help people to identify what they truly want in life and to teach them how to manifest it for themselves. The workshops and retreats are based on the law of attraction and on the retreat weekends people have the additional benefit of SRT clearing work with Jo.

~ * ~

Life continues to excite me and is more and more rewarding with each new day and, of course, I'm truly grateful that I was born into this time and place.

I am a busy lady, but I replenish my energy with regular massages and acupuncture treatments, as well as yoga and meditation sessions.

Andy and I continue to be dear friends and support each other on our journey of life.

Over the past couple of years, my spare time has been dedicated to writing this book and Andy has been extremely supportive and helpful with the project. He has made a positive impact on my decisions regarding the book and it would have been a different book without his input.

I am thrilled that, as I turned 50, I celebrated not only with a wonderful weekend away, but by sending my manuscript for proofreading.

My 50th birthday weekend in October 2012 was an amazing event, full of love and joy and a total celebration of my life. I hired Mockbeggars Hall, a nine-bedroom Jacobean house in Sussex and was joined there by 16 of my wonderful friends for the long weekend. On the Saturday evening, we all dressed up in ball gowns and tiaras, dress suits and bow ties and had a formal sit down dinner at the house. I felt like a total princess, with the camera's clicking away at me, the beautiful table decoration (thanks, Sonya) and the huge birthday cake (again, thanks to Sonya). Everyone took it in turns to say wonderful things about being my friend and I had a total of 72 birthday cards from friends, family and clients. The love I felt was overwhelming and every day I thank the Universe for the love and positivity in my life.

I also had a wonderful meal with my family at the Boathouse in Leigh-on-sea and a delicious lunch with the Treatment Triangle ladies at a Michelin star restaurant, Chapter One in Orpington. I am truly blessed to have had such a wonderful time.

I have signed up for my next challenge. Sonya and I will trek the Inca Trail to Machu Picchu in October 2013. Sonya is raising money for Animals Asia and I'm raising more for Huntington's Disease. We are funding the trip ourselves so all donations will go straight to the charities.

Chapter 66

How to live with joy

There are no challenges, issues or crises that do not contain within them seeds of opportunity that could not have otherwise existed – Mike Dooley, Notes From The Universe

I've learned a lot on my highly emotional-but-exceptional journey to find my happiness and joy. It's been a rollercoaster ride of highs and lows, but it's been amazing. The people I've met, the things I've learned, the experiences I've had, it would never have happened without the push I have felt to heal myself of the sadness of my life.

After the little hummingbird died and I came back from Costa Rica suffering from depression, I didn't know which way to turn. If you are at this point in your life and are looking for direction, my advice to you is to seek help. Different things work for different people, but the important thing is to recognise and accept that you don't have to go it alone. There are many people and organisations that can help you to get back onto the path of wellness and often a number of different approaches can be beneficial.

Take responsibility. Make the decision to change. Whatever path you chose, remember this: if nothing changes, things will stay the same and if you bury your head in the sand – well, I guess that (at best) you will always be in the desert, along with your anger, hurt, frustration and negative emotions and feelings. At worst, your mental, spiritual, emotional and physical health will spiral downwards.

So, firstly get the support of someone who will listen to you, with kindness and love. This could be a friend or a therapist of some kind (there are many types of complimentary and holistic therapies, counsellors, life coaches, NLP practitioners, journey therapists, etc), then make a pact with yourself to take some control over your own wellbeing. Eat a healthy organic diet, avoid toxic chemicals, take regular exercise and make sure that you are not spending your life around negative people or influences. Being around positive energy will lift you up.

Take positive steps towards a less stressful lifestyle.

At the end of the day, happiness is an inside job. We can't rely on others to make us feel happy. Why? Because if they leave us, let us down in any way or pass away, our happiness will disappear with them. Don't get me wrong, it's important to connect with people, to love and be loved, but the happiness bit – that's your job!

Every day, give thanks for your life. Practicing an attitude of gratitude works wonders. Say to yourself each day: "What am I going to do with my precious day today? How am I going to spend it? How do I choose to feel today?" And then remind yourself that you will never get this day back again and then make the most of it. Find something each day to be grateful for and you will gradually begin to let the joy back into your heart and your life again. A joy that is always and forever with you, even when you are experiencing the more challenging times of your life.

Be gentle on yourself and allow yourself to have some fun. Take regular exercise, at least go for a daily walk. Train your mind to think positive thoughts and focus on the things that will take you towards a more happier and healthier you.

Notice the good things about yourself and get into the habit of paying yourself and others regular compliments. If you don't love and value yourself, how can you expect others to?

Choose to use gentle remedies to heal yourself (rather than modern medicines that have side-effects), such as aromatherapy oils, homeopathy, herbal remedies, good nutrition and flower essences. And always drink plenty of water every day.

Remember, life is all about the journey, not the destination. Make wonderful memories.

~ * ~

Kindness is the language that the deaf can hear and the blind can see – Mark Twain

Be kind. It costs nothing and brings great rewards. If you act with kindness and love it will be sure to return to you.

Choose to be happy. Don't focus on the negative things that may happen in your life, but on the positive and good things that may happen. Remember: the law of attraction means that the quality of the energy we put out there will be the same level of energy that will return to us. So, make sure it's good!

Spend some time alone and get to know yourself better. If you find it difficult to be alone, ask yourself why.

Pain is inevitable. Suffering is optional – Dalai Lama

Don't be afraid of emotional pain, it serves to makes us stronger. The challenges of our lives give us an opportunity to grow both spiritually and emotionally.

There are many ways to climb a mountain and many varied routes we can take. Every journey is unique and special in its own way. The most beneficial path is usually the steepest, longest and most difficult to climb, but the rewards of choosing this path are by far the greatest. An easy path is usually a quick fix to happiness and is not the true way to the summit. And not only that, it's usually the most boring and unchallenging route.

How do we know when we've reached the summit? I guess we can ask ourselves the following questions:

Do I feel healed in every area of my life?

Can I feel joy in my heart when life isn't going so well around me?

Do I have everything I need? (keep in mind that rich people are not always happy people)

What do I have in my life that I don't want? (including negative emotions)

Am I angry, hurt, sad or lonely?

Do I love and value myself?

Do I live with love and have an attitude of gratitude?

Are my actions coming from a place of fear or from a place of love?

Am I truly happy?

Namaste

Appendix A

A more positive attitude

Shana and Sarah

I love my mum very much and, even though she is sick she is still one of the most important people in my life – Shana Martin

I feel that it's important to represent another, more positive and uplifting insight into living with Huntington's disease. Not everyone feels as I did or as Nigel did. It's important to me that my readers understand that this is only my story and it doesn't reflect how it is for everyone.

Some children of HD sufferers, like the younger me, find it difficult to live a positive life, with the cloud of doubt hanging over them. But others, like Shana Martin and Sarah Winckless, drew strength and positivity from their situations.

Shana's mum was adopted at birth and had no idea about the family illness. She first showed signs of HD whilst giving birth to her daughter. She was diagnosed with the condition when Shana was just five years old.

Shana and her father cared for her mum until she could no longer stay at home.

Instead of having a negative attitude to life, Shana has worked exceptionally hard to accomplish many great things. Being physically strong and active is her way of coping and her passion for fitness and sport has led her to become the five-time log rolling and two-time boom running world champion.

As well as a fitness expert and world champion lumberjack athlete, Shana is a national spokesperson, fitness model, fitness competitor, gymnast, pole vaulter and runner. Her list of achievements goes on and on.

Shana says that, when her mum was diagnosed, they were hoping that it was going to be something less serious. Unfortunately, the diagnosis confirmed that her mum had Huntington's disease

"I was forced to grow up at a really young age," Shana said. "I was forced to be a mother to my mother. My dad and I spent almost all of our time taking care of her. She had lots of accidents - it was scary. I had a hard time with kids. I remember going home from school and I'd cry every day."

I can empathise with Shana and many others like her. I know that feeling so well. But where I spent my life feeling petrified of my future, Shana has an incredibly positive outlook.

"Even though I am at risk," she says, "I don't think about it. Every once in a while I'll trip or something and I think, 'Oh my gosh, I'm gonna have Huntington's disease,' but it's not something that I'm pre-occupied with."

"Sports and athletics and always having something to do, has kept my mind off of the whole situation. I really think that for anybody who has something hard going on in their life – to be able to stay busy and not have time to sit around and feel sorry for themselves, is probably the best way to go. Without sports and all the things I'm involved in, I don't know what I'd do."

Shana certainly does live her life to the full and I agree with her – it's a great strategy for coping.

Since the age of 16, Shana has been very active with the Huntington's Disease Society of America and she was also a founding member of the Huntington's Disease Society of America's National Youth Alliance.

Reading her resume makes me feel, well… proud. Proud and quite jealous. I haven't met Shana face-to-face yet, but I hope that one day I will.

She recently told me that her mum's name is Deborah.

"I believe I'm a stronger person because I've grown up around such other strong people," she revealed. "So there's always a silver lining to every cloud."

~ * ~

Shana's mum passed away in March 2013. She was about to attend a charity ball with her husband and daughter in aid of HD when she lost her battle with Huntington's disease.

Shana said, "She was all dressed up and so beautiful. She was able to see my dad one last time. Everything I do always has – and always will be – because of her.

We need to cure this awful disease."

Hummingbird

Everyone is going to die. Some of us just have more information about what that journey may look like – Sarah Winckless

Another lady who threw herself into sport is former British rower, Sarah Winckless. Sarah watched as her mother suffered the effects of Huntington's disease, stumbling awkwardly, slurring her speech and experiencing mood swings, changing from happy to angry in an instant.

Sometimes other people thought that Sarah's mum was drunk and the family had to cope with that. When her friends hadn't seen her mum for a while, they noticed the changes and would ask what was wrong with her. Sarah would say to them, "that's just Mum."

Sarah's mother's symptoms went undiagnosed for more than a decade. They had no idea what the matter was because the changes were gradual and slow. Her mother was always very emotional but Sarah knew that her behaviour wasn't right – just as my mum knew that there was something wrong with my dad.

As is often the case with sufferers of HD, Sarah's mother must have sensed that there was something wrong but remained in denial. When she finally agreed to be tested, and was diagnosed in 1996, it was a huge relief to Sarah. She finally understood her mum's behaviour – it all made sense to her.

Their relationship had been tough but once they understood what the problem was, the difficulties were instantly forgiven.

Sarah wanted to know if she had inherited the disease and decided to take the genetic test. Her test showed that she had indeed inherited the faulty gene. Despite her diagnosis, she remains positive and believes that a cure will be found.

Sarah continues to raise awareness of Huntington's Disease, and - like Shana and myself – she also trekked to the top of Mount Kilimanjaro to raise money for the cause.

"Mum has taught me that life does not stop the day you get the diagnosis," Sarah said in an interview with the Mail Newspaper.

Sarah was passionate about rowing and focused on her studies and her sport. She won a bronze medal for Great Britain at the 2004 Olympic Games and was twice world champion (2005 and 2006).

"My Olympic effort was nothing compared to what my mum battles with every day of her life," Sarah said in an emotional interview with the

Daily record in September 2010.

"Mum is my inspiration. Finding out I also carry the faulty gene that will lead to Huntington's was hard but it's just meant that I see the colours in life more brightly. If you can't fight it, there's no point in being scared of it.

Huntington's is a very complex disease. It is different in every case. It's tough and the problem with this disease is, every time you think you've reached a status quo, something changes.

For me, it was a really simple decision. Knowledge was power. If you look at the end result which is Huntington's, that can be a very scary place.

I've always had a great love of life. I want people to see how families with Huntington's can still play and have fun together. If you keep your mind active and your spirit light, it helps."

Sarah is patron of the Scottish Huntington's Association.

~ * ~

I thank Shana and Sarah for allowing me to include their stories in my book as examples of a more positive way of looking at the disease. I really think that it's important for anyone with HD in their family to be able to read positive things in relation to the illness. But of course you don't have to be an amazing sports person to be positive about your life and your future if you are at risk. These are two exceptional women. As long as you have a focus and a purpose, your life can be fulfilling and meaningful and a positive attitude can carry you a long way in life, whatever your challenges.

Appendix B

American folk singer, Woody Guthrie

Woody Guthrie was born in 1912. When he was a young boy, there were several fires at his home, one of which killed his sister (he was seven years old when this happened) and one which severely burned his father. In another fire the family home burned down. It wasn't known at the time that Woody's Mother was suffering from Huntington's Disease and it's questionable as to whether her illness was responsible for the fires.

I can only try to imagine what it must have been like for Woody Guthrie as a young boy. I know only too well how the symptoms of the undiagnosed illness can affect the whole family.

Woody's maternal grandfather drowned and, because of this, researchers suspect that it's likely that he also suffered from HD.

It wasn't until Woody Guthrie's health began to deteriorate that the disease was finally diagnosed. Woody had become moody, violent and unpredictable. He was hospitalised several times, picked up for 'vagrancy' and incorrectly diagnosed with alcoholism and schizophrenia before his erratic behaviour was finally understood.

Like Woody, his mother also had a love of singing and after she died Guthrie wrote a song about her, entitled 'I hear you sing again'. The lyrics are moving and in the song Woody conveys how much he misses his mother and wishes that he could 'close his eyes and hear her voice again'. He talks about the troubled times that turned her hair grey and all the tears and sorrows that followed her to her grave.

Woody's lyrics about his mother came to life after his death, when Janice Ian put them to music and recorded the song so beautifully. I listened to it on YouTube and it's extremely moving. Whilst I was listening to the song I sent up a prayer for the Guthrie family.

Woody wrote many other lyrics that had no music to accompany them and after his death his daughter, Nora, approached the English alternative rock musician, Billy Bragg, and asked him to write new music to her late father's undiscovered lyrics. Billy agreed and 'Mermaid Avenue' was released in June, 1998.

Appendix C

Infant massage instructor, Mia Elmsäter

If you understood the extraordinary gifts that every single challenge in your life makes possible, even inevitable, you'd celebrate your challenges, new and old alike, as the omens that they are of new beginnings and spectacular change – Mike Dooley, Notes from the Universe

Mia, my infant massage instructor, turned out to be an extraordinary woman. She discovered the power of infant massage for herself when she had given birth to a boy with Downs syndrome. Her story is not only moving but inspirational and I wanted to share it with you because it's a story that teaches us a valuable lesson about how we can look at our life in a more positive light. Mia kindly agreed to relay her remarkable story for us and I thank her deeply for that.

~ * ~

Mia's story, in her own words

Early in the morning of the third of August, 1986 – after an amazing pregnancy and a quick and easy birth – the midwife laid my third son on my chest, covered us both in a blanket, and put her hand over mine.

"I think that your son has Downs syndrome," she said, in the kindest way she possibly could.

"No," I hastily replied. "That can't be possible. He can't have Downs syndrome, I'm a strict vegetarian."

Although her eyes looked sad, she smiled at me and insisted kindly.

"Well, that's certainly a healthy approach to food Mia, but I wouldn't tell you this if I didn't feel so strongly that your baby does have Downs syndrome. We'll need to run a test to confirm it, but I'm sure that I'm right. I'm sorry."

I was shocked and I felt numb. I was trying to take it all in when I was once again aware of the softly spoken voice of the midwife.

"Because of his weight and his difficulty in maintaining his body heat, we need to take him into the Neonatal Intensive Care Unit. They will monitor him in there and look after him."

I must have nodded to indicate that I understood. She left with my son and I laid there, no tummy and no baby.

I didn't see my new son Kim for a few hours. I tried to get my head around having a baby with special needs, and thought about all the questions that arose in my mind.

"Why me? I don't smoke, drink or take drugs. How am I going to manage? What will my family say? What is going to happen when he turns five, thirteen, when he gets married, when I die?

What if he can't talk, walk or go to school?" My head was spinning with questions.

I thought of the few people I had seen with Downs and they had disturbed me. They always had their tongue out and wanted to hug.

Later that day, I finally got the courage to go and see Kim. "He's so cute," I thought as I looked down at his beautiful blond hair. His lovely blue eyes stared right at me.

After another couple of days, I felt that I needed to hold him – or at least touch him – but I struggled. I remembered back to five years ago when one of my closest friends had taught me to massage my eldest son. I really didn't seem to get anything out of it back then but I was certainly ready to try it again, thinking that maybe I could massage the Downs syndrome away.

Although I couldn't remember everything my friend had taught me, I remembered some of the routine and so I started to massage my tiny baby boy. What happened was something amazing.

I took some oil in my hands and I looked at him.

"Hey little one," I said affectionately to my newborn son. "Welcome to the world. You have two brothers and two step-brothers you know." I paused before continuing. "But your dad has walked away from us all, so I'm not sure how it's all going to work."

I looked into his beautiful innocent blue eyes, as I presented my oiled hands to him.

"Would it be okay if I gave you a little massage?"

He looked right back at me and I took that for a yes.

I held one of his tiny, blue legs and began slowly, gently touching and stroking as I kept eye contact with him, soothing him with my words as I stroked. By the time I finished with the first leg, it was no longer blue, but a nice rosy pink colour.

"Hey!" I called to the nurses to come over and see what had happened. "Look at this!"

They came over to see what I was doing and I felt an arm slip around my shoulder.

"I don't know what you are doing," the nurse said, affectionately squeezing my shoulder a little, "but whatever it is, keep it up!"

I was delighted. Although the staff at the Neonatal Intensive Care Unit and I had disagreements on several occasions, this one simple act by a nurse opened my eyes to the fact that I was the most important person in my baby's life and I was doing a good job.

The bond was immediate.

While still in the birthing centre, I called my friend in Denmark, who had just become the first infant massage instructor trainer in Europe.

"I've had my baby," I told her. "I'm massaging him in the hospital and he really loves it."

"Oh, Mia, that's wonderful," she said, encouragingly. We talked for a while and then she had a thought. "We're having the very first infant massage instructors training here in Denmark in three months' time. Why don't you come along Mia? I think you would be a great instructor."

I signed up immediately. After hanging up, I had to call her back, as I had forgotten to tell her that Kim had Downs. All of a sudden, he wasn't a 'diagnose' any more. Downs syndrome may have been the label that the medical community needed to put on him, but he was a baby... my baby, and he was precious!

I couldn't stay away from him. Fortunately, we had a room together at the hospital and we spent the entire time getting to know each other.

By the time we left the hospital nine days later, I had not only quit wondering about Downs syndrome and the effects it would have on me, but had turned my thinking totally around.

Leading up to the months before Kim and I went to Denmark to do the instructor training, I massaged him every day.

After only three weeks, Kim was no longer hypotonic and the

Hummingbird

paediatrician couldn't believe what he was seeing.

"What have you been doing with him, Mia?" he asked me.

"I've been massaging him," I said. "He really enjoys it and so do I."

"I'm really interested to hear more about the massage," he said and I explained to him what I'd been doing and how Kim was responding.

I shared with him my news.

"I'm going to Denmark to train as an instructor. I'm going to come back and teach other parents to massage their babies this way."

Seeing how enthusiastic I was, the doctor was impressed.

"I want to help you to get the funding for the training," he told me. "I will personally see to it that every baby in the north of Sweden has the opportunity to be massaged by their parents... especially those babies having special needs."

After the instructor training, which Kim and I both attended in Copenhagen, I realised that this was what I wanted to do for the rest of my life. I wanted to teach infant massage, specifically to parents who had babies with special needs.

Thus began baby massage in Sweden. I like to think that Kim brought baby massage to Sweden when he came to me.

They say that when one door closes, another one opens. You just have to step back and see where that new door is, as it may not be in the same place as the old one. I was ready for a career change, and thanks to Kim, I found a new path.

Within three years of becoming an instructor, I was asked to become an instructor trainer with the IAIM. This has been my passion, hobby and work since then.

Today Kim lives in his own apartment (assisted by personnel) and has a job he goes to five days a week.

He speaks three languages fluently, bowls, lifts weights, dances and has a girlfriend with Downs.

"Mum, I have a great life," he told me. "We're going to get married and have dogs, not kids, because we have Downs."

At work on Mondays, he leads his colleagues in some kind of a massage on the back that he made up (or stole from me!).

How much of his development was due to infant massage and early intervention, I'll never know. What I do know is that it was infant massage that encouraged me to touch him and, through touch, I was able to heal whatever it was that needed healing... and do it immediately.

With the parents I taught in the years after having Kim, I saw similarities. When I could go in and talk to them before they left the hospital, it was the best. If I could get them to start doing infant massage when they came home, it was great. I saw changes week by week, and by the time the course of five to nine sessions was over, I saw things that brought tears to my eyes, every day.

I am fortunate to be doing this work. I have to thank Kim (and I do daily) because, had he not come to me, I certainly wouldn't have had the rich and wonderful life that I have now. His gifts to me were more than I could ever imagine, and I am a better person, mum, and infant massage instructor because of him.

Mia Elmsäter

~ * ~

When life gives you lemons, make lemonade – Elbert Hubbard

Mia's story is a wonderful and moving recollection straight from her heart and it teaches us many things. Again we are reminded that life doesn't always go according to plan, but that in fact a change of plan is not necessarily a bad thing at all. What we may initially feel to be a disappointment or a sad event, a shock or even a loss can turn out to be the most inspiring event that can change our lives for the better.

We are often sent blessings in disguise. We must remind ourselves that when life doesn't seem so good – that's when we have the opportunity to grow even greater and learn much more about ourselves.

Mia continued to grow. In 1990, she joined forces with a colleague and presented the infant massage program in Romania. This led to the start of the Sunrise Day Care Centre, which was the first centre in Romania to mainstream children with special needs. Mia created a sponsoring program for monetary support between Sweden and Romania.

She also created and co-created several massage and touch programs, including Tactile Stimulation for children and adults with special needs, Touch Therapy used in nursing homes and Child Massage used in day care centres. Additionally, the massage program for day care centres has been introduced into Germany.

Hummingbird

Mia has done volunteer work in neonatal units in Sweden, supporting parents and helping them to bond with their babies and she started a support group for parents who have babies born with Downs syndrome.

Not stopping there, Mia and her colleague, Sylvie Hétu, developed a program of bringing positive touch into schools. They believed that bringing a simple, non-invasive massage routine into schools all over the world would make a positive contribution in the lives of these children and I am sure that this is truly the case.

The Massage in Schools Programme (MISP) is a revolutionary approach which has spread throughout all of Europe and extends out to regions such as Asia and Latin America. It was introduced into the UK in 1999 and I'm so pleased because all we seem to hear these days is how healthy touch is being taken away from schools and nurseries.

What an amazing resume Mia has now! She's made an outstanding contribution to the world through the work she had done since the birth of her third son, Kim.

Her drive and determination is incredible. People like Mia are helping to make the world a better place to be.

Appendix D

The power of loving touch

Support World Peace… Massage your Children – International Association of Infant Massage

I was, and still am, extremely interested in the physical benefits of baby massage, but I have to admit that it's the psychological benefits that interest me the most.

Amongst the information I was given on the Infant Massage course was a hand-out entitled 'Can more touching lead to less violence in our society?' It looks to me as though my country is becoming more and more violent every day, with offenders getting younger and younger. Anything that would help this situation can only be a good thing.

An American developmental neuropsychologist, James W. Prescott, researched the origins of violence, particularly as it relates to a lack of mother-child bonding. Interestingly, Prescott said;

"I have devoted a great deal of study to the peculiar relationship between violence and pleasure. I am now convinced that the deprivation of physical sensory pleasure is the principal root cause of violence. Laboratory experiments with animals show that pleasure and violence have a reciprocal relationship, that is, the presence of one inhibits the other.

A raging, violent animal will abruptly calm down when electrodes stimulate the pleasure centres of its brain. Likewise, stimulating the violence centres in the brain can terminate the animal's sensual pleasure and peaceful behaviour. When the brain's pleasure circuits are 'on,' the violence circuits are 'off,' and vice versa.

Among human beings, a pleasure-prone personality rarely displays violence or aggressive behaviours, and a violent personality has little ability to tolerate, experience, or enjoy sensuously pleasing activities. As either violence or pleasure goes up, the other goes down."

So, from this evidence, we can see how important it is that we have sensory pleasure time with our children. Infant massage is a perfect way to learn how to give sensory pleasure and not only do our children benefit but we do as well.

Hummingbird

Infant massage classes are so much more than just learning the massage routine. They teach us about listening and responding to our babies' cues and signals, respecting our child's wish to say 'no' to the massage at any given time, and they empower a parent to feel confident when touching their new born baby – whatever their situation.

The classes teach us to better understand our babies and feel comfortable when our child cries. I have witnessed the most devoted earth mothers bond even closer to their babies and it has to make us wonder ..... what if everyone in the world was taught how to massage their babies, and continued to massage their children as they grew? What if we all learned about the benefits of the power of loving touch and grew up to be healthy, tactile adults? What kind of world would we be living in then? A much less violent one, I'm absolutely sure.

Appendix E

Cellular healing

The tuning fork massage and the Journey therapy were my first introductions to the concept of cellular healing. The idea that we can influence our cells and heal our bodies by releasing our suppressed emotions, thinking more positively and focusing on love is a subject that has captivated my interest for many years now.

My book would not be complete without a mention of some of the amazing discoveries that I have come across in my quest for healing myself and in my work as a holistic therapist. In this Appendix you will see how cellular healing isn't just an idea, it's a proven fact and that the healing power of love and gratitude can be proven through the amazing work of people such as Doctor Masaru Emoto, Fabien Maman and Bruce Lipton Ph.D

~ * ~

Hidden messages in water

The New York Times bestseller 'Hidden Messages in Water' by Dr Masaru Emoto (an internationally renowned Japanese scientist) illustrates the healing power of love and gratitude by showing us images of water crystals that have been exposed to different and specific concentrated thoughts and words.

Dr Masaru Emoto used high-speed photography to capture images of crystals formed from frozen water and to study the effects of the influence that words and energies had upon the water.

What Dr Emoto found to be true is that water from clear springs and water that had been exposed to loving words showed brilliant complex and colourful snowflake patterns whereas, in contrast, polluted water and water exposed to negative thoughts and words formed incomplete, asymmetrical patterns with dull colours.

The images in the book are remarkable and tell an interesting story. For example, the book contains images of crystals taken from lake water before and after a Buddhist healing prayer. The photograph taken before the prayer shows us a crystal that is deformed and discoloured, whereas the photograph taken after the prayer shows us a crystal that looks like a beautiful sparkling piece of jewelery!

Similarly we are shown pictures of crystals that have been exposed to the harmful effects of the electromagnetic waves of TV and Radio, beautiful radiant crystals that have been shown the words 'love and gratitude' and we can see the profoundly different effects that the words 'you're cute' and 'you fool' have upon the water crystals.

There are many pictorial examples in Dr Emoto's book of how loving words can change the quality of water and a great deal of information about why this is so important to us when we think about our health.

When we think about it, the average human body is seventy per cent water and so therefore it must follow that the quality of the words we use - and indeed hear - on a daily basis must surely affect our bodies.

~ * ~

Fabien Maman

The seed of the spiritual is found in the physical. In the heart of the cells, in the spiral of the DNA is written the divine story. When scientific research, spiritual practice and artistic expression work together, heaven and earth are in resonance. This is Tama-Do - The Way of the Soul – Excerpts copyrighted by Fabien Maman 1997, courtesy Tama-Do Academy. www.tama-do.com

In a similar vein, Fabien Maman (a musician, composer, acupuncturist, author, researcher, healer, teacher, bioenergetician and martial artist) conducted revolutionary biology experiments showing the impacts of acoustic sound on human cells and their energy fields. Fabien found that through a series of acoustic sounds, he could explode cancer cells, as well as energize and empower healthy ones.

Fabien Maman is one of the world's leading experts on vibrational sound healing. I was introduced to his work by therapist Chantal Fabrice. Chantal studied at the Tama-Do Academy and I was lucky enough to attend a presentation and evening of sound that she hosted at a complementary therapy event.

I was captivated by the presentation that Chantal gave about Fabien Maman's work. It re-affirmed everything that I had already learned about how our bodies can become 'out of tune' and how the energy of sound and vibration can alter our cells and heal us.

Chantal showed us images (taken by Fabien Maman with a Kirlian Camera) of healthy blood cells that had been exposed to a chromatic scale of sound frequencies. The images showed how the colour and shape of each cell and its subtle energy field (Aura) changed according to the pitch and timbre of each musical note. The pictures were truly magical.

> Taken from www.tama-do.com

> He also discovered that when the cell felt a 'vibratory affinity' with a certain note, the cell's aura would transform into a mandala shape with vibrant colors of pinks and blues. Maman concluded this was the cell's 'fundamental note', and if the person 'tuned' with it, harmony could be achieved within the cells, the energy field of the person and the outside world.

> If physical cells and their energy fields can recognize and respond favorably to vibration, is it possible that cells have consciousness? What is the link between cells and the Soul? Is it possible that vibration is the key?

Please take time to visit the website www.Tama-Do.com and see some of the amazing images for yourself.

~ * ~

Bruce Lipton Ph.D

The third person I would like to tell you about is Bruce Lipton Ph.D. Rather than re-invent the wheel, I thought I'd give it to you straight from the horse's mouth!

> Taken from www.brucelipton.com

> Dr. Bruce Lipton is a former medical school professor and research scientist. His experiments, and that of other leading edge scientists, have examined in great detail the processes by which cells receive information. The implications of this research radically change our understanding of life. It shows that genes and DNA do not control our biology; that instead DNA is controlled by signals from outside the cell, including the energetic messages emanating from our positive and negative thoughts. Dr. Lipton's profoundly hopeful synthesis of the

Hummingbird

latest and best research in cell biology and quantum physics is being hailed as a major breakthrough showing that our bodies can be changed as we retrain our thinking.

Bruce Lipton's amazing discoveries, along with the work of Brandon Bays, Fabien Maman, Dr Masaru Emoto and no doubt many others just like them, not only show us, but *prove* to us, just how important it is to our physical health that we live with love, joy and a positive attitude. A healthy lifestyle if not just about exercise and diet but about so much more.

Thank you

Thank you for taking the time to read my book. If you have enjoyed it or found it beneficial in any way, please give me a positive review on Amazon. The reviews make a big difference to how many people get to read Hummingbird, learn about Huntington's disease and connect with my story.

I have created a Facebook page to accompany my book. Please visit www.facebook.com/HummingbirdBook to see photos of my fundraising events, my treks, my 50th birthday weekend, a link to Lavender Man's CD, my workshops and retreats, to make a donation to the HDA and various other information.

With love, from my heart.

Deborah x

Useful websites

Hummingbird Facebook Page	www.facebook.com/HummingbirdBook
Make a donation to the HDA	www.justgiving.com/HummingbirdBook
The Huntington's Disease Association UK	www.hda.org.uk
The Scottish Huntington's Association	www.hdscotland.org
The HD Society of America	www.hdsa.org
Dignity in Dying	www.dignityindying.org.uk
Notes from The Universe	www.tut.com
The Secret	www.thesecret.tv
Bruce Lipton	www.brucelipton.com
Tama-Do	www.tama-do.com
Jo Constantinou (SRT)	www.yournewlifepath.co.uk
Sivananda Yoga	www.sivananda.org
Shana Martin	www.shanamartin.com
Sarah Winckless	www.sarahwinckless.co.uk
Amy Kate Wolfe	www.amykatewolfe.com
The Messenger CD, Native American Flute (Lavender Man)	http://www.youtube.com/watch?v=26Brr0dJ2Dc&feature=share

25131236R00164

Made in the USA
Lexington, KY
13 August 2013